P9-BJP-236

PARISH PRIEST

EUGÈNE MASURE

PARISH PRIEST

TRANSLATED BY

ANGELINE BOUCHARD

FIDES PUBLISHERS ASSOCIATION

CHICAGO, ILLINOIS

Library of Congress Catalog Card Number: 55-11502

NIHIL OBSTAT: Rev. George C. Bernard, C.S.C., S.T.D.
University of Notre Dame

IMPRIMATUR: Leo A. Pursley, D.D., Apostolic Administrator,
Fort Wayne, Indiana

COPYRIGHT: 1955
Fides Publishers Association
Chicago, Illinois

Manufactured by American Book–Stratford Press, Inc., New York

55

TO THE SWEET,

LASTING, AND PROUD MEMORY

OF OUR FORMER STUDENTS,

WHO DIED BEFORE THEIR TEACHERS,

IN THE SERVICE OF THE CHURCH AND OF FRANCE,

IN 1914–1918

IN 1939–1945

AND DURING THE INTERVAL BETWEEN THE WARS,

FOR WHOM AND SOMETIMES WITH WHOM

THESE PAGES WERE SLOWLY WRITTEN.

E. M.

Contents

PART ONE

THE PRIESTHOOD

Introduction

THE PRESENT English translation of Canon E. Masure's *Prêtres Diocésains,* by Angeline Bouchard, is both a valuable and a timely contribution to the ever growing literature on the secular, or diocesan, priest, a subject often neglected or grossly misrepresented in the past.

The anxiety expressed by the author with regard to conditions prevailing now in France begins to be felt in many other countries, including our own. Young men with a divine vocation hesitate before choosing the way to a diocesan seminary, because the great ideal of a practical apostolate, as realized in the vocation to the secular priesthood, has never been sufficiently explained to them. In the present work Canon Masure offers the needed explanation with the purpose of recruiting more men for the oldest and most glorious of Christ's armies, the only active army that without interruption goes back to the days of the apostles, the presbyters or *elders,* the ordinary collaborators of the Bishops from the beginning.

While trying to create enthusiasm in the candidates for the secular priesthood, the book does not fail to offer inspiration to the priests themselves. The secular priest is not ordained solely for the purpose of offering the Holy Sacrifice of the

Mass—a most sublime and Christlike duty in itself—but in addition to share actively in the religious and apostolic function of his bishop. "The priest"—according to the author—"is a Christian who participates in the religious and apostolic powers, duties, and graces of the bishop, in dependence upon him within the limits of Order and jurisdiction fixed by the bishop and by the Church." This definition clearly determines the position of the secular priest. He is at the side of his ordinary bishop to assist him in the pastoral work of the diocese, who without such help and assistance would be crushed under the weight of his duties.

It is a well known fact that the biblical terminology—in the epistles of St. Paul and in the Acts of the Apostles—is undecided and unfixed with regard to the terms ἐπίδκοπος, bishop, and πζεδβύτεζος, *elder* or priest. These two terms are often used as synonyms. This indecision seems to have lasted as long as the Apostles lived, and as long as the churches, which they had founded, were directly dependent upon them. With the death of the Apostles, the bishops became their successors in the government of those churches and the presbyters became their immediate and subordinate collaborators in the very same apostolic work of salvation as pastors and teachers. These were the first diocesan priests, and for many centuries there were no other priests.

In order not to create confusion between the priests of the Old Testament, the Levitical priests, and those of the New Testament, the word ἱεζεύς, which recalled both Levitical and pagan priests, was discarded from the beginning in the Church of Jerusalem in favor of the term πζεσβύτεζος. This word was familiar to both Hebrews and Greeks who in civil and religious matters were governed by a council of *elders* or presbyters. This term while not excluding the sacrificial character which is proper to ἱεζεύς, stresses the other apostolic activities of pastoral administration.

Canon Masure, with a few other modern writers, disdains as unsuitable the appellative "secular" with regard to priests and prefers to call them "diocesan." One may wonder what he would call those secular priests who served in this country when it was still under Propaganda and there were no dioceses, or diocesan bishops. If historical and canonical reasons are taken into consideration the appellative "secular" should be retained and be preferred to "diocesan." The code of canon law and other Ecclesiastical documents use the appellative "secular" almost exclusively. Secular refers to *saeculum,* which in late ecclesiastical Latin means the world and worldly things. The Divine Savior wanted his disciples and their successors, our priests, in the world in order to save it: "Go into the whole world, and preach the gospel to every creature." Mark, 16:15. "I do not pray that thou take them out of the world, but that thou keep them from evil." John, 17:15. The priests are secular because they are in the world but not because they are worldly or of the world. Everybody knows that the Lord wanted his disciples to be the light of the world, the salt of the earth. They are ordained to minister to men living in the world, exposed to the attacks of the Devil and his cohorts. The ministers of Christ must remain at the side of those who are in the arena for the supreme test. No remote-control service for the salvation of souls has yet been found. The secular priest is in the arena of this world, on the front line of battle, in active duty to the end of his life, day and night answering the call of souls at the expense of rest and comfort, often risking his own life. This is the life of a secular priest and if anyone uses the word secular in a slighting and disparaging sense in order to discredit the proper helpers and collaborators of bishops, the secular priests, such a one betrays lack of charity and ignorance of the facts. In recruiting young men for religious communities some went so far as to tell such candidates that if they should enter the diocesan seminary they would be lacking in generosity towards God. The present book shows the fallacy of their argument.

In order to check the downward trend of the Jewish Christians of Palestine, before the fall of Jerusalem, at a time when many Hebrew Christians were on the verge of apostasy, the Apostle Paul wrote the famous Epistle to the Hebrews. This is a sublime analysis and explanation of the Priesthood of Christ with the purpose of lifting the fallen spirits of many Christians and inspiring them with courage in the face of imminent catastrophe. In our present generation three Supreme Pontiffs have issued three great Encyclicals on the Priesthood in order to inspire all faithful with more confidence in their spiritual leaders during these calamitous days. The priesthood remains even today the one great inspiration in the face of a widespread apostasy and of threatening dangers.

In his book Canon Masure returns to the Pauline doctrine of the Epistle to the Hebrews in order to revive faith in Christ, the eternal Priest, the great mediator between God and man, ever present with his power in the humble person of his anointed ones. In analyzing this doctrine the author follows the Berullian method, the method of the so-called French School which is substantially a revival of Pauline mysticism.

To conclude, this book has made a valuable contribution to the solution of an old problem, the problem of the state of perfection of the secular priest, and of the specific ascetical means at his disposal for the attainment of his spiritual perfection. Canon Masure makes it clear that the secular priest is engaged, under his bishop, in the apostolic exercise of practical charity, as dispenser of the mysteries of God to the members of his parish. Since the work of charity is a work of perfection, his state, like his work, is a state of perfection, a perfection of service under the Bishop: "If the priest whose profession is to exercise charity fulfills his task with the help of God in the spirit we have tried to analyze, then his whole existence . . . all his actions, considered at once as means and ends, will help him more each day to establish himself in the interior and exterior state which will be the very state of perfection."

As supplementary reading on this subject we would like to recommend a scholarly work—a doctoral dissertation—of recent publication: *State of Perfection and the Secular Priest,* by C. H. Dukehart, S.S., S.T.D. (*The Grail,* St. Meinrad, Ind., 1952).

This English translation of Canon Masure has a great mission and should be a real inspiration to priests and seminarians, and a practical guide to young men who wish to dedicate their life to the service of God but are still undecided on what course to follow for the proper realization of their divine call.

Pascal P. Parente, S.T.D.
The Catholic University of America

Washington, D.C.
December 27, 1954.

Special Preface to the American Edition

THE PURPOSE of this little book, addressed to the diocesan clergy, is to reinstate the dignity of the priesthood in the eyes of priests, to instill in them a greater sense of the nobility of their ecclesiastical state, and to point out its demands. To prove these points, it relies upon the highest of authorities on this subject, that is to say, upon the *Epistle to the Hebrews,* together with the testimony of the *Gospels* and of the *Acts of the Apostles.* It then enters, a little rashly perhaps, into the very heart of current concern about diocesan spirituality. Encouraged by the patronage of several contemporary bishops, it ventures, with less right than they, to sketch the structural outline of a problem that is constantly being solved and yet always remains open, namely, the problem of the best means to assure the Christian perfection of the priestly state.

We have looked to St. Thomas for the principles of doctrine, and have found them in IIa IIae, q. 184. At the same time we have not hesitated to prolong the Angelic Doctor's theses in the same direction as his own teaching. We have also tried to take advantage of the supplementary light provided by the history of the Catholic clergy in the last few centuries. There are so many circumstances that modify the conditions of the problem from day to day, and usually for the better. The Seventeenth Century and the French School of seminary-founders contributed much to the progress toward a solution. At the present time, the missionary atmosphere that surrounds even the most firmly established of our churches, gives greater assurance of priestly vocations of a high quality. Since candidates to the priesthood can no longer expect any material advantage from governments or from civil institutions, their vocations are purer than ever. The clergy is no longer, as it was during the various "ancien régimes," one of the great bodies of the State, and the priesthood is no longer a "career." In many countries, benefices are only a memory, whose very name is incomprehensible to younger members of the clergy. The use of the word "secular" to designate a poor, needy, apostolic, missionary, and "consumed" clergy, in the words of Father Chevrier, a clergy that has scarcely enough to eat—this ill-advised adjective is becoming an anachronism and even an injustice, at least in the country that the author knows best. The time is no more when Boileau dared to write:

> La déesse en entrant qui voit la nappe mise,
> Admire un si bel ordre, et reconnait l'Église.[1]

We may thank God that today the Church and her ecclesiastics are recognized by other marks. We should have liked to point out and describe some of these signs of the presence of Christ in the midst of His own, of His friends.

The service of God and the service of men: we hope to show that herein lies the whole reason for being and even the essence of the Christian priesthood, and that these two principles united as one are the foundation of ecclesiastical spirituality.

Eugène Masure

---

[1] "When the goddess enters and sees the table set, she admires such splendid order and recognizes the Church."

Foreword to the Reader

THIS LITTLE BOOK was born of anxiety and regret. The anxiety of the director of a seminary who, in his long career, has had many a young man, rich or poor, come to him with remarks equivalent to the following: "I want to give myself to God in a state of perfection. It doesn't matter to me whether I obey this vocation here or there, in the diocese or elsewhere. I am attracted only by the total gift of self. Should I leave you and seek elsewhere?" Let us suppose, to complicate or simplify the case, that the visitor is generous and intelligent enough so as, by normal human estimates, not to seem to need the protection of a rigid ascetic plan of life. What am I to answer?

The problem becomes still more difficult when the tall seminarian adds: "I should like to fulfill this total gift in the apostolate. I dream of a fatherhood of contact with the faithful and unbelievers, with children and adults. It is in this direction that I conceive abandoning myself to others and to God. And yet, must I not renounce this desire and this joy of universal service if I am to follow a particular and regular vocation that, so I am told, is more perfect?" Again, let us suppose that here is a youth capable of bringing the greatest spiritual

assistance to his diocese and to his bishop, and—who knows?
—competent later on to accept the heaviest apostolic responsibilities in his turn. What then?

We spoke also of regret, the regret of a professor of dogma
who has always been amazed at the small place given to the
theology of the priesthood in the general scheme of ecclesiastical studies. Fortunately, the manuals speak of the priesthood
of Christ at the end of the Treatise on the Incarnation. However, when the various authors, much later on, reach the
Treatise on Holy Orders, at the end of the Tract on the
Sacraments, they do not take the trouble to give an exact definition of this ministerial or participated priesthood which is
conferred on priests by ordination. They allow themselves
even less time and space to study at length the grace proper
to the sacrament of Order. Whence the paradox that a student can become a priest and leave the seminary without ever
having learned in class just what his priesthood is. Books of
spirituality and retreat sermons do make up for this lack, but
they do so in their own way, which is more edifying and
exhortative than precise and truly scientific. They intermin-
gle, without properly ordering them, ascetic and mystical considerations borrowed from schools or from masters without
having the time to compare, discuss, and differentiate them.
As a result, on this subject which is most personal to him,
the priest runs the risk of being content with inadequate
approximations.

It was in order to answer the questions of his exacting students that the author of this little book was obliged, as were
so many before him, to consult Scripture and Tradition and
to extract from them a small treatise on the priesthood and on
the priestly state. The *Epistle to the Hebrews*—which, thanks
to the *Acts of the Apostles,* has been placed once again within
the framework of the origins of the Church and of the episcopacy, which are better known at the present time—obviously continues to support the fundamental doctrine by its
irreplaceable authority. We have looked to St. Thomas for

the principle of the doctrine of the state of the priestly life. At the same time, we have taken the liberty of prolonging the theses of the holy Doctor in the light of his own teaching. We have also tried to profit by the supplementary light provided by the history of the Catholic priesthood during the past centuries. Thanks to the great reforms carried out in the education and in the apostolic life of the clergy, we are perhaps gaining a better understanding of the Savior's intentions when He said to the first priests whom He had just ordained: "Go forth to teach and to baptize; I have not come to be served but to serve, do as I have done."

The service of God and the service of men—we hope to show that herein lies the whole reason for being and the very essence of the Christian priesthood.

This work is in part a new, corrected and enlarged edition of another book which appeared a few years back but which is now out of print, entitled *L'Eminente Dignité du Sacerdoce Diocésain*.[1] Realizing that he was entering unexplored territory, the author pointed out in the preface of that earlier book the possible need of future corrections and even of retractions. Both have been made easy for him by the views expressed to him both in public and in private. He has tried to keep these views in mind, and he now wishes to thank both his critics and his correspondents.

---

[1] Our first publishers, Messrs. Bloud & Gay, have graciously authorized us to reproduce large portions of a text that was their property. We wish to thank them, as well as *L'Office français du Livre,* which has permitted us to transcribe an entire chapter from our essay "Vers une spiritualité de l'action," which appeared in the collection *Amor.*

PART ONE

THE PRIESTHOOD

CHAPTER I

The Priesthood of Christ

CHRIST JESUS, true God and true man, is the sole priest of the
new covenant, that is, of the perfect religion. This is a proposition of faith. It had already been presented to the Fathers of
the Council of Ephesus in 431, in the tenth anathematization
of St. Cyril of Alexandria against Nestorius, in terms borrowed from St. Paul's own Epistles.[1] Although the thesis was
not defined at that time, it continued to be a part of the purest
tradition. It is accepted by all the Eastern churches, by all the
Protestant churches that are faithful to the doctrinal principles
of their origins, and, obviously, also by the Catholic Church.
The Council of Trent expresses this thesis in passing with
reference to the Eucharist, in the solemn words of the opening
Chapter of the Twenty-Second Session. The *Epistle to the
Hebrews,* speaking of Christ's priesthood, had said that it was
a profound doctrine and one that was difficult to explain:
grandis sermo et ininterpretabilis ad dicendum, or as it is
even better expressed in the Greek: πολὺς ὁ λόγος καὶ
δυσερμήνευτος λέγειν.[2] Relying precisely on this Epistle, the

---

[1] Denzinger-B., 122.
[2] Heb. 5:11. English translation in the Confraternity of Christian Doctrine edition (Paterson, N. J.: St. Anthony Guild Press, 1947): "On this
point we have much to say, and it is difficult to explain it."

3

Church has not renounced the task of explaining to us the mystery of this unique priesthood. Just as St. Paul had done, she has shown that Christ's priesthood is a consequence of the hypostatic union of the two natures in a single person, and that it is in reality a formula for the same mystery inasmuch as this mystery culminates in the institution of a new religion and of a perfect sacrifice.

As in the case of the dogma of the divinity of Christ, there will always be two ways open for the demonstration of the thesis of the priesthood of Christ, the path of history and the path of faith. History's way is that of visible facts and spoken words recorded in documents, a touching and powerful reality whose developmental stages can be described. The other way or source is that of dogmatic teaching, interpreting these facts in order to translate them into doctrinal propositions wherein the Church defines the truths to be believed as they are revealed by the same Scripture or recorded in Tradition. Modernism has tried to oppose these two methods, alleging that their conclusions do not agree. Supposedly, there would have been a Jesus of history and a Jesus of faith, and an opposition between the truths of the former and the theses of the latter. On the contrary, the demonstration of the dogma of the priesthood of Christ gives us the joy of seeing the perfect concordance between history and faith, or—if we prefer to simplify—between the Jesus of the Gospels and the Christ of the *Epistle to the Hebrews.* In the one as in the other, we recognize, beneath the symbols of different vocabularies, the same Mediator between God and men, the same Priest, the Son of God among us, because He unites in Himself all the privileges and the riches of divinity, and all the duties as well as all the sufferings of humanity.

The first path of demonstration is therefore the path of historic realities, and this is the one that the Gospels invite us to follow. The Gospels show us Christ exercising during His whole life, and especially during His public ministry, the functions of religion and salvation that make Him the supreme

Mediator: the intermediary between God and men at every instant in all the manifestations of His religious activity. He claims for Himself the monopoly of this unique position: *sine me nihil potestis facere,* and more explicitly: *nemo venit ad Patrem, nisi per me,* or still more clearly: *qui videt me, videt et Patrem.* Except for the title of priest which He does not use, He takes on—by virtue of a personal privilege which is that of His divinity united to our humanity—all the qualities and all the functions that precisely constitute the definitive priesthood. Moreover, He suppresses in His favor, by His mere presence, all the priestly or pontifical institutions that existed before. Moses and Elias, the law and the prophets, all the giants of sacred history who formerly brought men close to God and brought God close to men, render Him homage in the great scene of the Transfiguration, bowing before His transcendence.

This demonstration by history and by texts has been repeated often, to the great joy of devout souls. We shall merely point out here the more recent authors who have resumed the use of this method.[3]

By a careful study of the evangelical labors of Jesus of Nazareth, this method shows that the deep-seated intention and will of Him whom we call Christ is to fulfill all obligations toward His Father, in the name of all men as represented by the small flock of His disciples: respect, adoration, thanksgiving, praise, and above all love—to all of which God has a natural right. It is likewise demonstrated that at the same time He brings these hesitant, wretched, benighted sons of Adam, these sinners, closer to this infinitely good Father who has sent His Son to them. Truly, Christ is between God and men, between heaven and earth, so that He may bring them to-

---

[3] Gaston Brillet, Superior General of the Oratory, *Méditations sur le sacerdoce* (Bruges: Desclée De Brouwer, 1942); Canon Thellier De Poncheville, *L'histoire sacerdotale de Jésus* (Paris: Editions Spes, 1945); Rev. Georges Lemaître, *Notre sacerdoce* (Bruges: Desclée De Brouwer, 1945).

gether in His Person; for His Person is the bond, the mediation, the revelation, the intercession—in short, the religion,
the religion of charity, of the immense charity from above to
which the pitiful and suffering love of earth must answer.

This historical demonstration finds expression in several
literary styles, to which correspond various types of spirituality. The primitive vocabulary of the Synoptics is messianic.
It is a messianism that is progressively enriched by the good
tidings brought by Jesus. The Prologue of St. John has taken
both from the Old Testament and from Hellenism the name
that best sums up the whole theology of mediation: Jesus is
the Word of Yahveh, the Logos of God. Much, much later,
from the Greek Platonistic Fathers to the logicians and jurists
of an exacting and sound scholasticism, from the tender ef-
fusions of the Franciscans to the splendors of the French
School, this theology of the priesthood of Jesus has been maintained by all the mediators and contemplators of the life of
Christ, passing through the entire dogmatics of the Incarnation like an electric wire conductor. What is Christianity, if
not a religion? It is nothing but that, and yet all of that. Who
is Christ, therefore, if not the perfect priest?

It is to our interest, in order to strengthen our grasp of the
meaning of the Gospels, not to overwork the increasingly
marked distinction which our modern manuals have been
making for teaching purposes between the mystery of the
Incarnation and the mystery of the Redemption—as if Jesus
Himself had first taught that He was the Son of God made
man, and then later taught that He was to be our Saviour.
Actually, it has almost always been for our sakes and in order
to stress the work of our redemption that Jesus has shown
Himself as He is. This is precisely what explains the intimate
relationship between the dogma of the Incarnation and that
of the priesthood of Christ. It is in the exercise of His functions that Jesus manifested to us His powers and His unique
title, which consists in His being the eternal Son of God
among us. He proclaimed He was the Messias, bringing hope

of salvation; He set Himself up as God in the center of these hopes in order to fulfill them; and He later transformed these overly temporal visions into an interior religion, into a spiritual contact with the heavenly Father. It was thus that Jesus gave to the biblical title of Son of God, which He claimed for Himself alone, a strictly divine and therefore eternal meaning. All in all, it is impossible to say whether Jesus presented Himself first as the Second Person of the Blessed Trinity, incarnate among us, or as the one and only intermediary between His Father and men, and therefore as the priest of the definitive religion.

If we are to be faithful to texts and to facts, we must not make too great a separation, as we shall see, between the thesis of the priesthood of Christ and the thesis of the Sacrifice of the Cross. Obviously, it was Jesus' death which made of His agony on Calvary the sacrifice of the new alliance; but equally important is the fact that the victim was the Son of God made man. Thus, the priesthood and the sacrifice of Christ mutually justify each other by a kind of reciprocal causality, the former explaining why this death fulfilled the perfect sacrifice, and the latter giving to the personal priesthood of Christ its reason for being and its value. This is the way the *Epistle to the Hebrews* presents all these mysteries in order to organize them into theses of faith.

The reason this doctrine is so solid is because from the start it was founded on the enduring text of the *Epistle of the Hebrews,* which teaches and explains it. In constructing the thesis of the priesthood of Christ on the basis of an inquiring and exacting scriptural argumentation, the writer of the Epistle has left almost nothing for future theologians to discover or even to seek. Obviously, he had been thoroughly trained in the dialectical methods of the synagogue, and under the inspiration of the Holy Ghost he was now placing these methods at the service of the new faith. It is impossible to get away from these great texts; it is difficult to add anything to them. All that anyone can do is to understand them correctly, or merely to repeat them accurately.

When these Paulinian pages appeared for the first time, while they brought no innovation to evangelical doctrine, they did present it in the framework of the new vocabulary.

Never during His mortal life had Jesus of Nazareth accepted or demanded for Himself the title of priest or pontiff. Never had the great apostolic Epistles given Him this name until then. Even the Johannic literature that was to come later did not use this terminology. And we believe we know the reason why. The priesthood of Israel had either fallen or remained far too low for that, in the formalistic regions where the priest and the Levite were mere salaried executors of exterior rites, and sometimes the rivals of the prophets, the competitors of the men of God, and even persecutors of the saints. Indeed, it was at an assembly presided over by the chief priest that the man who was to be the first Christian martyr cried out: "Which of the prophets have not your fathers persecuted?" [4] Jesus Himself, the greatest of the divine envoys, died a victim of a coalition plotted by the synagogue and the sanctuary, by the Pharisees and the priests. If He had accepted the name of priest too soon, even in the singular, if He had appropriated it so as to allow Himself to be defined by it, He would have been putting new wine in an archaic goatskin, He would have been placing religion in spirit and in truth on the same level as the Mosaic observances, and this would have made it even harder to liberate it from them. If He had taken the name of priest before it was time, He would have blinded heedless eyes to the transcendence and to the spiritual purity of Christian revelation which had come to renew the face of the earth.

What infinite precautions the *Epistle to the Hebrews* took when it finally claimed for Jesus of Nazareth a title that really

---

[4] Acts 7:52.

belongs to Him alone, a title that until then men had assumed
only in counterfeit, or at best as remote and inadequate figures.
A vigorous dialectician might begin by distinguishing between
two priesthoods, the priesthood that the Old Law had known,
that of Aaron and of the Levites, and another also recorded
in Scripture but with mysterious and until then uncompre-
hended marks, that of Melchisedech. Even so, St. Paul would
not explain Jesus through the King of Salem. The latter remained a convenient and even admirable, but still an annun-
ciatory figure; whereas Jesus alone, bearing within Himself
His mystery and His privilege, was capable of constituting and
of defining His own priesthood in His Person and in His twofold divine and human nature. Christ's priesthood admits of
no precedent or answer: "but He, because He continues forever, has an everlasting priesthood." [5]

Regardless of long oratorical usage which has been tolerated
by an indulgent theology, it would be erroneous to seek in
Hebrews 5:1 a definition of the priesthood in general, that
might serve as a major premise in a syllogism concluding to
the priesthood of Christ in particular. In the first place, this
verse must not be separated from the two following verses
that explain it and that in developing it make it irreconcilable
with the perfect holiness of Jesus. Actually, the famous sentence: *omnis pontifex ex hominibus assumptus . . .* [6] defines
only the Hebrew high priest and the first alliance. Now, "that
which is obsolete and has grown old is near its end." [7] It is
not upon such ruins that the Christian priesthood rests. Moreover, the author of *Hebrews* does not proceed by way of
Aristotelian syllogisms; he uses a method of argumentation
a fortiori by *quanto magis,* in which there is neither major nor
minor, but only imperfect figure or symbol and transcendent

---

[5] Heb. 7:24.
[6] Heb. 5:1. "For every high priest taken from among men . . ."
[7] Heb. 8:13.

realization.[8] Christ is a priest because He is much more of a priest than Aaron and a much better one, because He fulfills

---

[8] It is possible to transcribe the *Epistle to the Hebrews* almost in its entirety in two parallel columns, and thus demonstrate the author's mode of reasoning:

The high priest of the Hebrews (5:1)	Jesus Christ, the Son of God and our high priest, (5:5)
taken from among men (*Ibid.*)	during His earthly life among His brothers (2:17; 5:7)
whose weaknesses and sins he shares, (5:2-3)	shared our weaknesses but not our sins, (4:15; 7:26)
has been chosen and called by God (5:4)	has been proclaimed a priest by God (5:5-6)
but without an oath, (7:20)	with an oath, (7:28)
that he may offer sacrifices (5:1)	having offered the sacrifice of His sufferings
each day (7:27)	once for all (7:27)
for himself and for the people. (5:1; 7:27)	for the sins of the people.
Since he belongs to the tribe of Levi, he is not a king (7:5, 14)	He is of the tribe of Juda. (7:14) He is a king as well as a priest (king of peace, of justice) (7:2)
moreover, he is subject to death; (7:23)	and He lives forever. (7:24-25)
and since his priesthood is not eternal, (*Ibid.*)	Therefore His priesthood is eternal, (7:24)
it can be transmitted to others. (*Ibid.*)	and cannot be transmitted. (7:28)
In the person of Abraham, Aaron bowed before another, (7:4-10)	It is before Him that Aaron bowed, (7:4-10)
for his priesthood is imperfect and provisory (*Ibid.*)	for His is the definitive priesthood (7:28)
as is carnal law. (7:27-28)	for eternal salvation. (7:19; 9:28)
He never definitively takes away sins, (10:11)	He has taken away all sins, (9:28)

all the conditions of the latter and exceeds them to such a degree that in the end He is the one and only pontiff. As far as we are concerned, if some of us do become priests in some manner, by participation, it is by attaching ourselves to Christ and not by simply fulfilling the definition of the Hebrew high priest.

This critique and the reading that it presupposes would have no great importance if they did not also provide us, by means of a precise example, with the method by which we must understand the *Epistle to the Hebrews* in order to appraise it at its full value. Coming before St. John's Prologue, this great doctrinal letter does not tell us about the mystery of Christ in its entirety, from His divinity to His humanity (except perhaps in 1:2-3, which is a kind of outline of the theology of the Fourth Gospel). It does not descend from eternity into time to show us the Incarnation first, and then the Redemption. Conversely, it teaches us that the way the Redemption terminates,—in the Resurrection and the Ascension, and in the admission of the sacred humanity of the Son to the right hand of the Father,—is a proof of the divinity of Jesus, that is, a proof of the Incarnation. Thus, Christ's historical life unfolded a priestly mystery that is explained by the Incarnation: Jesus is a priest because events have proven that He is the Son of God present in our midst, and (abstracting from the sacrifice of the Redemption and the dogma of the Mystical Body with its divine Head) because He unites in one person the nature of God and the nature of man.

Throughout its sumptuous biblical demonstration in which the mysterious image of Melchisedech upheld with its shadow a proof that was greater than itself, the *Epistle to the Hebrews*

---

and, obsolete like the first alliance, (7:11, 19)	and established the eternal alliance (10:14)
he is but the earthly shadow of the good things to come. (10:1)	in the imperishable tabernacle, namely, heaven. (4:14; 6:20)
etc., etc.	etc., etc.

rediscovered these titles of priest and pontiff which were henceforth purified of any legalistic or Mosaic connotation. Pauline theology finally did what Jesus had not wanted to do Himself, namely, to take the time to change the fundamental meaning of the Levitical names. Thanks to the earlier writings of the Apostle, thanks to their doctrinal vigor and precision, thanks, too, to the passing years, Pauline theology could at last joyfully announce that Jesus is the sole priest of God His Father, and of men, His brothers. And it thus enriched the language of Christianity (we do not say Christian dogma) with a definitive priestly vocabulary. The Jewish priesthood did not survive this formidable transmutation of values.

For a long time, however, everyday language kept the marks —and even today it preserves the memory—of the precautions taken in the beginning to prevent the ministers of the new covenant from being confused with the last survivors of the old alliance. The founders of the Church and of the Churches, the mandatories of Christ, were not called pontiffs at first, but apostles; then they were called episcopes, and finally bishops. Their auxiliaries did not take the name of ἱερεύς, or *sacerdos,* but of *presbyter-episcopus,* from which we have derived the specifically Christian words of "priest" and "priesthood."

This is how the passage from the old to the new alliance came about in this field. It was neither a transmission nor an evolution, but a revolution within the continuum itself.

We can now return to the *Epistle to the Hebrews* and in-quire of it wherein essentially consists this new priesthood, which the *Epistle* has succeeded in distinguishing from all other divine or human institutions that once bore that name. Actually, the *Epistle* has already informed us of this. Jesus is the sole priest because He is the consummate intermediary, the perfect mediator between God and men, as the Son of God incarnate among us. He alone is a priest by nature, or rather by His twofold nature, divine and human. Through the centuries the language of Christianity has orchestrated this doctrine into magnificent periods, for it is a doctrine that lends itself easily to oratorical developments. The most beautiful of these texts can be found in Thomassin's *Dogmata Theologica, De Incarnatione,* lib. X, *De Christo sacerdote.* May it suffice for the disciples of the French School if we cite the sumptuous words of the young Bossuet, summarizing the doctrine of his masters, Bérulle, Condren, Vincent de Paul, and Olier: "Through the dignity of His unction Jesus Christ was to unite the kingship and the priesthood, which had been separated in the first people. Christians, do not look upon this as a kind of corporeal unction: the unction of our pontiff is the divinity of God the Word. . . . In uniting itself to the humanity of Jesus, the divinity of the Word first of all poured itself upon the whole of this humanity and upon all its parts. Divinity penetrated humanity so completely that it became effectively incarnate in this humanity. Thus, out of the divinity and humanity there emerged a single whole, the result of their ineffable union. That is why Jesus our Saviour is called the Anointed One *par excellence,* Christ; it is because of this divine and miraculous unction."[9]

Nowadays, we should doubtless prefer to speak with less lyricism and return simply to the evangelical facts lived in the light of the *Epistle to the Hebrews.* We have the right to consider Jesus the perfect priest whom we had sought for centuries to unite us to God; the One who was called Rabbi, Prophet, Son of man, Christ, that is to say King Messias, and lastly, Son of God. Men have always needed a man superior to themselves to whom they could yield up their whole souls in this great business of salvation. Let him be a leader, certainly! Let him lead them to war and walk before them; be the judge who settles their disputes; the master who teaches them; the hero whom they admire without reservation and therefore obey unflinchingly. But above all he must be the man of God

---

[9] Bossuet, *Premier Sermon pour le deuxième dimanche de l'Avent,* Metz, 1653 (Lebarcq, Urbain et Levesque), Vol. I, p. 467. Cf. Bossuet, *Sermon pour la fête de l'Ascension,* Metz, 1654 (*ibid.,* p. 522 ff.), and *Elévations sur les Mystères,* The Thirteenth Week.

who knows both divine secrets and human sorrows, who can inject these divine secrets into human sorrows, soothe our anxiety, fill our solitude, and speak to us of hope in the name of his own certitudes, of his own powers and rights. Now, Jesus of Nazareth, as we can well see now, is this man of religion whom we have been seeking: a priest to His innermost depths, filled with God, both to give Him to us and to pray to Him in our name, thus giving us a twofold protection. He is a priest in His actions, that cure and sanctify us, that fill our darkness with light and peace, exercise our terrors, and bring down our pride, that erect a bridge between ourselves and the Infinite who attracts us and yet frightens us. Jesus answers all these exigencies in His person in a most unexpected way, but it is a way that is very dear to our modern views, to our psychological tastes, and to our desire for a pure spirituality and for historical reality. As the Son of God and Founder of the true religion, as the envoy from on high who is also a mortal like ourselves, this Head, of whom we are so proud and who belongs to us, unites us to God from whom He comes and carries up to God the suffering and adoration of men. He is the priest of a truly new order.

As we have already said, there is another conclusion to draw from the doctrine of St. Paul, and in particular from the pages of the Epistle to the Hebrews which are devoted to establishing at the present moment the dogma of the single sacrifice of Christ on the Cross and in heaven. This inspired author teaches us that Christ is a priest because Jesus offered up the sacrifice of the Cross, and inversely that the death of Christ on the Cross is a sacrifice or the beginning of a sacrifice (inasmuch as this sacrifice is consummated in heaven), because Christ is a priest. There exists a reciprocal causality.

And yet how could the death of a man, even the purest and most innocent, be a sacrifice in itself, and the perfect sacrifice? At best it would be a lamentable judicial error, a great injustice, a crime, an assassination. But how could it be a sacrifice of religion? Religious sacrifice, moreover, ordinarily demands a liturgy, rituals, and exterior, sacred conditions that are not to be found on Golgotha. Let us not forget, however, the method and the doctrine of the *Epistle to the Hebrews,* strengthened by a vocabulary of sacrifice already used in earlier Epistles of St. Paul and also by Jesus Himself at the Last Supper: the death of Christ on Calvary and its glorious acceptance in heaven by the Father constitute the perfect sacrifice, because, while they begin by imitating ancient sacrifice with respect to the immolation, the spilling of blood, the religious oblation, and the divine acceptance, they far surpass the ancient rites by reason of the irreplaceable, transcendent, spiritual and unique value of the Victim, who is the incarnate Son of God.[10]

We have distinguished the priesthood, which is a state (and in Christ a state which involves the union of His two natures

---

[10] Using the same method as before, we could summarize this point of doctrine in the *Epistle* as follows:

The high priest of the Hebrews (5:1)	Christ the Redeemer, (1:2; 3:1, etc.)
of the carnal and provisional order, (10:1)	for the sake of the good things to come (9:11)
once a year, (9:7; 10:1)	once for all, (9:25-28; 10:14)
with the blood of goats and bulls (9:13)	by virtue of His own blood, (9:12)
that he offers for his own and the people's sins, (9:7)	that He offers not for Himself but for us,
enters the Holy of Holies (9:3, 7)	enters eternal heaven, (9:24; 10:12)
that is perishable, made by human hands, (8:13; 9:24)	
without bringing anyone else with him (9:7)	bringing us in with Him, (10:14)
only to come forth and start over again. (10:4)	and remaining forever at the right hand of God (8:1)
etc., etc.	etc., etc.

in a single person), from sacrifice, which is an act. We must now show the close relationship and coordination between the priesthood and sacrifice. While the priesthood is logically anterior to sacrifice, and exists in order to make sacrifice possible, how much would it amount to if it never fulfilled its purpose by offering up and immolating a victim? It is in the celebration of sacrifice that the priesthood affirms and fulfills itself, and in a certain sense passes from potency into act. Being broader in its scope than transitory sacrifice, the priesthood is permanent and multiform. The priest is an intermediary and a mediator on many different occasions and in many different ways. And yet at the hour of sacrifice, the priesthood recollects itself to its innermost depths. If it did not do this, it would lose its consistency. The instant the priest is looked upon as an intermediary, it follows that, since sacrifice is essentially the efficacious rite of mediation, the priest alone has the right to celebrate sacrifice. At the moment of sacrifice, his priesthood is in fullest possible activity. Nonetheless, the notion of the priesthood goes beyond the idea of sacrifice in terms both of time and metaphysics. The priesthood endures, it is a state. Sacrifice is accomplished and completed, it is an act. And yet the two institutions are correlative.

This interrelation is the remote source of a conception of the priesthood that is too narrow, and that we have already condemned with respect to the Jewish religion. According to this view, the priest would be simply the minister in charge of the sacrificial rite. Beside and above him would be other men of God who would also serve as religious intermediaries on a higher spiritual or intellectual level—the level of the prophets, like Elias for example, or of the leaders of the people like Moses, or in the level of the ascetics and mystics. This approach would result in an overspecialized priesthood, always in danger of falling back into liturgical formalism and decadence.

In the religion of Jesus, however, or at least in His person (and in Him religion and person are intimately united!), the priest is the sole intermediary. It might be better to say that it is Jesus who assumes all mediatorial functions at once, for in His mystery they cannot be dissociated. He simultaneously assumes all the functions of Moses and Aaron, and before them of Abraham and Melchisedech. Jesus never ceased exercising His priesthood, that is, His mediation, when He preached, baptized, forgave sins, or cured the sick. As for His sacrifice, it was the history of His agony and the very fact of His death, before we began repeating it in the Eucharistic rite. When Christ died, He killed formalism as well as sin. After Him, the priesthood could be nothing if not a participation in His interior and exterior religion, before being the power to exercise the sacramental functions instituted by Him.

For it is not only at the Last Supper and on Calvary that Jesus was a priest. He is a priest forever, inasmuch as His priesthood is coextensive with the Incarnation itself. He continues to exercise His mediatory functions without interruption. Since He is a living and substantial sacrament, He is a priest in all of His relations with God and men. As Father Salet says, "The instant the Word becomes incarnate—the Word who is at once the perfect image of the Father and the exemplar of creation—He must of necessity be the Mediator, the religious bond between God and man, and consequently *the Priest*. His ordination is the Incarnation itself. He is consecrated not by a transitory and accidental act, not by an unction received on a certain day, but by God Himself uniting Himself to His humanity and thereby conferring upon Him the incommunicable name of 'Christ.' That is to say, He is a Priest in His substance, by all that He is, by His entire being. It also means that all His actions are necessarily priestly acts." [11]

---

[11] Gaston Salet, S. J., *Le Christ notre vie* (Paris: Casterman, 1937), p. 53.

NOTE

For many years manuals of theology and sermons to the faithful have been divided into two opposing camps in their efforts to explain and prove that the death of Christ on the Cross (followed by His Resurrection) and the Eucharist are sacrifices, or better, a single sacrifice, or the perfect sacrifice.

The first method prefers to choose as the major premise of its deductive demonstration a definition of sacrifice in general, which it seeks to find in the history of religions, in the Old Testament, in the dialectics of the School, or even in the *Epistle to the Hebrews*. It then demonstrates in its minor that the death of Christ and the Eucharist each individually more than fulfills all the conditions required by this general conception, and the conclusion is then drawn.

The second method protests against this mode of argumentation. If the sacrifice of the Cross was and remains the perfect sacrifice, of which all others have been merely inadequate outlines or sterile caricatures, we must start from Calvary to construct the general idea which proceeds from it. The sacrifice of Christ is its own definition, and by setting itself up as a solution, it explains after the fact what its remote figures in the Old Testament or its counterfeits in other religions are trying to do.

Actually, these two methods need to be completed by one another, or rather contained within a third, for they err in not following the true path of Scripture and of Revelation. This path initiates us into the thoughts and desires of God by the constant use of anterior institutions which do not define the supreme and decisive institution, but outline its direction beforehand and to some extent its structure, even if only through the yearnings which they betray. Throughout its history, Revelation, and evangelical Revelation in particular, has had its symbols which have preceded it, and which it has used to explain itself by progressively making them more sublime; but it has never identified itself with the definitions of any of these symbols. The *Epistle to the Hebrews* is the perfect model of this method. It chooses figures from the Old Testament, uses them to reach out beyond them, and concludes by declaring them inadequate and obsolete. This method, which is more Platonistic than syllogistic, runs counter to our scholastic habits of reasoning, but it is nevertheless the traditional, efficacious, and irreplaceable way.

Father Bouyer of the Oratory has written a very penetrating article on this subject, an article that is very "new" because it is so old.[12] In the dialectic of the notion of sacrifice that he has presented, he may even have gone beyond the results of the method; for while rightly showing that the sacrifice of the Cross is a spiritual sacrifice, he has not mentioned that the Eucharist continues to make a liturgical sacrifice of this spiritual (and historical) sacrifice. But that was not his subject. Moreover, he has simply imitated to the limit the *Epistle to the Hebrews,* which did not mention the Eucharist in its synthesis because it was not within its scope.

---

[12] L. Bouyer, "Liturgie et exégèse spirituelle," in *La Maison-Dieu,* 1946, no. 7.

CHAPTER II

The Priesthood in the Church

IN BUILDING THE THESIS of the priesthood of Christ in the light of the Gospels and of the *Epistle to the Hebrews,* we used the terms "privilege" and "monopoly" several times to designate the supreme pontifical function of the only-begotten Son of God. Will not these words, which we were happy to write, now turn against the very title of the present chapter? Is it still conceivable that there can henceforth exist other priests besides Jesus? Is the priesthood of Christ communicable to others since His departure? The cited texts seem to answer "No"; and so does the doctrine that we thought we had culled from them. Hebrews 7:24 [1] even speaks of a ἀπαράβατον ἱερωσύνην, which is translated by the Latin Vulgate by: *sempiternum sacerdotium.* It would be better to say: permanent priesthood, that is, a priesthood that cannot be transmitted, as is explained by the preceding passage: *eo quod maneat in aeternum.* There is indeed only one Son, only one Son of God, and we have seen that this only-sonship, together with the Incarnation, is an essential part of the one and only priesthood of Christ.

---

[1] The Confraternity of Christian Doctrine edition reads: "but He, because He continues forever, has an everlasting priesthood."

And yet when we examine this problem more closely, we notice that the difficulty of prolonging one or another of Christ's mysteries in His Church already existed with regard to filial or supernatural grace in general, and that this latter queston was solved affirmatively by divine mercy. The grace that we call baptismal because it is normally communicated to us through baptism was already the property of the Son on a lower level than that of the priesthood, and yet it is granted to all men. There is only one Son by eternal nature, but through historical grace there are millions of adopted sons who participate in the life of the only Son. Now, can we not affirm the same thing of this sonship when it becomes a mediation and a priesthood as we dare to do of it insofar as it makes the Son and the sons personally pleasing to God?

On both levels, we must first of all maintain the privilege, and if we prefer, the monopoly of Christ, who is the only Son and consequently the only Priest. This mystery which is personal to Him thus becomes for us a principle and a point of departure. We would never have been called to sonship, if Jesus were not *the* Son; but granted that He is the Son, we can hope to become sons through Him. There would never have been any genuine priesthood in this world if Jesus had not been *the* Priest; but granted that He is the Priest, we can become priests thanks to Him. His priesthood is the foundation of ours. The converse is not true, of course. That is why Aaron had nothing real to communicate to Jesus.

There is only one Son of God; and yet we are all sons of God through baptism. There is only one Head of the body of the Church; and yet the pope and the bishops are heads of the Church, too. There is only one Priest, the Word incarnate, and yet there are thousands of priests dispersed over the face of the earth. Such is the will and permission of the dogma of grace, by reason of which grace is a participation in the mystery of Christ, and not a copy of it or a new and multiplied edition of this mystery, for this mystery is unique. Christ is the author and principle of the Redemption, and in this sense

He is the only Son, the only Head, the only Priest. We are beneficiaries, and not founders. We profit from the grace of another; we exercise the functions of another; but He is the one Lord, together with the Father and the Holy Spirit.

It is in this sense and on this condition that we can speak of the priesthood of bishops and priests. Christ's priesthood is a mystery, the mystery of the Incarnation and of the Redemption. The priesthood of His priests is rather an institution, within the limits set by their potentialities and by the will of Christ.[2]

The Church, inasmuch as she is the body of Christ and receives her life from Him, can aspire to certain functions as well as to certain graces of her Head, provided she recognizes that He is their principle, that she receives them only because of Him, and that she therefore does not enjoy them in the same manner nor by the same right as He. But this inferiority is an added cause for joy, pride, and gratitude. For although the Church possesses nothing in her own right on these levels, she participates all the more perfectly in the riches of Christ in the measure that she brings nothing of her own dowry or of her own resources.

It follows that if we base the entire economy of salvation upon Christ and on that account reserve for Him alone the names that imply the idea of cause and principle, such as the titles of Redeemer, King, and even of Head, we can hope that the attributes that presuppose a dependence, a heredity, a participation, and that for that very reason rest upon an analogy and upon a grace, such as the names of son and priest, may also become ours thanks to a fitting initiation of which Christ Himself has been the author.[3]

---

[2] The Collect of the votive Mass of our Lord Jesus Christ, the supreme Priest, teaches this very exactly when it says with reference to priests: *quos ministros et mysteriorum suorum dispensatores elegit* [Christus], *in accepto ministerio adimplendo fideles inveniantur.*

[3] Christian terminology, which is both traditional and theological, seems to have considerable flexibility in this matter. Christ has certain

In the following chapters we shall see how Jesus initiated His Apostles into the ministry and the grace of His own priesthood. In the end, it was through the institution of a sacrament. This is the favorite means used by the Saviour when He wants to obtain for us, through grace and participation, gifts and favors that we do not possess by nature. Since we are neither sons nor priests by right of birth, it is normally necessary, if we are to become sons or priests gratuitously, that when we receive this superabundance an external sign should show that we are receiving what we did not possess before. That is one of the ends of the sacraments. In a society that is organized by the presence and use of the sacraments, they must appear as collations and octroi in the ancient and feudal meanings of these words, or, in theological language, as efficacious signs.

---

titles and names that God bears because He is man, such as prophet, servant (παις), religious, lamb, etc., and He has other names and titles that man bears because He is God, such as king, head, redeemer, master (magister). The former are transmissible to men by way of grace; the latter are not communicable. The former are usually used with a divine term in the genitive: prophet of the Most High, Thy servant Jesus, religious of the Father, lamb of God, etc.; the latter customarily appear with a term denoting a creature: king of the world, head of the Church, redeemer of men, master of disciples and of brothers.

There are other titles, however, whose meaning depends upon the adjective that modifies them: eternal Son, only-begotten Son, and even first-born Son (for there are adopted sons also); sovereign Priest (in contrast to the priests of Christ).

Lastly, there are names whose meaning is indefinite, that must at times be reserved for Christ alone and at others applied to men through grace, depending on the degree to which they are given their fullest and principal (in the Latin sense) meaning. Such is the title of mediator. In a sense there is only one Mediator, as St. Paul says (I Tim. 2:5). Twenty centuries later, the Encyclical of Pope Pius XI on the Catholic Priesthood, following the evolution of language and the history of the word, used the word in the plural in applying it to Catholic priests. The same remarks could be made concerning the name "pastor," and even the word "bishop" (I Pet. 2:25). The important thing is not to apply these names to Jesus and to His disciples in a univocal sense. There is the priesthood of the Redeemer and the priesthood of His ministers, the latter deriving from the former.

CHAPTER III

The Priesthood of the Apostles

IN THE GOSPEL Jesus devoted all His activities to reconciling men with God, serving as an intermediary between His Father and ourselves, fulfilling in all perfection and beyond every hope the definition of the priest that St. Thomas was later to give: *proprie officium sacerdotii est esse mediatorem inter Deum et homines, inquantum scilicet divina populo tradit (sacerdos = sacra dans), et iterum inquantum preces populi Deo offert, et pro eorum peccatis Deo aliquatenus satisfacit.—* "The office proper to a priest is to be a mediator between God and the people: to wit, inasmuch as he bestows divine things on the people, wherefore sacerdos (priest) means a giver of sacred things, . . . and again, forasmuch as he offers up the people's prayers to God, and, in a manner, makes satisfaction to God for their sins." [1]

And yet, if we may dare say so, Jesus was not jealous of His role, and His greatest desire was to see His twelve favorite disciples acquire the habit of helping Him, of imitating Him, and even on occasion of substituting for Him in His apostolic and religious tasks. The Gospel is also the account of an

---

[1] *Summa,* IIIa, q. 22, a. 2, c. (English translation by the Fathers of the English Dominican Province, published by Benziger Brothers, 1947.)

24

education and an initiation, that of the Apostles to their future ministerial life, their duties, and their powers. It was a progressive transmission of a spiritual heritage in which the pupils followed their Master step by step, so that they would be able to succeed Him in the majority of His functions that are solely concerned with the communication of graces of which Jesus is the author. As for the Redemption itself, it is the personal work of Christ and the consequence of His incommunicable title as only-begotten Son. However, He permitted the Twelve to participate in His prayer and in His ministry, to distribute together with Him the religion of which He is the principle, to join Him in spreading the kingdom that He established.

The Apostles were therefore candidates for the evangelical succession. All that was needed was a supreme gesture which would consecrate them definitively and visibly, two or three words that would establish them in this state, and the Gospel, insofar as it is a religion, would continue in their persons. The redemptive principle had been set down by Christ alone, but He provided for a universal application that presupposed powers like His own and graces derived from His grace.

Succeeding Christ under these conditions, the Apostles adored, prayed, taught, preached, cured, governed, and presided over "the breaking of bread," [2] which, as we shall see, is both the sacramental sign of their powers and the efficacious sign of the redemptive religion of Jesus.

The institution of the priesthood, therefore, is not to be traced from the election of the seventy-two disciples, of which St. Luke speaks.[3] (The pontifical was to cite this episode only in the preliminary advice to the ordinands, and then merely as a figure.) Actually, our Lord gradually entrusted His religious powers not to the disciples but to the twelve Apostles. Whenever there was question, not of the personal conditions

---

[2] Acts 2:42.
[3] Cf. Luke 10:1, 17.

of their perfection and salvation, but of the salvation and the conditions for the salvation of other men, Christ placed the Apostles on His side, on the side of the Mediator that He Himself was. And just as in the messianic visions, He had them sit about Him on the twelve judges' seat, so He entrusted to them upon earth all His functions of liaison, service, teaching, ruling, and authority. The texts that affirm this are the same that serve to prove the foundation of the Church. This is not surprising, inasmuch as the Apostles, as priests, were to be—after Christ—the heads of this mystical, spiritual, but visibly organized body.[4]

The Apostles were assimilated to Christ the Priest in all His ministerial duties. In order to be an intermediary between His Father and men, Jesus had prayed, baptized, sanctified, forgiven sins, exhorted, consoled. He had announced the good news and organized the Church. The Apostles were delegated to all these functions necessary for the extension and exploitation of redemptive grace. The first time St. Peter wanted to define himself as a priest, he as yet possessed no theological vocabulary and so he lisped words destined to resound through the centuries—words that are worth as much as all the theses in our manuals: *nos vero orationi et ministerio verbi instantes erimus.*[5] *Orationi,* that was his priesthood orientated toward God, to adore Him, pray to Him, supplicate Him in the name of men; *ministerio verbi,* this was the preaching of the Gospel, evangelization, the priestly ministry as oriented toward men, to instruct, enlighten, convince, and sanctify them, to unite them to God. There is no isolated theocentrism or anthropocentrism about the priesthood, which is poised between the two, or rather exists for both, adoring God in the name of men, watching over men in order to give them to

---

[4] This demonstration is very well given in the *Dictionnaire de Théologie* (Vacant-Amann), under the word "Ordre," columns 1198 and 1199.

[5] Acts 6:4. "But we will devote ourselves to prayer and to the ministry of the word."

God, and giving God to humanity. Such was the apostolate in the days of the Apostle Peter, when the two words "apostle" and "apostolate" had not yet taken on the narrower meaning they have today, which designates preaching in all its forms, the evangelization of men. It then designated all the combined religious functions of Peter and of the Eleven, through which they prolonged all the religious functions of Jesus, the one and only Pontiff of the New Alliance.

CHAPTER IV

The Institution of the Eucharist and Its Sacerdotal Significance

ON THE NIGHT of Holy Thursday, a few hours before the opening of the Passion—or more exactly at the very beginning of this mystery— the eternal priesthood of Christ and His sacrifice of the following day were inscribed in an institution that was to remain their sacrament or efficacious sign until the end of time. At that moment all these spiritual values became incarnate in a rite in which the Church would always find them under the liturgical vesture that would contain them for us in its own way, at once symbolic and real.

To understand this marvel, we must contemplate it at close range. We must not give the ritual sign the rank of a principle, for this belongs to the mysteries that it contains. Nor must we forget that the institution of the sacrament of the Eucharist assures the invisible and spiritual realities of the Redemption an everyday permanence in our lives, by favoring contact between them and humanity. Jesus was winning His hard-won victory over the religious formalism of the pharisees of all ages, replacing what He destroyed, fulfilling and purifying the hopes and dreams of men, substituting for all our hypocritical magic, for all our ritualistic affectations, the purest and most transparent of all sensible signs. After having for three years preached and established the religion in spirit and in truth, and now that He was about to die for this religion, He had the right to institute upon earth the most powerful of all sacramentalisms which would contain the whole of this religion, which would enable men to see and to touch the invisible, the sacred, and the divine.

He found a liturgical sign that would place the Redemption perpetually before the eyes and in the hands of men—the Redemption that had lasted all His life and was to find its supreme consummation on Calvary, the Redemption that was historical, real, efficacious, that was a sacrifice but not yet a liturgy. Now, all at once He exercised the mysterious, eternal priesthood that had always been His but that He had until then expressed only by veiled interventions into the affairs of daily life. He exercised it with gestures and words wherein the Apostles clearly discerned the heir and the successor to all the pontiffs, priests, and Levites of Israel's long liturgical history: "This is My blood of the new covenant." [1]

But Jesus added: "Do this in remembrance of Me." [2] Until then the priesthood, that we have briefly outlined in the preceding chapter, had lacked consistency. Insofar as it was defined by its resemblance to and its dependence upon the Master's priesthood, it was already filled with all the spiritual values of Christ; however it was neither declared, nor affirmed, nor visibly constituted. The instant Jesus spoke these words, this priesthood became incarnate in its turn in the gesture of the Eucharistic transmission, wherein it too found its efficacious sign.

Lest we fall back into the levitical and pharasaical formalism from which Christ delivered us by His life and His death, we must vigorously seek to understand these great evangelical institutions. We must therefore begin by grasping the significance of a sign in the hands of Jesus and of His Church.

---

[1] Matt. 26:28; Mark 14:24.
[2] Luke 22:19; I Cor. 11:24.

1. *The Sacramental Sign*

The notion of the sign appears at least twice in theology: first, to define miracles; later to define the sacraments. In both cases, manuals seem to take for granted that this term is known, and they do not take the trouble to explain it before they use it. A few oversimplified and sometimes childish examples take the place of psychology, criteriology, and metaphysics, which we might have a right to hope for. What is called for is a presentation of the origin and the use of signs in human life, the method of reasoning and the mode of knowledge to which they give rise, and finally the deep-seated causes that enable us to understand them and to legitimize their importance.

It is the human composite that explains the presence of the sign in the world. Man is an embodied spirit, or if we prefer, a body animated by a soul. The union between these two elements of our nature is so close that the flesh is at the service of the soul, to give it a means of expression and in so doing to become in a sense rational; and on the other hand the intelligence sheds its light upon the slightest movements of our muscles, making them intelligible. When man was thrown upon the earth naked, in his primitive indigence, he already could, because of the unity that reigned within him, find in his body, in the movements that he commanded it to make, in the sounds that he drew out of it, in the attitudes and gestures that he imposed upon it, the means of putting into pictures or at least into symbols his most secret thoughts, and even his sentiments, his emotions, the interior states of his conscience, his wants and desires.

As the intelligence and the will are very intimately related in man, sociologists are following the wrong lead when they ask too insistently whether the sign proceeds from one or the other of these two faculties. To explain the sign and its insertion in the history of rites, beliefs, and civilizations, it is more useful to consider the human body reduced to its outlines, its cries, to see it wholly in the service of ideas, and as being put into motion, animated, and modified by them. Animals have only reflexes, or at most associations of images. Man, on the other hand, with a similar activity of his muscles and vocal cords, makes use of signs. Through the centuries he has made infinite combinations of symbols or words, until he has placed the entire visible world at the service of his field of consciousness. He has succeeded so well in doing this that present-day manuals take for granted that signs are objects outside of us. It is true, they are; but they are always animated in their source by our minds.

In the beginning, signs were our very bodies, the movements of our limbs, the sounds brought forth from our throats. Later on, they were tatooings or necklaces, that is, ornaments inscribed in the flesh or laid upon it. Even then, when the sign moved away from the arms a little, it merely prolonged them. Take for example the flag as we know it today. Did it not come forth in the first place from the human body, from the extremities of the hands and fingers that waved it one day, to stress their pride or their anguish, their will to rally or to call others to their cause, like the white handkerchief on the raft of *La Meduse?* Then the flag detached itself from us, attached itself to a pole, and the pole in turn planted itself in the ground or affixed itself to a wall. In the folds of the material there continues to subsist the invisible idea, and even, if we dare say so, the human mind.

The sign, therefore, is a reality that subsists on two levels, the level of the flesh and the level of the spirit, and its visible portion serves as a symbol of the invisible part. It is a composite value, whose material element represents and can reveal its spiritual content, thanks to a more or less indissoluble similarity between the two, thanks also, as in the human composite for example, to a more or less reciprocal causality between the two.

However, we must insist upon the presence of spirit in matter.

If the sign is really in its origins no more than a muscle

or a vocal cord raised to the dignity of the life of the intelligence and of the will, then it does not distinguish itself by its own signification; or rather it is defined at once by its carnal element and by its spiritual value. It would be a misuse of the sign, ensuing from the use of badly chosen and childish examples that have already been emptied of their psychological meaning, to restrict it to its sensible species, and to say, for example: the tricolor is the emblem of France, smoke is the sign of fire, words are the symbols of ideas, etc. Signs do indeed consist in these objects that are perceptible to the senses, this piece of material, this word, but they also consist in the invisible riches of the mind and will, that are represented, expressed, and contained within the signs. The sign is a synthesis of the visible and the invisible, just like man, who is its author and its subject. A sign is a piece of the human composite that can become intelligible to another human composite. The sign has its own body and soul, a portion that is perceptible to the senses and another that is not, and it consists of the two together.

Thus the sign becomes a language and a means of transmission of human thought for those who already know its signification beforehand and who see the thought under the symbols that represent it. In the beginning, symbolism had to be very natural, in order to be understood quickly. It is said that it afterward became conventional, in the measure that it became separated from its principles, and that memory was obliged to help or take the place of the intelligence in grasping the meaning of symbols.

But in man the intelligence is often balanced by the will: the son of Adam often wants his own thought, he always thinks about what he desires. Moreover, his body is an instrument of action as well as a means of expression. Man therefore makes signs, too, in order to realize what he is intending. A blow on the cheek is as much the effect as the expression of anger. It is the symbol of anger, but it is also the executive agent of this passion.

By all these paths, prolonged into the eminently invisible and spiritual order of the supernatural and divine world, the sign has become man's supreme means of signifying and realizing his religious life, his relations with Divinity, his hope of influencing it through sacrifice and of obtaining its favors through the sacraments. Here again and more than ever, the body of man is at the origin of this action that is both dangerous and sublime, sometimes painful, almost always disturbing, and always respectable. Man has used his poor carnal body, as Péguy would have expressed it, in order to enter into contact with Spirit. He has subjected his body to untold ablutions, incantations, rhythms, and even mutilations, in the wild, incoercible hope of making spirit out of matter—or at any rate of translating into a gesture, a word, or an unction of oil, all the invisible powers that he dreams of expressing, channeling, exorcising, or utilizing!

Under the name of sign (or of sacrament, to use Christian terminology), we sometimes designate both the visible and the invisible parts of the signifying composite, and at other times we designate only its visible portion. The former meaning seems to have been the primitive one, for in the human composite, the body is a sign only on condition of forming a single whole with the soul, of being what it is in union with the soul, that is, an animated body. Otherwise, it dies, it disintegrates, it ceases being a human body. In its origins, the sign signifies what it is, the body of a soul, the movement of a will, the carnal expression of an idea without which it would not exist.

At this point, the human mind's incoercible power of rational distinction intervenes. It dissociates the sign and its signification. By isolating the sign, it causes it to express what it did not express in the beginning. It varies or modifies the meaning that the sign naturally carries within itself. At the utmost limit, we find the lie, the word that says the opposite of what actually is. Between the two extremes, we meet all the varieties of flirtation, diplomacy, worldly conventions,

human expressions that have a double meaning and indefinite
signification. It is behind these subterfuges that the sly, the
hesitant, and the weak take refuge.

Religious sentiment has perhaps taken advantage of this
hiatus between the exterior sign and its signification, to ask
divine power to put into a gesture more than its natural content. It might be better to say that in this great matter, man
has pushed the principle of the gesture beyond its original
limits. The sign has the power to contain the intelligible, that
is, the spiritual, in a muscular or vocal movement. Why should
we not try to encompass the divine itself, or at least the sacred,
in an assemblage of visible signs in which the body would
lend its irreplaceable bodily emotion and its evocative power
to the invisible supernatural? From this have come the idea
and the institution of the efficacious religious rite,—efficacious
of transmitting a value that exceeds it but which divine power
permits it to contain even while it symbolizes or represents it.

We have said: *that exceeds it,* and by this we mean "that
is superior and anterior to it," for this sacred reality already
existed somewhere in the invisible world. But the rite, thanks
to its divine institution, has succeeded in channeling this mystery in order to give it to us, and by showing us that the rite
communicates the mystery to us, it has succeeded in rallying
all our powers of sensibility around the result thus made
tangible. In this way the sign, that we may call the sacrament,
is much more efficacious than was the natural sign in the
beginning. The natural sign contained what it represented
because it was in a way identical with it, and so it was one
with its signification. The sacramental sign, on the other hand,
though sterile by itself when it is merely magic and human,
becomes fruitful and efficacious by reason of a value that is
far superior to it, thanks to the divine institution transmitted
by man's ancestors and by the community.

This value, which was formerly foreign to the sign, is now
within the sign itself. The sign communicates this value to us
ex opere operato. And yet in a sense the value does not come

from the sign. It existed before the sign, and continues to exist without the sign, and God can communicate the value to us without the sign, if He so wills, *ex opere operantis*.

The end result is that the original values are reversed. At the corporeal beginning of the sign, the visible element signified what it was, the body showed that it was animated and therefore that it was a be-souled body. At the other end of the history of the sign the relationship is reversed, but the result is all the more wonderful. By virtue of the omnipotence of God which passes through the word of Christ and of the Church, the sign or the sacrament of bread is what it signifies, it is the body of Christ.

Thus in this singular composite of flesh and spirit, of human and divine, of visible and invisible, whose unity and indissolubility we have been trying to stress, we must also note the different position of the two values. The material element is completely encompassed by the sign of which it is a part. It constitutes exactly and exhaustively the sign's visible portion, and it is indistinguishable from this portion. The spiritual element, on the contrary, is not necessarily contained in the synthesis in which it is included. It lends or rather exchanges itself more than it gives itself, for it possesses a superior existence elsewhere.

The signification, or rather the religious reality signified by the sacramental symbol, is independent of the symbol which momentarily incarnates it, which makes it visible by reason of their union, but does not create it. The grace of baptism may be anterior to the baptism itself. The body of Christ and the redemptive principle of fraternal charity are anterior to the Eucharist, and so on. The sensible symbol and its signification are not two values of the same order that can be added together or substituted for each other. They do not form a single sum, because they do not have a common genus or specific unity and the one does not equal the other. There is no better formula to express their metaphysical relationship than the one Cardinal Billot used to translate his conception of the Eucharistic sacrifice with reference to the sacrifice of the Cross: it is a relationship from the *representative* to the *represented,* from the *multiple* to the *unique.* There is no need to make a pronouncement here on this disputed theology of the Mass. Suffice it to say that this vocabulary seems most usable for providing an understanding of what the symbol is, the nature of its extraordinary dignity and also of its singular humility in the presence of the reality that for a moment becomes incarnate in the lines of the symbol's design, in the words of its formulary.

We always come back to the formula of the Council of Trent: The sacraments contain what they represent, they produce and even cause [in the soul] what they signify.[3] But what they contain is anterior to themselves, for it is the riches of God Himself, overflowing them on all sides. Indeed, the sacraments are obligatory, necessary for salvation, as the Council of Trent also declares.[4] And yet God is not encompassed within the obligations of which He is the author, in the necessities of which He is the legislator. He can give His grace as He pleases, by Himself and without any sacrament, for grace is a participation in His life and the sacraments have created neither this life nor the principle of this participation. While the sacraments are irreplaceable values from the viewpoint of our poor human nature, which feeds upon signs as the food most appropriate to its twofold essence, they are trifles by comparison with the infinite divine riches that they distribute to us drop by drop without ever exhausting them. Even the Eucharist is only a pledge, a token, for there is another way of possessing Christ that surpasses it:

> *ut te revelata cernens facie,*
> *visu sim beatus tuae gloriae.*[5]

---

[3] Cf. Session VII, Canon 6.
[4] Cf. Session VII.
[5] "That I may see Thy countenance unfolding,
    And may be blest Thy glory in beholding."

Now that we have completed our analysis, do we not possess all the secrets of the institution of the sacraments and all the elements of the definition of the sacrament? John of St. Thomas protested in the name of tradition against his fellow theologians who were dazzled by the hylomorphic theory and wanted to see in divine signs simply their matter and their form. "I beg your pardon!" said he, "you are forgetting the signification. You do not see that this matter and this form between them compose still another matter with relation to the spiritual and divine content that they represent, more or less satisfactorily, but which they give us with absolute certainty."[6] In short, we can conclude that the sacraments resemble the Church which they serve perpetually to organize and recreate: *they have a body and a soul.* And the relation of soul and body in the sacrament is the same as that between the soul and body of the Church. According to Christ's will, they should coincide perfectly in mutually edifying each another in the sense of *building* each other. For the Church is a spirit and it is a society; it is at once invisible and visible. Likewise, the sacrament that explains this mystery of unity and realizes it is a spiritual grace and a corporeal gesture, the one in the other, the former anterior to the other and in itself, as in God, independent of the other, but always jealous of incarnating itself in the corporeal, of acting only in union with it, so that the sublime dream of unity that Christ allowed us to glimpse before His departure may at last be fulfilled in man, in the world, and in history. It is the dream that the Church may be so holy and so completely composed of saints, so Catholic and so human, that her body shall be coextensive with her soul, and vice versa; it is the dream that all the sons of God shall

---

[6] *"Verba et res compositum faciunt cui supervenit significatio sacramentalis . . ."* And elsewhere: *"conjunctio realis materiae et formae in sacramentis est ordo fundamentalis quo ista duo ordinatur, ut sint unum subjectum reale significationis sacramentalis . . . cum significatum ejus sit gratio . . ."* John of St. Thomas, *Cursus theologicus, de Sacramentis in genere,* q. 40, a. 6, *dubium secundum.*

be baptized and instructed in the truth; that all visible creatures shall belong to God as much as does the heavenly kingdom. And in all this there is the primacy of charity: an unbeliever in good faith and in the state of grace is worth infinitely more than a baptized Christian in the state of mortal sin. And while our first wish must be that baptized Christians shall also be Christians in grace, the supreme triumph of the Incarnation and of the sacramental institution that prolongs it would be that all the sons of God should be reached in their flesh by the historical Church and by the corporeal gestures of the Son of God—in other words, that they be baptized, anointed, nourished by the sacraments, so that out of their bodies and souls a single being would be supernaturally produced—a being that belongs wholly to God: *ut sint unum*.

Now we begin to understand what the priesthood means in the Church and what is the exact value of the sacrament that confers the priesthood upon men.

2. *The Sacramental Sign of the Priesthood of Christ*

Let us apply our analysis of signs to the great matters that concern us. Jesus was a priest before the institution of the Eucharist, and even without the Eucharist Christ's death on the Cross would still have been the perfect and redemptive sacrifice. And yet the Eucharist contains, within the rite of offering up bread and wine, the sacrifice and therefore the oblation and immolation of the sacrifice of the Cross. Without the sacrifice of Calvary, the Eucharist would be nothing but a sterile liturgy. But this symbolic liturgy reminds us that the death of Christ which is contained within it was a sacrifice. By providing the victim, the Eucharistic liturgy permits us to profit from the fruits of Calvary which are necessary for our daily needs.

Jesus was not constituted a priest by His priestly demeanor at the Last Supper, or by the words He pronounced and the sacrificial gestures He made. He had been a priest since His

Incarnation. And yet it was at this moment that He revealed His priesthood, by informing His Apostles that the following day He would accept death upon the Cross as the priest of His own sacrifice.

The institution of the Eucharist which just a moment ago revealed to us, applied to us, and realized for us the sacrifice of the Cross, now discloses to us the priesthood of Christ, and continues to keep this priesthood in action for our spiritual profit.

But we can and must go further, pursuing the same methods of reasoning until we come to the institution of the priesthood of the Apostles. While the collation of the power to celebrate, which was transmitted to them by the words of the institution of the Eucharist, does not of itself define their priesthood, it is an efficacious sign of it. Since they had no title or personal right to this function which was beyond their capacities, they needed to be admitted to it by God before they would dare to exercise it, and they needed to be initiated into it in a visible and organized Church, by a visible, liturgical, ritual sign, in which would be recognized the reality and regularity of the transmission of this and other powers they would henceforth exercise in the name of Christ.

And so the priesthood of Christ became a sacrament thanks to the institution of the Eucharist, but it was anterior to this institution in which it finally became liturgically incarnate. It already existed without this rite, that does not define it and therefore does not constitute it. Moreover, it is because of this incontestable truth that the author of the *Epistle to the Hebrews* was able to construct an entire theology, and even an entire metaphysics of the priesthood and sacrifice of Christ, without once alluding to the Eucharist. He accepted the challenge of constructing the synthesis of the mystery of the Redemption without speaking of the sacrament in which this mystery is given to us each morning upon our altars. And it is even in this lawful independence of any liturgy that he saw one of the causes for the transcendence of the priesthood of

Christ, *secundum ordinem Melchisedech,* by comparison with the ritualistic priesthood of the Hebrew high priest, *secundum ordinem Aaron.* Christ is a priest in His two natures, the divine and the human, which, in the unity of the Person of the Son, make of Him the one Mediator and eternal intercessor. He was also a priest, therefore, on the day when He immolated Himself on the Cross and prepared His triumphant entry into heaven at the right hand of the Father. Christ is a priest because He is God and man; He is Priest, Saviour, Redeemer, because, through His death and Resurrection, He has reconciled us with God, because He has merited life for us and given it to us; but since He is a priest by nature, by His twofold nature, He began His work with the Incarnation, through which He continues to sanctify us. For Him, being a priest does not mean first of all the performing of certain rites, but adoring God and saving the world; and this is the purpose of His priesthood. This priesthood presupposes the exercise of all religious, apostolic, and redemptive functions, with the exalted charity of salvation which Christ has never ceased showing for His Father and His brothers.

The priesthood of the only-begotten Son, therefore, is not a Levitical priesthood; and its sacrifice, which is identical with the supreme act of the Redemption, is not first of all a ritual sacrifice. The similarities that the author of the *Epistle to the Hebrews* has so strongly emphasized between the mystery of Jesus and the priestly and sacrificial institutions of the Old Testament, in order to establish the dogma of Christ, both Priest and Victim, lead in the end to the thesis of the transcendence of Jesus. Jesus is a perfect Priest and Victim only because He is not a priest and victim after the manner of Aaron and of the holocausts. This rather delicately shaded doctrinal position might almost be repugnant to our Western theology which rests entirely on the opposition between "yes" and "no," but which must in this case acquiesce to a more flexible view of the mystery. After all, we are already familiar with this paradox of Christianity, which is a sacramentalist religion only because it is now and wants to continue to be a religion in spirit and in truth. Here again we return to the mystery of the sacraments.

To repeat, what is a sacrament if not a rite that contains riches anterior to itself, and without which it be nothing but a vain gesture of magic or formalism? Without these riches, it would still be a value that we could not reach except through it, because of the exigencies of our nature: our animal and sensible nature, which remains what is even when it is under the influence of spirit, our own and God's; a nature that can live by the invisible life of God only by agreeing to pass through the visible symbols that transmit God's life to us. Inversely, the Incarnation and the Redemption, divine mysteries that were historically realized once and for all, take on ritual species, even though they are not rites, so as to be better adapted to our nature.

We know through the *Synoptic Gospels* and through the *First Epistle to the Corinthians* that Christ has sacramentally represented this mystery of the Redemption and enclosed it in an efficacious sign, the Eucharist. We know that it suffices for us to celebrate the mystery of the Eucharist in order to participate in all the effects of Calvary. When Christ instituted this liturgy, He gave ritual expression to a priesthood which was not predominantly concerned with rites, and which in itself is not so concerned even now. For the death of Christ on the Cross and His entrance into heaven at the right hand of the Father constitute a sacrifice, and even the only sacrifice; a sacrifice that is more beautiful and greater than the liturgical sacrifices of the old law and even of all the superior religions. And yet Christ's death and Resurrection do not constitute a liturgy. Now, by reason of the Last Supper, they can become incarnate in a sacramental rite which is at our service. Here we find again all the relationships we have already studied between soul and body, between signification and sign, between reality and sacrament.

The liturgical or unbloody sacrifice of the Eucharist is a

sign: *sacrificium sacrificii invisibilis sacramentum visibile, id est, sacrum signum est,* as St. Augustine expressed it. Now, a sacramental sign is related as a symbol to the hidden reality that it outwardly expresses and that it produces in men's souls thanks to its institution by Christ. It is not related to this reality as a complement, and even less as a value of the same order that could be added to this invisible content. It is an efficacious symbol of this reality, therefore a copy, an image, a figure, and an operative figure. The grace of baptism and baptism itself do not constitute two graces, any more than a man and his portrait make two men. In scholastic terms, these two values are contraries, and this does not mean that they are opposed to each other but that that they do not have a common genus. One of them may serve to give the picture or to bring up the memory of the other, or even to give the other, but it cannot define the other. The portrait of a man allows our eyes to see and to evoke him, but it does not express his essence, any more than the thing that represents defines the thing it represents, or the ambassador the king who has sent him.[7]

This position is neither scandalous nor disconcerting. It is illuminating. It merely shows that the Eucharist depends upon Calvary, and not the contrary. It shows also that the Church can add this sacrament to the Redemption, provided Jesus has instituted the Eucharist in efficacious remembrance of Calvary. Ontologically speaking, however, the historical Redemption comes first and is sufficient to itself without its sacrament. It may be that the Redemption alone would not suffice for the psychology of human nature, as the Council of

---

[7] Father Danielou holds that this idea of the coexistence of two spiritual values, one depending upon the other and not the contrary, making it impossible to add them together or to replace one by the other, is the point on which the Catholic mind and the Protestant mind are most profoundly opposed, the Catholics affirming it and the Protestants denying it. Cf. his essay, "Protestantisme français," in the collection *Présences* (Paris: Plon, 1945), p. 438.

Trent has indicated,[8] but that is another matter. If Jesus had not instituted the breaking of the bread, He would still have been the Priest and Victim of the New Alliance on Calvary. We might have seen it less clearly, and understood it less explicitly. But the fact of which the author of the *Epistle to the Hebrews* spoke is no less certain.

The sacrifice of the altar has value, reality, significance, and efficacy only because of the anterior sacrifice of the Cross, to which it is identified. Now, it was first of all on Calvary that Christ exercised His pontificate. The priesthood of Christ, therefore, while it has its own rite, is not primarily ritualistic, but historically redemptive. The Eucharistic sacrifice, which is a sacrament, presupposes an anterior reality which it incarnates but does not create. Christian rites presuppose a spiritual and historical content, and not the opposite.

Such is the exact place of sacramentalism in the religion of Jesus Christ: The Eucharist is an obligatory institution for us, and in conformity with our ritualistic nature; it is dependent upon an anterior reality that is not ritual, but concrete and historical, as well as moral and spiritual.

This entire doctrine is to be found in the Council of Trent, Session XXII, Chapter 1, in which, as Cardinal Billot has so well remarked, the two strong conjunctions *etsi* and *tamen* place in juxtaposition ("in opposition" in the sense Aristotle gave these words in his logic) an historical sacrifice that is valid by itself, and a sacramental sacrifice that multiplies the historical sacrifice without wronging it, since it owes all its value to it.

Now, we need only draw our conclusions. The priesthood of

---

[8] Council of Trent, Session XXII, Chap. 1: *"Sicut hominum natura exigit."*—The notion of rite implies an obligation, imposed upon men by God, of following exactly certain material conditions in order to obtain the spiritual result that is sought. Now, since Christ, through the hypostatic union, is the sacrament personally and permanently, He needs no rites in order to save us. He is subject to no order anterior or exterior to Himself.

Christ is anterior to the institution of the Eucharist, and the sacrifice of Calvary had no need of the Eucharist in order to exist and to save us. And yet the Eucharist, which would not have existed without the sacrifice of the Cross, contains this sacrifice, whereas the Cross did not necessitate the Eucharist. Thus the order of all these sacred values is explained and respected.

For the same motives, the priesthood of Christ, which was communicated to the Apostles through the right that Christ granted them of consecrating the Eucharist, extends far beyond this power, not only in Christ but even in the Apostles. For the power to consecrate is but the sign of the realities it contains but which extend beyond it.

If we reread the first chapter of the Twenty-second Session of the Council of Trent, we shall see that the priesthood of Christ is anterior to the Eucharist, that the Eucharist would not exist without Calvary, and that nonetheless it is in and through the institution of the Eucharist that Christ declared Himself and therefore revealed Himself to be a priest. Likewise, the Apostles, in their quality as cooperating disciples and co-founders, were able to be initiated into the apostolic and priestly functions of Christ before the institution of the Eucharist. However it was the institution of the Eucharist, inasmuch as it conferred precise sacramental and sacrificial powers, that not only declared but actually instituted them as priests.

This is all very logical.

Before the granting of these powers, everything was amorphous, indefinite, confused. These powers specify, organize, and establish *order*. Indeed, this is the very name of these powers. It is an admirable thing. By their very presence they constitute a hierarchy, for the Apostles, who possessed these powers in their totality, could communicate them in greater or lesser degree, in part, dependently and subordinately. The twelve founders imitated and made incarnate in the sacramental institution the differences in authority that, while they did not exist among themselves with the exception of Peter, existed between them and the other disciples.

The priesthood of Christ, which is indivisible in His person, is divisible in the sacrament in which He is signified: It is possible to participate more or less in the priestly and apostolic functions of the Lord, in the measure that one participates more or less in the sacrament of His priesthood. Again, the reason is not that this priesthood is defined by its sacramental powers or that its essence is completely encompassed by them. It is because these powers render the essence of the priesthood visible and organize it, thereby creating a hierarchy among the members who participate in it. Thus, in the Church there is participation in the priesthood of the Apostles in the measure that the powers of Order, that is the sacramental powers, are received from them.

If the Twelve, anticipating the problems that were really to arise only at their death, communicated to others all their powers at once, as did happen for Matthias and later for Paul, they were really creating other apostles, later to be called bishops, their successors. If on the other hand, they kept their superior functions for themselves and imposed hands only to give over a part of their powers, they ordained simple priests. And even if these priests had in the beginning received, under the name of *presbyteri-episcopi,* all the powers of Order, including the power to impose hands in their turn, they would still have received these powers in sacramental dependence upon the authority of the ordaining Apostle, and consequently at a subordinate level. In short, they would not be truly bishops. Finally, the deacons received even less, but what they possess is still magnificent. For, dependent upon the priests, they also participate in the priestly functions of Christ Himself. Beyond that, abstracting from the lesser ministers who were created only much later under sacramental conditions that are still under discussion today, there is in the Church, in the diffused state, only the priesthood in the broad sense of I Peter 2:9.

CHAPTER V

The Priesthood of the Bishop

OUR LORD JESUS CHRIST instituted His Apostles priests when He said: *hoc facite in meam commemorationem*. He then laid the foundation stone of a priestly or hierarchical sacrament that is called Order or Orders.

These propositions are of faith. They are defined by the Council of Trent, Session XXII, Canon 2, and Session XXIII, Canons 3 and 6. In Session XXII, the Council's precise intention was to affirm that the Eucharist is a sacrifice, and in this perspective it taught that the ministers of this sacrament are really priests when they offer it up and because they offer it up. In Session XXIII, the Council sought first of all to teach that the Christian priesthood is hierarchical, that it, shared in inferior and superior degrees that are rightly called *Orders*. It did not then specify the number of these orders, but informed us that they are at least three in number: the episcopacy, the presbyterate (or priesthood), and the ministers. The Council also affirmed that this priesthood is not merely a ministry of preaching, but also a sacrificial and sacramental power. It tied the priesthood in its entirety to its institution by our Lord, and thus placed Order or Orders among the seven sacraments of the New Law.

There are two different theological methods of presenting

and demonstrating this vast thesis, which presupposes the existence of two somewhat dissimilar definitions of the priesthood within the very doctrine taught by the Council of Trent. By extension, this would imply two divergent views on the sacramental relationships between the episcopacy and the presbyterate or priesthood. One of these views is less favorable to the communitarian concept, the other favors it much more.

All authors agree with the Council of Trent that our Lord ordained His Apostles priests when He said to them: "Do this in remembrance of Me." But some consider this Eucharistic gesture to be the conclusion and the efficacious sign of a reality long since prefigured in the souls of the Apostles, somewhat the way the baptism of adult catechumens simply establishes and regularizes a life of grace and faith that has already been granted invisibly to these neophytes in the course of their long preparation. For other theologians, however, this gesture and these words of Jesus on Holy Thursday suffice in themselves to exhaust the definition of the priesthood. They see in them the beginning as well as the terminating point of the work of institution. And since there is no mention of the episcopacy in this text, bishops would presumably have been instituted in another manner and at another time. For these authors, the principle of the priesthood is to be found in the simple priest and in the power to celebrate the Eucharist. In the position that is more favorable to the concept of community, it is the episcopate that comes first in the definition of the priesthood, just as it comes first in the hierarchy.

We shall review these two opinions in detail beginning with the more individualistic one.

I.

Among theologians, there are some who rightly stress that the celebration of the Eucharist is the sacramental sign of the sacrifice of the Cross, which is the one and only Christian sacrifice. But they take advantage of this fact to relate and even to reduce the priesthood essentially to the power to consecrate the Eucharist and to administer the other sacraments that prepare for or prolong the Eucharist. And starting from this point of view, they present the institution of the sacrament of Order as follows:

The Apostles were ordained priests in the Cenacle, when the Saviour permitted and commanded them to renew, in His memory, the breaking of the bread or the Last Supper, more exactly, when He said to them: *hoc facite in meam commemorationem*. Earlier (and also later, for example in John 20:23) they received other powers, those that made them, in addition, the heads of the Church.

Driven to its ultimate conclusion, this position presupposes that bishops and priests are equal with respect to their essential priestly power, and that the hierarchic functions of the bishops are added to this primary power from without and yet do not go beyond it. The partisans of this view are led to hold that the episcopacy is not an Order. *Episcopatus magis est dignitas quam ordo,* says St. Thomas in his fourth opuscule, *De articulis fidei et Ecclesiae sacramentis.* And the Commentary on the Sentences says clearly: *Episcopatus non est ordo.*[1] The passage that is of interest to us is, moreover, rather disturbing. St. Thomas begins by excluding the episcopacy from the list of the seven Orders, which are, according to him, the priesthood, the diaconate, the sub-diaconate, and the four minor Orders. Then he makes a distinction: as a sacrament, that is, as a power over the Eucharist the episcopacy is equal to the priesthood and is not a new Order; but insofar as it is an office concerned with sacred actions exercised over the mystical body, it exceeds the priesthood and it is even a superior Order. This view has the disadvantage of presupposing that there is no parallelism between the powers over the Eucharistic body and the powers over the mystical body.

---

[1] *In IV Sent.,* q. 40, a. 5. This is a work of St. Thomas' youth, which was transformed by the editors of his works into a Supplement to the *Summa Theologica*.

The thought of St. Thomas in this delicate matter does not have the rigorism that we are criticizing. We are attributing such rigorism to this theological view in order to criticize it more easily; but we are doing this without attributing it to any particular person. We hold that this conception involves the following consequences: the sacrament of Order impresses a character; it gives powers, rather than communicates a grace, that is, a participation in the holiness of Christ. To be more exact: it gives a grace only because the powers that it confers demand holiness. Is this not an edulcoration of the definition of the sacraments—*which are efficacious signs of grace*—that would apply to the sacrament of Order only indirectly, *in obliquo.*

And yet this presentation is quite widespread. It is of a nature to frighten many priests and above all candidates for the priesthood. From St. John Chrysostom, who in his youth enumerated in his *De sacerdotio libri sex* all the formidable perils of the priesthood and of the episcopacy with the intention of escaping these burdens himself, to the famous dictum of the author of the *Imitation of Christ: non alleviasti onus tuum,*[2] an atmosphere of holy terror surrounds this conception of a priesthood that confers powers before conferring a grace, powers that are definite and crushing, and an uncertain, indefinable grace.

The partisans of this position may answer by saying: it is an uncontested thesis of the Church that an ordinand in the state of mortal sin does not receive the grace of the sacrament, but receives notwithstanding its character and powers. To this we reply that an ordination received in this way is an accident and even a sacrilege, and that we must not define the institutions of Christ by the monstrous and rare exceptions to which our sins sometimes drive them, for then the intention of the Saviour is ignored and His will is violated.

We can go further in refuting the opinion under discussion.

[2] Book IV, Chapter 5.

Pushed to the limit in its more or less avowed theological retrenchments, this view suppresses a part of the doctrines that we hoped we had solidly established in the earlier chapters of this book. Not only is the priesthood of bishops and priests, which is considered equal in both, reduced to the celebration of the Eucharistic sacrifice; but by way of consequence or of principle, the priesthood of Christ Himself, instead of animating His entire evangelical ministry and His whole life, is said to have been exercised only on Calvary and at most also at the Last Supper.[3] Other authors do not seem to hesitate before this extreme reduction, which is unfortunately logical with their point of departure, and which has the disadvantage of requiring a complete reorganization of our ideas concerning the mystery of Christ, and a much sharper separation between the Saviour's various names and titles.

Following this path, some even go so far as to distinguish between Christ the Priest, the source of the priesthood, and Christ the Pontiff, the source of the episcopacy. It would follow that Jesus does not exercise His priesthood at all times, but at certain moments is content to exercise His functions as doctor, founder, or legislator. It is as if Christianity in His person sometimes ceased being a religion, as if this doctrine, this institution, these laws and this moral teaching—indeed, as if this society which is the Church were not always and essentially religious, that is, indissolubly bound to the priesthood of the Head, who Himself is defined by the Incarnation of the Son of God!

On the canonical and ascetic plane, this theology entails consequences that seem equally regrettable.

The state of life of the diocesan priest becomes very difficult to conceive, define, and organize. If the priesthood consists solely in the unadorned power to celebrate Mass and to administer the sacraments, if it does not presuppose, after ordina-

---

[3] Cf. *Dictionnaire de Théologie Catholique,* the word "Jésus-Christ," column 1240. The author does not insist upon this opinion, which he may be using only as an *obiter dictum.*

tion, any further relations with the episcopacy other than extra-sacramental relations of jurisdiction and obedience, then it leaves those who are clothed with these priestly powers somewhat in the air and without help. Ordinations become individual matters. The grace of the priesthood, correlative to personal and absolute powers, is also an individualized grace. The state of life of the priest is rooted elsewhere, upon another principle, upon the diocesan distribution of nominations or of posts (they were formerly called benefices), that has no intrinsic relation to the grace of the sacrament of Order. When the priesthood is conferred upon religious, these men already possess a state of life far better organized than that of the diocesan clergy, and an obligatory and far superior ascesis that saves them from this sacramental individualism.

While the so-called secular priest is placed in an inferior position by comparison with religious, he is no less separated from the laity because of the sanctity of his powers that require him to remain apart and to reserve himself for his special sublime functions.

Since the primary effect of ordination has been to confer upon the priest these isolated powers, he has no other resources with which to keep himself worthy of their demands than to borrow from ascetic rules, that is, from the state of life of religious, means of sanctification that his own state of life does not give him even though it obliges him to live the perfect life.

Let us stop here. But does logic stop, especially when it has started from too narrow a principle? Besides, the dialectical subconscious will continue to function. In the last analysis, are not these powers that the priest is to exercise conceived as merely ritual powers for the exercise of the cult? But is that not returning to the Old Testament, to a Levitical conception of the Christian priesthood, something that our Saviour would have wanted to avoid at all costs? Is not such a religion merely a religion of justice, a cult, rather than a religion of love that would encompass justice in a charity that overflows it and alone defines these relations with God which the Christian priest is supposed to establish? We have now turned away from the priesthood of Melchisedech, to which we had returned with the *Epistle to the Hebrews* in order to find Christ, and come back to the priesthood of Aaron, and we know what St. Paul said about Aaron's priesthood.

And do you not recognize this holiness by its very separation? It is another idea from the Old Testament, which the Gospels have left behind and replaced by a new and much more dynamic concept of holiness, conceived as a charitable action in the heart of the mass: *vos estis lux mundi, sal terrae. Non rogo ut tollas eos de mundo. Ite, docete, praedicate.*[4]

When the priesthood is separated from the episcopacy, it ends by emptying itself of Christian vigor. Let us face the facts. Without denying the Old Testament, which is a shadow and a figure for us, we must go beyond it.

2.

The other group of theologians also remember—and if possible even more vividly—that the celebration of the Eucharist is a sign, the sign of a deeper reality, namely, the Redemption. They do not forget that the Redemption is possible only because Jesus Christ is the Son of God made man, that is to say, our mediator, and that in this capacity He is the supreme priest. Christ exercised this mediation during His whole life—a mediation that is a religion of love and adoration before God, an apostolate and salvation for men. With reference to both God and man, it is identified with the redemptive exercise of charity, in which the new law consists: charity toward God, charity that does not deny the cult we owe Him, His rights as Creator, and our obligations in justice, and yet ful-

---

[4] It is interesting to note that the first time the New Testament speaks of priests being "set apart" it is in order to separate them from their brother priests and to throw them into the mass to be conquered. (Cf. Acts 13:2.)

fills these obligations in a transcendent manner by submerging them in a sentiment, an attitude, indeed a love that is much deeper; charity toward men, for whom Christ wills the greatest good, namely, their salvation through union with God.

In this supernatural and as it were unlimited concept of mediation or of the priesthood, Christ's life is totally embraced—His prayers, lessons, examples, teaching, preaching, and finally His supreme gesture of charity for God and for men, namely, His death on the Cross, the greatest of sacrifices, and beyond that, His unending mediation in heaven. It is this entire ministry of religion and salvation that constitutes the priestly function of Jesus and that led Him to the obedience of the Cross, which is itself sacramentally and therefore efficaciously signified in and through the celebration of the Eucharist.

In Christ, the Eucharist is the sensible sign of the exercise of His mediatory function; and among us it is the efficacious sign of our participation in His holy religion. The celebration of the Eucharist does not by itself alone constitute the exercise of the priesthood. It presupposes the exercise of the priesthood, and it is its visible, ritual, and fruitful sacrament. A man appears to be a priest and he is a priest, under the new law, to the extent that he has the power to celebrate the Eucharist. Did not Christ Himself definitively reveal and manifest His priesthood in the very act by which He instituted the sacramental sacrifice? But just as His priesthood was not limited to this act, so the priesthood of His priests is not limited to this power that institutes them as priests, but which by itself does not constitute the priesthood.[5]

---

[5] Cf. G. Bardy, "Le sacerdoce chrétien d'après les Pères," in *La Vie Spirituelle* for October, 1937, pp. 22-23: "The mission [of the bishop in the epistles of St. Ignatius of Antioch] is incontestably more extensive [than that of the Jewish priest], since it also includes teaching of doctrine, spiritual government, control of morals, . . . [in addition to] the celebration of the Eucharist, which is the supremely sacerdotal function."

After Christ's example, the priesthood is defined among His successors and mandatories by the incessant exercise of this multiform mediatory function that we have just admired in Jesus and in which His successors participate through grace. Whereas the grace of baptism is shared among all of us on a level of equality, the grace of the priesthood is exercised as it were from above, from the level where he comes into contact with God to render to Him duties of adoration and love in the name of humanity, and thus to inaugurate, within the charity that is directed to God, the service of neighbor and charity toward him. The grace of the priesthood is exercised from above especially with respect to the neighbor, who is approached with authority[6] in order to make him rise to the supernatural plane and in order likewise to maintain toward him this attitude of mediation, that is at once superior, condescending, and charitable, and that is part of the Christian concept of the priesthood.

This conception of the Christian priesthood, in which the episcopate comes first and constitutes the historical and sacramental principle of all the orders, presupposes an entirely different demonstration of its institution by Christ—a demonstration that differs in its breadth and solidity from the one we have just discussed. It is the conception we had been using in the preceding chapters.

Just as the Eucharist is the sacrament of the Redemption, but is not itself the Redemption and does not constitute it, so the power to celebrate the Eucharist is the sacrament of the priesthood that it confers, but it does not exhaust the notion of the priesthood. Our Lord instituted His Apostles priests when he said: *Hoc facite in meam commemorationem.* But actually their priesthood is defined by their participation in the priesthood of Christ, that is, in His universal function as Mediator.

---

[6] Cf. II Cor. 5:20: "On behalf of Christ, therefore, we are acting as ambassadors, God, as it were, appealing through us."

Under these conditions, it is the Apostles as Apostles who were ordained priests. That is why the true sacramental priesthood, the complete and integral sacramental priesthood, is that of the Apostles and not that of priests.[7] The expression that attributes to the episcopacy the plenitude of the priesthood —an expression which has so often been left undefined and unexplained—now takes on its full force and lucidity. The episcopacy is not only an Order, it is the supreme Order. It consists, by virtue of a sensible, efficacious sign, in the power to celebrate Mass, to administer the sacraments, and in the power to give these powers to others; but it also consists in many other functions that constitute the apostolate properly speaking, that is, together with the service of God in prayer, the evangelization of the Jews and Gentiles, the preparation of believers for baptism and the other sacraments, the governing of the Church or the pastorate, in sum, the spiritual paternity that begets and preserves souls in the faith.

---

[7] Reduced to these proportions, namely, that the episcopacy is an Order and that it constitutes the fullness of the priesthood and of the sacrament of Order, this opinion is said to be that of the "moderns," that is, in the present case of the majority of theologians beginning with and including Bellarmine. Even the Dominicans are tending to accept it more and more. Father Périnelle, O.P., says: "The episcopacy really comes first. Everything was given to the Apostles, and the bishop is as it were their heir. The presbyterate derives from the apostolate-episcopate; it even makes its appearance after the diaconate, and with a less original aspect than the diaconate." (*Revue des Sciences philosophiques et théologiques* [de Kain], 1930, p. 250.) Later, Father Périnelle published a curious little book entitled *Le Sacerdoce* (Paris: Editions du Cerf, 1935), which, on the whole, is written in accordance with the views of the "ancients."— For a good discussion of this matter, see the *Dictionnaire de Théologie catholique* (Vacant-Amann), under the word "Ordre," column 1383.

This doctrinal problem is independent of the question whether the ordination of a deacon to the episcopacy, without having him pass through the priesthood, is valid. We must answer that it depends upon the intention of the Church, which no longer does this at the present time and probably no longer wants it done. But it seems very probable that it was otherwise in the beginning.

These functions are eminently holy and sanctifying in themselves. The bishop can and must, like all other Christians, seek elsewhere for extrinsic means of sanctification. But to become perfect, let him first of all exercise his functions, which are the exercise of charity toward God and neighbor, for perfection consists in this charity.

Now, although the episcopacy does not consist simply in the power to validly celebrate the rites of sacrifice and of the sacraments, it is no less true that apostolic and pastoral charity, which defines the episcopal state as well as the state of perfection proper to the bishop, possesses an efficacious sign in which it is sacramentally represented and realized. This sign is the Eucharist. The Eucharist contains charity and creates unity, because it is the body of Christ Himself, who reconciled God with man, and men among themselves. Moreover the Eucharist symbolizes this unity of the Church even as it produces it, because from all the scattered breads on all the altars of the world it brings forth a single body—the body that was born of the Virgin Mary and that was immolated on the Cross so that we might be one, as the Father and the Son are one.

When the bishop celebrates the Holy Sacrifice of the Mass, therefore, he does not interrupt this apostolic activity that requires him to spread the kingdom of God, everywhere, to disseminate the knowledge of the Father and of the Son, in which eternal life consists. But he concentrates this unity and charity which are in his care in an eminently efficacious as well as symbolic rite. Without ever ceasing to be a bishop anywhere or at any moment, he is never more a bishop, at least on the level of efficacious sacramental signs, than when he mounts the altar steps to begin once again the eternal mystery of charity, and to renew, thanks to the unique sacrifice, the unity of the mystical body, in the image of and through the virtue of the unity of the Eucharistic body.

The bishop must be holy and filled with charity everywhere and always—when he speaks, when he makes visits, when he commands, when he baptizes, when he confirms, when he administers the Church, when he presides over assemblies of priests and of the faithful. But he demonstrates ritually that he is holy, and he performs the sacramental act that makes him holy when he celebrates the mystery of the death of the Lord, the death that saved and sanctified us,—when he offers up the sacrifice that reconciles us to God and unites us to our brothers.

In this sense the Eucharist, regardless of how many definitions can be given of it, is the efficacious and exacting sign of the holiness of the bishop, who must be holy because he is heir to the redemptive charity of Christ.

Thus understood, this theory of the origins of the priesthood, identified with those of the episcopate and consecrated by the institution of the Eucharist—this theory is strong enough to take over the first opinion, to which it gives a very acceptable meaning. To conclude, we can reconcile the two theological views by interpreting one through the other. When it is clearly understood that a sacrament is a sensible sign that contains and consequently presupposes an anterior spiritual reality which it has the power to confer, there is no cause for astonishment that the power of consecrating the Eucharist, which is itself a sacrament, presupposes, as does the Eucharist, an anterior reality that it transmits. And in the case of the sacrament of Order, this anterior reality, this real spiritual value, is precisely the ministerial participation in the mediatory functions of the Word incarnate for the salvation of the world.

It is true that before the sacrament, and in the present instance before the institution of the Eucharist (or before the ordination, in the case of the priest), nothing has been done for our benefit or for that of the visible Church. We cannot say, however, that nothing at all has been done. For a spiritual reality already exists, namely, the sacerdotal grace; and this grace is not exhausted but efficaciously signified by the power to celebrate the Eucharist. Since the sacerdotal grace and the Eucharistic power are not of the same order, they cannot be added together. It no longer makes sense to ask, as we had agreed to do in the beginning, whether a man is a priest by reason of the power to celebrate *or* by participation in the mediatory functions and graces of Christ. For a man is a priest by reason of both, in two different senses, on two parallel levels, the level of the sign and that of its content. Consequently, a man who has received the power to celebrate the Eucharist can and even must *ipso facto* regularly exercise all the apostolic functions of Christ. Conversely, no one can legitimately take Christ's place in His ministry of mediation unless he has received the power to consecrate the Eucharistic body.

The marvel of Catholicism is that a sign should contain and require a grace. But then, we must be sure to keep the two values, the sign and the grace, and by this we do not get two different definitions but two necessarily complementary definitions of the priesthood, the one within the other. The hypothesis of a personal priesthood anterior to ordination is moreover impossible, because Order is a hierarchical sacrament, that is conferred only by transmission from superior to inferior, in contradistinction to baptism that can be conferred by a person who has not even received it himself. The fact remains, however, that it is not the rite that constitutes the priesthood, for the priesthood is defined as a participation in the sacerdotal grace and functions of Christ before it is conferred by the power to celebrate the Eucharist. Conversely, the ritual power to celebrate the Eucharist presupposes, when it is thoroughly understood with all that it contains, that the one who exercises this liturgical function participates in the totality of Christ's sacerdotal grace and priestly functions.[8]

---

[8] This would be one of the deep meanings of the recommendation of the pontifical at the ordination of priests, which has been commented upon so often: *agnoscite quod agitis, imitamini quod tractatis.*—On the successive and progressive meanings of the verb *tractare,* culminating in this text of the pontifical, we can find an excellent memorandum by Canon Bardy in *Recherches de Sciences religieuses,* April, May, June, 1946, No. 25, Tome 33.

While the proofs of this book were being corrected, the great com-

By straining the habitual sense of these words a little, we might dare to say that each day the priest offers up the sacrifice of Christ twice, or perhaps that he exercises the priesthood of Christ in two ways. He exercises this priesthood once ritually, and indeed really, when he celebrates Mass. He exercises it in another way the rest of the day, as he accomplishes the works of his ministry of priestly charity—a ministry that is subordinated to that of the bishop, as we shall see in the following chapter. These two modes cannot be added together, nor do they replace one another. The celebration of the Holy Sacrifice of the Mass is the sacramental sign of the apostolic ministry, the latter being normally and necessarily the principle as well as the consequence of the former.

---

mentary of Father Spicq, O.P., on the Pastoral Epistles was published: *The Mystery of Godliness,* Ceslaus Spicq, O.P., Fides Publishers, Chicago 10, Ill. In dealing with the origins of the episcopate it would seem to confirm the positions here presented. There is another excellent article on priestly spirituality in the New Testament in *La Vie Spirituelle* for November, 1947.

CHAPTER VI

The Priesthood of the Simple Priest

THE DEFINITION of the priesthood of simple priests evidently depends upon the conception of the episcopal priesthood in the preceding chapter. Let us for the sake of clarity review the distinction between the two theories as we have explained them.

The first theological view seems to have the highest esteem for the presbyteral priesthood, which we ordinarily call the priesthood, for it sets it up as the highest level of the sacrament of Order, thus putting it on an equal footing with the episcopacy. But this honor costs the one to whom it is attributed very dearly! And how strangely it diminishes his office! Above all, how terrifying is his resultant solitude! The priesthood would thus consist essentially in the personal and absolute power to consecrate the Eucharist and to administer the sacraments, with no other sacramental relation to the bishop than the original ordination by which these powers are granted to the priest. This individualistic theory presupposes that from the moment the pontiff has communicated a part of his own powers by the imposition of hands, he has only a right of jurisdiction, *reverentiam et obedientiam,* upon the priest ordained. The power of Order, although it is originally derived from that of the ordaining bishop, is to be exercised henceforth, as Order, independently of the bishop's power of Order. The priest is a Christian who has the power to say Mass. But he is not essentially, by reason of his Order, a collaborator with the bishop or in his pastoral functions. True, an administrative nomination may afterward attribute to the priest, as an additional power, certain pastoral functions. However, these pastoral functions do not have their sacramental principle in his ordination. He will exercise them by virtue of canonical obedience, rather than by virtue of the character that he received by the imposition of hands. His pastoral ministry depends upon the power of jurisdiction possessed by the bishop, but it is not at the same time the manifestation of the pastoral character, subordinate to that of the bishop, that the priest already possesses himself. A few moments ago, we said the priest, according to this view, is a Christian who has the power to celebrate Mass. Now we say that the pastor is a priest who has powers of jurisdiction. This approach parcels and fragments the concept of the priesthood. All sense of unity is lost, and with it perhaps also the charity which ceases to be considered as the principle of the priestly state.

The duties of pastoral charity, as conceived by this system, appear to have been imposed after the fact, and as it were from without. The canonical nomination does not merely specify these duties, but in a sense creates them, for ordination alone would not have sufficed to establish the priest in the pastoral state of charity.

Considered within the framework of this conception, the priestly state is plainly inferior to the religious state, or at least to that of religious priests. While the latter are equal to diocesan priests in their power to celebrate Mass, they are superior to them by reason of their asceticism. Thus, the state of the diocesan priest, instead of being parallel to and different from that of the religious priest, is inferior to it, well deserving the adjective "secular," which has come to be applied to the diocesan priest in a depreciatory sense, as if to imply that he is an inferior clergyman, not only with relation to the bishop, which is certainly true—but also in the second rank with regard to generosity and duty, halfway between God and the world, between perfection and compromise. This is shocking.

We must say very plainly that if this conception were to win out completely, we would lose our wits and our courage.

. Not long ago, His Eminence Cardinal Liénart said equivalently in an allocution given during the retreat for the ordinands of his diocese: "In wanting to limit our priesthood to personal powers of Order, independent of those of the bishop who conferred them upon us, we have greatly restricted the value and exigencies of our priesthood,—and this theological and sacramental individualism has been fatal to the dignity of our presbyteral state."

That is why, in order to see clearly within ourselves, in order to respect ourselves by respecting our state, we have returned to the origins, to Scripture and to the Pontifical, and there we have found an entirely different doctrine, one that goes beyond the preceding one, without however suppressing it: *non tollere, non solvere, sed adimplere.*

The presbyteral priesthood does not consist first of all nor solely in the individualized power to consecrate the body of Christ and to administer the sacraments validly, but in the priest's subordinate participation in the religious and apostolic functions of his bishop. It is the bishop who ordained the priest to be his collaborator, because he was crushed by the weight of his obligations. Finding he had to reconcile the unity of his church incarnate in his person with the overwhelming multiplicity of his ministries, he has hit upon no other solution than that of entrusting a part of his ministries to priests having the necessary powers, to collaborators who would exercise these functions only in dependence upon him, and therefore in a subordinate manner. The priest is a Christian who participates in the religious and apostolic powers, duties, and graces of the bishop, in dependence upon him, within the limits of Order and jurisdiction fixed by the bishop and by the Church.

The priesthood is not an institution separate from the episcopate, consistent by itself even though incapable of perpetuating itself, and attached to an intention of Christ that is distinct from that by which He created the Apostles and the bishops. If it were, the priesthood, after having obtained its powers from the episcopate, would owe it nothing more than obedience, instead of owing it its *raison d'être* and its definition.

On the contrary, the priesthood has sprung historically and theologically from the episcopate, or rather from the Apostolate, in the primitive sense of the latter word that designated the powers and the functions of the Twelve. The Apostles conferred upon inferiors a portion of their obligations, so that these inferior priests might exercise them in dependence upon them: it was a participated, derived, and subordinate priesthood.

Thus, there is not only a hierarchy of jurisdiction, but also a hierarchy of Order. This does not mean merely that the inferiors have fewer powers than the superiors, but it signifies that the inferiors exercise their powers only in dependence upon their superiors. Strictly speaking, even if they had the same powers of Order, as is the case today of the auxiliary bishop by the side of the titular bishop, that would not lessen their dependence in the exercise of their powers. In fact, so great is the dependence with respect to certain of these powers, that they would cease to be valid if the superiors so decided.[1]

---

[1] The presbyteral priesthood is therefore a partial and subordinate participation in the episcopal priesthood. It is conferred by a partial and subordinate participation in the Eucharistic powers of the bishop. The priest participates, under the direction of and within the limits fixed by the bishop, in the sacerdotal duties of the latter, which are, as we have said, holy and sanctifying. Inasmuch as the priest participates only partially and in a discontinuous way in these episcopal functions, he can seek means of sanctification elsewhere, as for example in the ascetic state of life of the religious. But he will first of all make use of the means that flow from his own state, which is that of the participated and subordinate exercise of the sacerdotal charity of the bishop.

The priestly state must be related to the episcopal state, not only as the part to the whole, but as the subordinate and dependent to its principle. The priest accomplishes in an imperfect manner, limited in time, space, and power, what the bishop does in a perfect, absolute, and independent manner. That is why the priestly state must be defined through the episcopal state if it is to be rightly understood. The presbyteral priesthood consists essentially in the subordinate participation in the religious and apostolic functions of the bishop. Seeing himself in this light, the priest will find once again all his value, his eminent dignity, as well as a state and a law of life.

In support of this affirmation, we have a number of excellent proofs, none of which, taken separately, may be decisive (as often happens in freely discussed theological questions), but which in their totality are impressive and concordant.

1. *Proofs from Scripture*

There is no text on the ordaining of the first priests by the Apostles as detailed as the one telling of the institution of the first deacons (Acts 6:1-7). But it is permissible to reason from the text on the diaconate *a fortiori*. Now, in the *Acts of the Apostles,* the diaconate from its very origins does not seem to have been solely limited to the right and duty of serving the Apostle at the Eucharistic altar, but also involved the right and duty of acting for him in a subordinate capacity in whatever communal functions the Apostle may have chosen to entrust to his deacon. That is all the more reason why the

Within these limits, therefore, the priest is an apostle by state and sacramentally, much more than any layman can be. He has nothing to envy in *Catholic Action,* for he goes beyond it. Let him be an apostle in his own way and in accordance with the concrete needs of his own time, well and good! But he is twice an apostle—through the sacraments of baptism and Order which each bring him their own particular grace. These ideas will be taken up again in one of the following chapters, and in the second part of this book.

first priests must have been chosen and ordained to accomplish, under the direction and control of the bishops, all the apostolic functions that it may have pleased the latter to entrust to them. Among these functions was that of consecrating the body of Christ, but it did not suffice to define the presbyteral priesthood, which would be much more adequately defined as a subordinate and limited episcopacy, limited to the functions permitted by the bishop, but deriving its origin, its power, its grace, and its reason for existing from the episcopacy proper.

We all know the beautiful text which is so often cited, taken from St. Paul's farewell discourse to the presbyters of the Church of Ephesus, who had flocked to Miletus to greet him for the last time: "Take heed to yourselves and to the whole flock in which the Holy Spirit has placed you as bishops to rule the Church of God, which He has purchased with His own blood." [2] The essential words of these instructions—*posuit episcopos regere ecclesiam*—left by the founder-Apostle to his mandatories, to his inferiors, to these *presbyteri-episcopi* whose college was to replace him during his absence, must be understood to refer to a subordinate power of Order. It was so that they might feed and govern the Church of Ephesus that the Holy Ghost, through the grace of ordination, had made of these men auxiliaries of the Apostle, the *episcopi*

---

[2] Acts 20:28. Concerning the primitive hierarchy and how the presbyterate depends on the episcopate, see I Clem. 42:1-4; 44:2-3, cited and translated by G. Bardy in *La Vie Spirituelle* for February, 1937, pp. 109-110. On the origins of the Christian priesthood, see also G. Bardy in *La Vie Spirituelle,* April 1, 1936, p. 12, and "L'épiscopat et le presbytérat," by Lemonnyer, O.P., in *La Vie Spirituelle* for March 1 and April 1, 1936.

There is a very good summary of all the discussions and conclusions of modern criticism concerning the origins of the unitary episcopacy in the recent edition of the Letters of St. Ignatius of Antioch by Father Camelot. Cf. *Lettres de saint Ignace d'Antioche* (Paris: Sources chrétiennes, 1944), Introduction, p. 30.

(in the plural), the collaborators of the founder-*episcopus* (in the singular).

For this very reason their powers as well as their graces extend beyond the celebration of the Eucharist, to an all-embracing pastoral ministry that places under their care the spiritual interests of the faithful. Is that not what is meant by feeding the lambs? Does it not mean taking care of them in all their needs, leading, feeding, sheltering, and defending them, making them grow and increase in number: *ars artium*. ... Thus, the first Scriptural text, after the Gospels, that speaks of the priesthood, defines the priesthood as we have done it. Formerly, this text was weakened because of the mystery surrounding the identity of the *episcopi* and of the elders-presbyters. Today, however, there is no hesitation in the exegesis of this text. These *presbyteri-episcopi* of Miletus were simple priests.

Later on came the pastoral *Epistles* and the portrait they gave us of the qualities required of the *episcopus*. The *episcopus* was neither the Apostle himself, nor the bishop, his sucessor. He was the auxiliary to the bishop, doubtless Timothy or Titus. Now, it was this auxiliary who had the responsibility for this good work—*opus bonum*—that is entrusted to the Church. There was no mention of the Eucharist.[3]

Finally, there is the beautiful passage of I Pet. 5:1-4, written from the same point of view: "Now I exhort the presbyters among you—I, your fellow-presbyter and witness of the sufferings of Christ, . . . tend the flock of God which is among you, governing [the Greek word used is *episcopating*][4] not under constraint, but willingly, . . . nor yet as lording it over your charges, but becoming from the heart a pattern to the flock. And when the Prince of the shepherds appears, you will receive the unfading crown of glory."

---

[3] Cf. I Tim. 3:1-7; 5:17-22; I Tit. 1:5-9.

[4] We must note, however, that this word: ἐπισχοποῦντες is missing in several of the reliable manuscripts.

2. *Historical Proof*

If we generalize this conception of the origins of the *presbyteri-episcopi,* we shall immediately be rid of many artificial difficulties found in the primitive texts. This is an example of an hypothesis which, once it is admitted, explains all the rest in its entirety and in its details. It enables us to understand that:

(a) In the New Testament, the words *episcopi* (in the plural) and *presbyteri* are used interchangeably to designate the same persons.

(b) These *presbyteri-episcopi* are distinct from the founder-Apostle, who established them, and who remains the head of the Church even in his absence, and upon whom they are closely dependent. Whence the unity and hierarchy in each urban community.

(c) Even if these *presbyteri-episcopi* assembled in a college (the *presbyterium*), should have the same sacramental powers and powers of order as the founder-Apostle, they do not possess them in the same way as he does. He is accountable only to the supreme college of the Twelve and to God; the others depend upon their head in all their functions.

(d) This explains how, at the death of the Apostle or shortly afterwards, the bishop-successor is chosen by way of election, to replace the deceased (in a different and total sense), and as such becomes superior to the *presbyteri-episcopi,* who have been his colleagues until that moment.

3. *Liturgical Proof (Lex orandi, lex credendi)*

It is a remarkable fact that the ancient prayers for the consecration of priests and deacons, at the Pontifical when the imposition of hands originally took place, do not speak of the Eucharistic powers (for the deacons there is a simple

allusion to the altar; for the priests, nothing whatever is said),
but strongly emphasize their quality as *subordinate auxiliaries
of the bishop*. This is their great title to glory, their definition:
they are charged, by virtue of their intimate dependence upon
the bishop, together with him and under his direction, to
extend the Redemption (including the Eucharist) throughout
the world by the exercise of apostolic charity.

Seen in this light, the various sources all agree: the texts of
the *Acts of the Apostles* and of the *Epistles* of St. Paul, concerning the *presbyteri-episcopi;* the information given by St.
Ignatius of Antioch on the organization of the churches of
the second and third generations; and the texts of the Pontifical. The short formula: *Accipe potestatem celebrandi missas,*
is of more recent date, Latin and medieval, whereas on the
contrary the Eucharistic prayer of the imposition of hands, in
which there is not even any allusion to the power to celebrate
the Mass, places strong emphasis on apostolic collaboration.
When we go back to the origins, it all becomes clear, necessary, and coordinated. By reason of his Order, the priest is
the collaborator of the bishop. This is his true definition.

4. *Canonical Proofs*

There are a few indications pointing in the same direction to
be gleaned from Canon Law. Canon 948 of the Code reads as
follows: "Ordo ex Christi institutione clericos a laïcis in
Ecclesia distinguit *ad fidelium regimen* et cultus divini ministerium." This is a distant echo of: *posuit Spiritus Sanctus
episcopos regere ecclesiam Christi.* The Council of Trent had
already said in Session VII, *de Sacramentis,* canon 10: "si
quis dixerit Christianos omnes *in verbo* et omnibus sacramentis
administrandis habere potestatem, A.S." And again we are
reminded of another text from the *Acts:* "nos vero orationi et
ministerio verbi," [5] which we are to understand as meaning
the ministry of evangelization.

---

[5] Acts 6:4.

And now to close, without leaving the Canon Law of the sacraments, this flexible and solid concept, which in the beginning would perhaps grant to the *presbyteri-episcopi* the same powers of Order as to the bishops, but in a subordinate and dependent way, would reassure us in the face of certain historical facts that seem probable, if not certain. It would seem that the highest powers of Order were taken away from the simple presbyters little by little, precisely by virtue of the original subordination that placed them under the sacramental dependence of the bishops. And from time to time history reveals to us the transitions toward these increased restrictions. The distinction between the powers of priests and bishops has not always been exactly the same. It is not the same in the East as in the West, for instance in the case of confirmation. The fact that the priests of the Latin Church have the theoretical right but not the practical capacity to administer the sacrament of confirmation without first receiving an indult would seem to be the proof that they efficaciously exercise certain of their powers of Order only if their bishop (the Bishop of Rome) so wills.[6] In other words, certain of their powers

---

[6] The patriarch of Alexandria is consecrated by his electors, the members of the *presbyterium*. Cf. Magnin, *Dict. de Droit canonique* (Letouzey), the word "Alexandrie"; and also Dom Cabrol, in *Dict. d'Archéologie et de Liturgie,* on the word "Alexandrie (élection du patriarche)," column 1208: "The bishop possesses the fullness of the priesthood, the priest possesses the same priesthood, but in a lesser degree. There is no substantial difference between them. Could it not be admitted that specifically the presbyters of Alexandria all enjoyed the fullness of the priesthood? One of them, designated by election, thus became bishop naturally, as it were, without undergoing a new ordination. The same hypothesis was originally proposed to solve the difficulties that arise from the confusion between the terms *presbyter* and *episcopus;* and the same solution would apply in particular to the texts of St. Jerome that seem, as we have said, to imply a kind of identity in the beginning between the two degrees of the hierarchy. In spite of the difficulties that this opinion would still present, to our mind it is the only possible one, if we admit the reality of the fact of the election

of Order remain, even after collation, in the hands of the bishop. We grant they are priests, and even *episcopi* in the beginning, but subordinate even in their essential priesthood.

The recent authorization given to pastors by the Sacred Roman Congregation on the Discipline of the Sacraments (September 14, 1946) by which they may validly administer the sacrament of confirmation to the dying within the limits of the parish, has made this problem once again a matter of current interest. How can a simple priest be at once so powerful and so weak with regard to sacramentally administering the Holy Ghost? So powerful, since a mere indult, and in the present case a remote decree, permits him to exercise this great function validly. So weak, since outside certain stipulated conditions he cannot do it—and by this is meant (1) that he

---

and of the consecration of the patriarch by the priests of Alexandria. But is this a real fact? Setting aside all theological consideration, it still leaves room for many doubts. . . ."

It appears that the abbot of Cîteaux, from the 16th century until the Revolution, enjoyed the right to confer the diaconate and the sub-diaconate upon his monks. Cf. Dom Joseph-Marie Canivez, *L'Ordre de Cîteaux en Belgique,* pp. 426-429, and also Cardinal Lépicier, *Institutiones theologicae speculativae, cursus brevior* (Turin: Marietti, 1932), Tome III, p. 316. Cf. *Revue d'Histoire eccl.* (Louvain: 1946), Tome XII, p. 255.

Two other Cistercian examples are cited: a bull by Martin V, dated November 16, 1427, to the abbot of Altzell, and a privilege granted in 1400 by Boniface IX to the abbot of Osyth in Essex. Cf. K. A. Fink, "Zur spendung der höheren Weihen, durch den Priester," in Zeitschrifte Savigny-Stiftung Rechtsgesch, 63, Kanon. Abt. (1943), 506-508; and *Bulletin de Théologie ancienne et médiévale* [de Louvain], 1946, No. 241.

The ingenious institution of the *chorepiscopus* might be considered in this connection. This institution was very widespread during antiquity and historical light still remains to be shed on it. It is quite apparent that in the beginning and for a long time afterward they were far more than the simple prelates they are tending to become today under the pressure of present-day Latin canon law. Cf. *Dict. d'Archéologie et de Liturgie,* edited by Dom Cabrol, under the word: "Chorévêques."

does not have the permission to do it (this would involve the illicit administration of a sacrament); and (2) that he does not have the power to do it (this would involve the invalid administration of a sacrament).

How can we explain that all of a sudden a document that has come by post from Rome, can, without any new imposition of hands, confer upon a priest not only the right but also the power to exercise an episcopal function?

The manuals hesitate, equivocate, and propose controversial explanations.

We can boldly answer that it is because the simple priest already had this power by virtue of his ordination to the priesthood, but since he had neither the permission nor the faculty to make use of it, any attempt to use it would have been vain, that is, invalid. The decree presently in force also specifies that if a pastor exercises this function outside the limits of his parish, the sacrament is nonexistent. "Si hujusmodi mandati limites iidem ministri praetergrediantur, probe sciant se perperam et sacramentum nullum conficere."

We may, if we wish, speak of a "bound" power, but that is perhaps only a metaphor that hides our ignorance. I should prefer to speak of a power subordinated to another, inasmuch as the intention of the minister is necessary for the validity of a sacrament. In this case we would speak of the intention of the priest, subordinated to the intention of the Church. And if the Church does not have the intention that priests should utilize their power, or, if you prefer, if she does not support it from above by her sacramental authority, then the priestly act in question is null. If this explanation is accepted, then we must renounce the individualistic conception of the priesthood, which would make of each priest an independent, isolated, absolute personage—in short, solitary.

Do you remember de Vigny's Moses, "powerful and solitary"? And his Joshua, "pensive and pale," for he, too, was "the elect of the Almighty"? The truth is much more beautiful and much deeper: in the one body of Christ, which is the

Church, we are articulated to one another, and first of all to our superiors. Priests exercise their powers in community, in subordination, hierarchically, under the conditions willed and foreseen by the heads of the entire organism of which they are members. When they legitimately exercise their functions, they are never alone. The whole Church is present, expressing her approval. Perhaps it is better to say that the Church acts through the ministry of her priests, which rests upon hers and prolongs it in the particular daily cases in which their action intervenes. If the Church draws back her hand, then the priest is really alone, but also powerless, because in this great body of charity which is the Church of Christ, a separated member, a branch that has been cut off, loses all its vitality. In the sacramental order, just as in the order of grace pure and simple, Christ says: "Without Me, and without My Spouse, the Church, you can do nothing."

It is true that the Church rarely uses this right of hers to draw back her hand. In ordinary circumstances, she prefers the general order and the moral security of her faithful to the absolute perfection of the sacramental regime. She lets unworthy ministers exercise their powers validly, even though sacrilegiously, for the good of the people. But in certain general cases, as in that of confirmation in the Latin Church, she reserves for certain ministers, namely the bishops, the power to exercise functions which the priests never use except under the authority, in the name and in place of their superiors and of the entire body of Christ.

We possess—or at any rate we once possessed—signs of this doctrine that made it incarnate in our liturgy and institutions. Formerly, better than today, one could roughly judge the hierarchical status of a cleric in the Church by the extent of his Eucharistic powers.

Indeed, the co-celebration of the Eucharistic sacrifice in the first centuries of the Church must have given a much better picture and idea of hierarchized sacerdotal realities than do the Low Masses of today. When the bishop, in the middle and at the top of the single altar, but surrounded by the *presbyterium,* that is, by the priests of his diocese or of the city, they in turn surrounded by deacons and inferior ministers,— when the bishop thus surrounded offered together with them the one Sunday Mass before the assembly of the participating faithful, the spectator could actually see the priestly hierarchy in all its degrees inscribed in the visible rites of the liturgy as well as in the ordering of this sacred choir. And each and every one exercised together with the others, but in his respective place, the powers which he possessed. Sacramental functions were subordinated to one another as were apostolic duties, and they were rigorously kept in their respective Orders. Each one, by reason of the place he occupied at the altar, and by the Eucharistic capacities that he put into action, knew and manifested his exact position with relation to the ministry of the bishop and to the priesthood of Christ.[7]

The very extension of Christianity has fragmented this unity, without however destroying this dogma. The dependence of priests upon their bishops continues to define them, and in defining them, to sustain them. It is through this that they know what they can do and what they must do, and therefore understand what they are.

It is unfortunate that the doctrinal individualism of the last centuries has replaced this hierarchized theology by a compartmentalized concept of the priesthood, as if a man could

---

[7] The holiness of the bishop at the altar is not a holiness that is his individually. It is the holiness of the Church of which he is the head, a holiness that the sacrifice realizes in the person of the pontiff and of his collaborators and of the participants. The bishop is officially vowed to charity in the service of God and of souls. It is this profession of charity that designates him as the organ of command from the moment of his consecration, as the living principle of the cult, the head that commands the mystical body by uniting it to God. Since charity is his state in life, he is the president of the "agape," where he completes the Christian community by his primacy of charity, in the capacity of head. The Holy Sacrifice of the Mass, and above all the episcopal High Mass, is, in this sense, the sacrifice of the head.

be a priest in an absolute manner, without being the priest of a church, and without being a priest for a bishop, for the purpose of performing the functions that the latter may see fit to give him or even to take away from him.[8]

When the priest celebrates Mass, he does so only by virtue of a delegation, and in a way in the bishop's place. And in participating in the mystery of unity, charity, and perfection, he must raise himself up to the exigencies of episcopal holiness, or, if you prefer, of Eucharistic holiness.

The prevalence of individual, separate, Low Masses—one might call them closed and isolated Masses—has long since made us lose sight of this unity of the *presbyterium,* of the presbyteral body associated with the bishop in the celebration of the holy mysteries. We no longer have any picture, except on the day of ordination, of what the ancient co-celebration must have been like, when the bishop consecrated the Eucharist on the single altar of his church, at the one solemn Sunday Mass, with all his presbyteral clergy around him participating in his powers, and affirming the sacrificial unity by the position occupied, the actions performed, and the liturgical services rendered.

And it is not too certain that the co-celebration of ordination Masses—which is said to be of rather recent liturgical date (since about the end of the Middle Ages)—gives us an exact

---

[8] Cf. the following comment taken from *L'Ouvrier de la Moisson,* for July, 1937, concerning a work on the priesthood that had just been published: "The author started out, as many do, from the presbyteral priesthood considered as the power to celebrate Mass, in order to reach the summit, the episcopacy. Does not this approach lead to a concept of the priesthood that is too individualistic, that would make the priesthood seem to be sufficient to itself once ordination has been conferred? A somewhat ambiguous sentence says that the humblest village curate possesses the power to say Mass as fully as the Sovereign Pontiff: 'He validly exercises it in complete independence, through the virtue and in the name of the Word incarnate alone.' But the Word incarnate is never severed from His mystical body, which is the hierarchic Church."

idea or picture of the ancient rite. For it consists rather in several Masses joined into one, as might be done at certain pilgrimage shrines in order to save time or space, if present-day Canon Law authorized it. The ancient co-celebration, on which we have little information, must have presented the figure of a single Mass, the Mass of the bishop or of the church, celebrated by several ministers, each in his own place and in accordance with his powers collaborating with the powers of the bishop rather than being added to them. There is no certainty, for example, that all the priests pronounced the words of co-celebration: the words of the bishop could have sufficed. Nevertheless, on other days, these priests went out individually in lieu of the bishop to celebrate in country churches for the needs of the faithful, with the very vivid awareness that they were doing it in the bishop's place. Dom Leclerq has collected texts that indicate this for the article on "Concélébration" of the *Dictionnaire d'Archéologie et de Liturgie*. In a letter to a certain Decentius,[9] Pope St. Innocent, during the beginning of the fifth century, said that on Sunday priests were dispensed from assisting the bishop at the altar because they were supposed to go out among the parishes: *quia die ipsa propter plebem sibi creditam nobiscum convenire non possunt*. But so as to maintain the principle of unity, the pope sent to them, through his acolytes, the Eucharist which he himself had consecrated: *idcirco fermentum a nobis confectum per acolythos accipiant ut se a nostra communione, maxime illa die, non judicent separatos*. Finally, in parishes that were too remote to be reached by the acolytes, the titular priests had the privilege of celebrating the Holy Eucharist by themselves on Sundays.[10]

---

[9] Cf. *Patrologia Latina*, Tome XX, column 556.

[10] Cf. *Dict. d'Arch. et de Lit.* (Dom Cabrol), Tome III, column 2474. It is very probable that the venerable gesture of the "commixtio et consecratio" performed by the priest after the *Pater Noster* and before the *Agnus Dei* is a liturgical commemoration of the sending of the *fermentum*: at that moment the priest mixed into the chalice

There is no question of wanting to re-establish these customs, if for no other reason than that the modern, personal piety of the priest, not to mention of the faithful, requires the daily and distinct Mass every day.[11] And yet, despite the evolution of Canon Law and of the liturgy, these ancient practices remind us that it is always in the name and in the place of the bishop, and in any case in union with him, that the priest celebrates Mass. And since the bishop celebrates Mass only to affirm, represent, and perpetually to produce and re-establish in the world the charity that defines his state and that defines perfection, each priest must, in participating in the bishop's powers, also participate in his graces and duties, that is, in the perfection of the episcopal state.

The true common life of the priest, therefore, is that of the altar, where he lives his Eucharistic life and his life of holiness in common with his bishop. In the primitive Christian basilicas, there was just one material altar, just as there was just one Sunday Mass. The unity of the altar was not only what it has continued to be: a theological and dogmatic truth because of the one Victim and of the one Spouse, the Church. It was a unity of marble or of wood, a symbol of spiritual unity. Now that the consecrated table has been fragmented into a multitude of altar stones distributed among as many churches and chapels—in accordance with an evolution of piety that, I repeat, is not to be turned back—the priest continues to remember the holiness of the bishop, which is none other than the holiness of the Church, in the name of which he celebrates the Mass each morning, repeating the gesture

---

consecrated by himself the parcel of the host previously consecrated by the bishop at the cathedral. Today this parcel is replaced by a fragment detached from the priest's own host. It is the supreme symbol of the unity of the Church and of the unity of the sacrifice: *a single altar, a single bishop.*

[11] On the co-celebration of the past, present, and the future, see the powerful and cautious article by Dom Bauduin, O.S.B., in *Maison-Dieu* (Paris: Editions du Cerf), Cahier 7, 1946.

of unity, symbolizing and bringing charity. And he knows that in this charity consists the incarnate perfection of the sacred body of Him who died through love on Calvary. How, then, could a priest dare, when he is accomplishing the mystery of charity in the name of his bishop who must practice this charity,—how could he dare not to participate in the holiness of the Church, brought forth from Christ's risen and living body that he immolates upon the altar?

It is now clear that we can reconcile the two theological approaches that, for the sake of clarity, we have distinguished and even juxtaposed in this chapter and the preceding one. We would build our synthesis this time, not upon the second of these views, the one we have adopted, namely, upon the episcopacy—but we would boldly start from the first view, from the Eucharist, taking into consideration how the priest celebrates it. He offers up sacrifice while he presides over the assembly: *sacerdotem oportet offerre, proeesse,* doing both at once. At least this is what he does at the ordinary and official Mass, at the real community Mass of the church, which of course is the Sunday Mass. The definition of the priesthood would then derive not only from the Eucharist, but also from the way in which the priest celebrates the Eucharist. It is as president, head, and pastor that he handles the Eucharist (*imitamini quod tractatis*). In celebrating it he affirms the powers and duties with which he is invested, the mandate that he executes, his substitution for the bishop, the delegation that he exercises, and all that the position he occupies presupposes, represents, and demands, the role entrusted to him, and the professional occupations that this function implies.

NOTE
Explanation of the Council of Trent, Session XXII
(de sacrificio missae), Canon 2 [12]

The Council declared that the Apostles had been instituted priests when our Lord gave them the power and the duty of

[12] *Denz.* 949.

offering up the Eucharist, because the Eucharist is a sacrifice, and no one is a priest unless he offers up sacrifice. The Apostles would not be priests, but simple pastors in the Protestant sense of the word, if the Last Supper had not been a sacrifice, and if they had not received the power to offer it up. These three truths, which are three revealed and defined dogmas, are mutually interdependent.

But the Council did not want to define the priesthood, nor in any case to limit it to the power to celebrate the Sacrifices of the Mass, since in another session (Session XXIII, Canon 1) it added to the essence of the Christian priesthood the power to remit sins, conferred at another time, without however affirming that it had yet exhausted the definition of the priesthood.

The Council did not want the priesthood to be restricted to the mere power to preach, with the consequent denial of the sacrificial character of the Last Supper and of the Mass.

In short, the act by which the Apostles were instituted priests does not exhaust the definition of their priesthood. The priesthood, which is a state, is not to be identified with the oblation of sacrifice, which is an act. In the case of Christ, His priesthood is traditionally defined by the Incarnation and by His mediation which embraces various exercises of religion and of the pastorate. The priest is also a mediator, and this he would not be if he did not have the power to offer up the sacrifice of Christ. And yet this power, which is the highest point and the signature as well as the sign of his priesthood, does not suffice to define it, any more than the signature which authenticates a letter, and is part of it, can replace or equal the contents of the letter.[13]

---

[13] The most recent commentator on the Canons of the Council of Trent takes the same approach: "In the preceding Session XXII, Chapter I and Canons 1 and 2, the Council of Trent had professed the institution of the Eucharistic sacrifice by Christ at the Last Supper, and the sacrificial character of the oblation made at Mass. Moreover, it had recalled that by the words *Do this in remembrance of Me,*

However, we surmise that the Council's definition, understood in a narrow sense, has influenced the oratorical and easily constructed position that would make the Christian priesthood consist wholly in the power to celebrate the Mass— the rest being unessential and not entering into the definition. As we have already said, this path leads to regrettable compartmentalizations in the Treatise on the Incarnation. Christ's titles, instead of being aspects or consequences of His one mystery, which is that of the hypostatic union, seem to be ministerial departments, independent of one another. He was a priest on Calvary, a teacher or doctor when He gave the Sermon on the Mount, a king when He governed, a prophet when He taught. But the *Epistle to the Hebrews* presents a far more synthetic view of the sacerdotal mystery of Christ: *Filius meus es tu.*

Christ had constituted His Apostles priests and had commanded them and all other priests to offer up His body and blood (Canon 2)." We know that this Canon 2 is not exclusive of the acts by which Jesus Christ was able to communicate other powers of the priesthood to His Apostles, for example the power to forgive or retain sins, conferred by the words: *Receive the Holy Spirit, . . .* (John 20:23)." Cf. on this point, Session XIV, Canon 3. (A. Michel, "Les décrets du Concile de Trente," in Héfelé-Leclercq, *Histoire des Conciles* (Paris: Letouzey, 1938), Tome X, Part I, p. 479.

CHAPTER VII

The Grace of the Sacrament of Order

THIS CHAPTER on the grace of the sacrament of Order is one of the most difficult to draft. The author who enters into this subject as into a forsaken forest receives little support or protection from the authority of the Church. In the fifteenth century, the Council of Florence, in its decree to the Armenians, had begun to write brief summaries on the grace proper to each sacrament. The Council of Trent, however, in the sixteenth century, in its concern to energetically affirm the dogmatic efficacy of our sacred rites rather than to specify their mystical effects, left this question open to theologians, and they have taken advantage of the permission.

A few of these theologians would almost go so far as to deny the existence of a particular grace proper to each sacrament, a grace distinct from general habitual or sanctifying grace. Instead of seven stained-glass windows, each with its own design and colors, we would thus possess only grisailles of the same tonality, in which only the sensible sign and the end in view would diversify the seven institutions of Christ. But God's gift would still be the same, accompanied by an acquired right to future actual graces, to eventual help to be distributed later through divine mercy at difficult moments, consonant with the spiritual goal of each of the sacraments.

This is all very vague. We get the impression that our manuals on sacramental theology are too often preoccupied with canonical questions concerning conditions of validity, at the expense of the essential subject, which is the knowledge and contemplation of the mystery of God. As we proceed down the sevenfold list, the state of unbalance becomes more marked. By the time we reach the sacrament of Order, the study of the character, that is, of the sacerdotal functions and powers, clearly prevails over the study of the effects of grace. Some authors, when they come to this concluding portion of their treatise, seem to forget the beginning, namely, that each sacrament is the efficacious sign of grace, and more probably of a specific grace.[1]

Fortunately, books on spirituality are much richer in this respect. They describe with great fervor, for ordinands and for the clergy in general, the graces that await priests when they receive Holy Orders. They lay great stress upon the supereminent perfection that consecrated ministers must have, a perfection that is sustained by the special grace of their state, and evidently received in principle on the day of their ordination: *admoneo ut resuscites gratiam Dei quae est in te per impositionem manuum episcopi,* according to I Tim. 4:14 and II Tim. 1:6.

But precisely what is this grace? Once again, we would like to dream of reconciling or rather of coupling the austerity of the theologians and the canonists with the mysticism of the spiritual writers. Who would dare to say, in a sermon to ecclesiastic retreatants, that the grace of Order is the same as the grace of marriage or of extreme unction?

---

[1] These controversies have been very competently unraveled by Father Roguet, O.P., in the volume on the sacraments in general of the *Summa Theologica* (Paris: La Revue des Jeunes), pages 60-65. The essential text of St. Thomas is IIIa, q. 62, a. 2. See Father Roguet's commentary, pp. 222 ff., and pp. 364-367. He sides with John of St. Thomas and Billuart against Cajetan, and professes to see in sacramental grace a contraction of habitual grace, in the sense in which the species contracts the genus.

Let us first say a word on the problem in general. If authors find it so hard, if not to admit, at least to explain the existence of a grace proper to each sacrament, it is perhaps because they are starting from an abstract definition of habitual grace, which they, with their legitimate concern as metaphysicians, have proposed to us in a way that is too exclusive. They have pushed aside innumerable Scriptural texts in which grace is presented as the life of Christ in us, and, as it were, an interior relation of our souls with the three Persons of the Blessed Trinity. Instead, they have clung almost unanimously to the famous passage of II Peter 1:4, in which Christians are said to be *divinae consortes naturae,* and the three Persons are not specifically named. Indeed, there can be no objection to this way of thinking and speaking. On condition that this view considers participation in the divine life an *accident,* a quality and not a substance, it has the merit of definitively repudiating any pantheistic conception of the supernatural and of the mystical life.[2]

In this presentation, however, the trinitarian aspect of grace is overshadowed, as well as its historical and Christological origins that flow from the Jesus of the Gospels. Now, in the incarnate mystery of the Son of God, there are, as St. John says, hours, successive moments, interior states that come to the visible surface of one or another event. There is a history of grace. And this history in turn becomes incarnate in sacraments which were not all instituted on the same day nor to signify the same interior and exterior attitude of Jesus. From this come a diversity and a specification of grace that were not apparent in the *divinae consortes naturae,* in which the participation ostensibly applied only to the one divine nature common to the three Persons and always identical with itself.

---

[2] We notice in certain austerely-inclined authors an incipient deviation, when they lay great stress on the fact that the priesthood demands holiness, but neglect to say that normally it also gives the necessary grace.

In short, in the evangelical and visible history of the Saviour, as in the life of each Christian, there are variations, episodes, which are—in time and in given circumstances—the incarnation of the mystery which, seen from God's point of view, always remains the same. And since Christ in His sacred humanity became one of us, *formam servi accipiens,* there are in His mortal life hours of grace that succeed one another and that to our eyes do not look alike. There are particular forms of this same divine life that we must ask for and obtain successively, so that, even during time and duration, the *vivo, jam non ego, vivit vero in me Christus,* of St. Paul may be realized.

Under these conditions, how should we try to picture the particular grace of the sacrament of Order?

The Council of Florence, in its famous decree to the Armenians which is for the most part inspired by St. Thomas, has expressed itself too laconically to satisfy our curiosity: *effectus [sacramenti Ordinis est] augmentum gratiae, ut quis sit idoneus minister.* That is all. Let us nonetheless start from this text to fill in the outlines.

Trinitarian grace, inasmuch as it is received by Christ in His sacred humanity and inasmuch as it is communicated to us for the first time germinally by baptism the day of our initiation into the Christian life, is a grace of filial charity. That is why St. Thomas calls the sacramental character that corresponds to it and that demands it a "passive character," in the scholastic sense of the word. To be a son is to receive or to have received life from another.

This grace of baptism is also a communitarian grace, since in Christ it blossomed into the grace of headship, and it makes us all live in Him with the same life. However, in the institution and practice of the Eucharist, which is its efficacious, perfect, and definitive sign, this grace is identified more and more with the fraternal charity that unites us all to one another on the same level in the holy Christian equality of sons of God. We might prefer to say—but this is only a trifling variation—that the grace of sacramental communion is a principle of fraternal charity and in a way equalitarian and horizontal. In any case, the Eucharist, exhausting all the powers of charity and unifying the mystical and visible body of Christ, is at the summit of the sacramental institution, as well as of the initiation of the Christian laity, gathering as equals around the same table, in the presence and under the influence of the immense charity of their Father who is in heaven.

But this same grace of Christ, inasmuch as it vivifies all His redemptive activity, inasmuch as it is at the root of the influence that He has upon us, as our head, our teacher, and our priest, can be communicated to certain Christians in particular. These Christians, in imitation of our Lord and participating in His priesthood as ministers, are called on to act spiritually, from above downward, upon their brothers, as pastors over their flocks, as teachers, and finally also as priests. The character that corresponds to this grace, says St. Thomas, is an "active character." We easily recognize it, for it is the grace of the priesthood. The charity of which it is the principle is exercised this time on an inclined plane. It is no longer horizontal, but hierarchical as befits the grace of one who represents God to his brothers. The *episcopi,* as the Greek root indicates, watch *over* their brothers from above: *posuit vos episcopos regere ecclesiam Dei.* Finally, priests are sons of God who have become in their own way the spiritual fathers of men. Their charity is no longer simply filial, like the charity of baptism, nor fraternal, like that of the Eucharist; it has become paternal. It is in this sense that we can understand the well-known text of their ordination: *accipe vestem sacerdotalem, per quam charitas intelligitur*—receive this chasuble, which symbolizes charity. And it symbolizes not charity in general, but the specialized charity for which we choose a particular word, one of the most beautiful in all human tongues, the name of God Himself in His First Person. It is a name that gives a true idea of what the priesthood must be in its profound mysticism, in its essential mystery. It is a fatherhood that permits and obliges the priest to say to God in his prayer, inspired by the famous text of St. Augustine: *da quod jubes.*

Who knows how many of our present-day bishops would not gladly renounce the titles of Lord, Excellency, painfully inherited from profane hierarchies, and cast aside all the external pomp which these solemn words symbolize, to hear themselves called by their true name, as in the days of St. Martin: *cur nos, Pater, deseris.*

How can we fail to recall here the great text of *Ephesians* 3:15, and its legitimate if perhaps too precise interpretation in the Latin Vulgate: *Pater Domini Nostri Jesu Christi, ex quo omnis paternitas in coelo et in terra nominatur.* That is what we mean. The fatherhood of the priest is a reflection as well as an overflow from the one divine fatherhood. Again, it takes St. Paul to explain it to us. We take the liberty of grouping here the principal texts of his Epistles, in which this paternal grace, winning out over modesty, betrays the secret of the virile emotions it has engendered in the Apostle's soul:

I Thess. 2:7-8. ". . . as if a nurse were cherishing her own children, so we in our love for you would gladly have imparted to you not only the Gospel of God, but also our own souls; because you had become most dear to us."

I Thess. 2:9. "For you remember, brethren, our labor and toil."

I Cor. 4:14-15. "I write these things . . . to admonish you as my dearest children. For although you have ten thousand tutors in Christ, yet you have not many fathers. For in Christ Jesus, through the Gospel, did I beget you."

II Cor. 12:15. "But I will most gladly spend and be spent myself for your souls, even though, loving you more, I be loved less."

Gal. 4:19. ". . . my dear children, with whom I am in labor again, until Christ is formed in you!"

Phil. 1:8. "For God is my witness how I long for you all in the heart of Christ Jesus."

Philem. 1:19. "I, Paul, write it with my own hand: I will repay it—not to say to thee that thou owest me thy very self."

Phil. 1:22-24. ". . . I do not know which to choose. Indeed I am hard pressed from both sides—desiring to depart and to be with Christ, a lot by far the better; yet to stay on in the flesh is necessary for your sake."

These beautiful texts are often cited by those seeking to fathom the mystery of the psychology and of the personal holiness of St. Paul. But do they not also reveal to us the spirit of an institution, of the apostolate whence the episcopate issued, of which the presbyterate in turn is a subordinate, fragmentary, and shared emanation? And this Spirit, whether written with a capital S or not, is a grace, the grace of fatherhood.

This is all perfectly clear when it is a question of the exercise of the priesthood from above, for the purpose of transmitting God's gifts to men.

This picture—and is it only a picture since we are dealing with a real grace—is likewise confirmed when the priest turns toward God and offers up to Him the adoration and sacrifices of men. For when he acts in this capacity, he is not acting in his own personal name, but in the place and at the request of his brothers. He acts in his quality as head of the community, as pastor of the faithful, and always as their father.

We have just used the word "community," which, with its exacting meaning, gives the final touch to the idea that we are trying to give of sacerdotal grace.

All the sacraments are communitarian because they not only give grace to men but also give the Church members grouped in various categories. And the two results are usually acquired one by the other, and the one within the other. The faithful do not first receive a grace which is theirs individually, and afterward, by way of supplement or consequence, are received into Christian society. The divine life that is communicated to them is the life of the Head who vivifies a single body. Spiritual birth, of which Scripture speaks so readily, is not a rupture, which breaks a bond and thereby brings about a separation and a new autonomy. Quite the contrary, without suppressing the personal responsibility of each individual, it is an insertion into a living being, a participation in a central life, an entrance into a communion. There is not first of all a grace, and then afterwards, because of this grace but distinct from it, an incorporation. The incorporation is the grace itself; or if we prefer, the life of grace is the very life of the community. One could not receive the grace without becoming a member of the Christian community, and vice versa. It is in this profound sense that the sacraments build up the Church at the same time that they sanctify Christians.

Among these sacraments, there is one whose purpose is to furnish the Church with the framework of her hierarchy as well as to assure the spiritual service of the faithful. Thus, this sacrament is communitarian twice or even three times over. First, because by its very existence it assures the Church the living mechanism that makes her an organized body. Secondly, because the purpose of the spiritual activities of this sacrament is to increase the community and its members in number and in vigor. Finally, because by sanctifying those who receive it, this sacrament increases their personal grace within them, for the ends of the society.

This is the sacrament of Order or Orders. It is the sacrament that confers the Christian priesthood in all its degrees. It is therefore at once an institution, a function, and a sacrament, and with reference to each of these aspects it is communitarian. Founded by Christ, organized by Him and by the Apostles, it has been from the start a hierarchy capable of begetting and of vivifying the society of the faithful, whose framework it constitutes. It is the internal skeleton and the external armature of the community. To this end, it communicates both powers to be exercised and graces that correspond to these functions. These duties are entrusted to bishops, priests, and to inferior ministers only for the spiritual good of their brothers. And these graces, which come from Christ, the Head of the body of the Church, are the prolongation of the divine fatherhood which is the principle of the vast Christian family.

A single word could sum up all these successive aspects of the same grace. This grace may be said to be communitarian by virtue of the doctrine on which this little book is based, because it is the grace of the bishop himself, or rather a participation, as we have repeatedly said, a partial and subordinate participation in the grace of the episcopacy. And the episcopacy, as our manuals tell us in their textbook terminology, is unitary and monarchical. It is unitary precisely because it is communitarian, because this single pastor recapitulates in the bonds of his charity as well as of his powers the one life of the community that he draws together, just as a father sums up in his person the spirit of his family, as the shepherd takes upon himself alone the sustenance of his flock.

St. Leo the Great has thrown light on this specification of the grace proper to the sacrament of Order. He gave this grace its other name—grace of service, grace of ministry—in a text in which he shows how this grace is superposed, added to the grace of baptism, thus contributing something new:

Omnes enim in Christo regeneratos, crucis signum efficit reges, sancti vero Spiritus unctio consecrat sacerdotes: ut *praeter istam specialem nostri ministerii servitutem,* universi spiritales et rationabiles Christiani agnoscant se regii generis et sacerdotalis officii esse consortes.[3]	All Christians regenerated in Christ by the sign of the cross that makes kings, and by the unction of the Holy Ghost that consecrates priests, can consider themselves participants of the royal race and of the priestly function, *outside of this special service that is proper to our ministry.*

---

[3] St. Leo the Great, *Sermon* IV, 1, P.L. Tome 54, col. 649.

This doctrine was also forcefully expressed in the beautiful text of St. Gregory of Nyssa, cited by M. Tixeront, and taken from the sermon "for the day of lights, on which our Lord was baptized": [4]

"In the beginning the bread is ordinary bread. But when the mystery has sacrificed it, it is said to be and it becomes the body of Christ. . . . This same virtue of the words also makes the priest august and venerable, separated from the common crowd by the newness of the blessing. Even yesterday and before that, he was lost in the multitude and among the vulgar, and all at once he becomes a guide, president, doctor of piety, and initiator into the hidden mysteries. And all this happens even though nothing in his body or form has changed, and his exterior appearance is the same as it was, only his invisible soul having been transformed for the better by an invisible force and by grace." [5]

It is perfectly clear that this grace and these powers that come to the priest through the sacrament and the imposition of the hands of a bishop, and that are a participation in the grace and the powers of the episcopacy, do not come from the personal holiness nor from the subjective grace of Bishop So-and-So who ordained him. To go from the level of institutions to that of persons would be renewing the old Donatist error in more modern dress; it would be implying that only the sacrament conferred by a saint is holy. The dogma of the Church, the dogma of *ex opere operato,* and all our certitudes would thus be called into question. We hope that no one is entertaining such a foolish thought.

---

[4] P.G. Tome 46, col. 581.

[5] This English translation is from Tixeront's French version in *L'Ordre et les Ordinations* (Paris: Gabalda, 1925), p. 181. Cf. also Henri Martin, P.S.S., *La Paternité Spirituelle du Prêtre, Commentaire du Pontificat* (Avignon: Aubanel, 1930).

APPENDIX

The Grace of the Christian Priesthood Seen Through
The Sacrament of Order That Confers It

IN THE sacrament of Order, we distinguish three elements, as was done in the Middle Ages:

1. *Sacramentum-et-non-res.*—This is the imposition of hands (or, according to St. Thomas, the porrection of the instruments). It is the sensible, efficacious sign *ex opere operato*. It produces, it always infallibly causes at least the powers, that is, the character.

2. *Sacramentum-et-res.*—These are the sacrifical power (to celebrate the Eucharist) and the sacramental power (to administer the sacraments), conferred by the sensible sign, powers that, like the sacrament itself, continue to be visible and even in their own way signs of the grace to come. But, just as St. Thomas dared to write concerning the most sacred body of our Lord, which is the *sacramentum-et-res* of the Eucharist:

Mors est malis,

we must say that the power to celebrate the Eucharist, which is the *sacramentum-et-res* of Order, while it is in its own way the sign of priestly holiness, that is, of grace, can be dissociated from such holiness and need not always coincide with it.

Consequently, there is between the *sacramentum-et-non-res* and the *sacramentum-et-res* the compensation that both are signs, but that the former is a cause rather than a sign, whereas the latter is a sign rather than a cause. The reason for this is that the former, while it is a sign of priestly grace, resembles it less than does the sacrifical power which is really the sensible expression of the priesthood; and the latter does not have the infallible relationship to grace that the *sacramentum-et-non-res* always has to the *sacramentum-et-res*.

But though this relationship is not infallible, it is nonetheless usual. The power to celebrate the Eucharist, while distinct from the grace of the priesthood, is to such a degree its sensible expression that we can understand how certain authors and certain schools of spirituality have come to confuse them and to identify the priesthood or the grace of the priesthood purely and simply with the power to celebrate Mass. The reason for this is that the Eucharist, the supreme divine institution, keeps its privilege here. Wherever the Eucharist is, as a sacrament, it establishes the reign of charity. As a sacrifice, it establishes the perfect religion that presupposes the perfect priesthood. The fact remains that because of sin, this relationship may be broken. It is possible to commune with the Real Presence without communing with the charity of Christ, just as it is possible to validly celebrate the Eucharist, and therefore to be a priest, without having the grace of the priesthood. The important thing is to know whether one prefers to define the priesthood by the powers it confers or by the grace that it presupposes. Here again we face the difference in approach between Canon Law and Christian spirituality. There will always be two vocabularies, with the canonical terminology predominating in practice.

3. *Res-et-non-sacramentum.*—But after all we must know whether a sacrament, as final principal cause, confers a character or gives a grace. The classical definition of sacraments does not permit any hesitation. Besides, we do not have a complete idea of a sacrament as long as we have not integrated into it the notion of the grace the sacrament brings.

Order, therefore, above all confers a grace. In the measure that the inward realities of the kingdom of God, for example the state of grace, are superior to the exterior organizations of the Church, and even to the sacraments, in the same measure does the grace of the priesthood surpass the powers of the priesthood. To be inwardly conformed to Jesus the Priest, to have through grace this priesthood which He possesses by nature, by His twofold nature, is far more important than to have the power to celebrate Mass. And indeed we cannot have one without the other. But there is no question here of separating what Christ has united. We are concerned with weighing notions, values, and of deciding which of them the Christian mind must esteem the more.

Now, there is no reason to hesitate. Just as the sacrifice of the Cross is more essential than the sacrifice of the altar, just as Jesus is a priest through the Cross before being a priest through the Last Supper (for without the Cross, the Last Supper ceases being a sacrifice, but the converse is not true); just as the grace of charity has greater value than Eucharistic communion; so does the grace of the priesthood excel the powers of the priesthood. And so we do not express the notion of the Christian priesthood perfectly when we say that it consists in the power to celebrate Mass, unless we immediately add that this power requires that the priest have by grace what Christ has by nature, that is, a personal relation with God and men that makes a priest of him by participation in the priesthood of Christ. And Christ's priesthood does not stem from the institution of the Eucharist nor does it consist solely in offering up the Eucharist, but it stems from the Incarnation which gave its essential fruit on Calvary and not at the Last Supper. Basically, if a priest had to choose, he should seek to understand his priesthood by meditating the mystery of the Incarnation-Redemption rather than the mystery of the Eucharistic sacrifice.

The point is that there must be no such choice, for these are values of different categories. There must be no choice between the supernatural reality and the sacramental or sacrificial sign that gives or realizes it. The two must be superposed. And the sign, which does not define grace, confers it. The power to celebrate, which does not define the priesthood (or the grace of the priesthood) confers them both. And to put this power into act by celebrating Mass is to give the priesthood a visible sign, and in so doing to renew, stimulate, resurrect, and exercise the grace of the priesthood. Indeed, one of the best ways, and in any case the best sacramental way, of resurrecting the grace (*res-et-non-sacramentum*) that is conferred by the imposition of the bishop's hands (*sacramentum-et-non-res*), is to use the power to celebrate Mass (*sacramentum-et-res*). Likewise, one of the best ways, and in any case the best sacramental way, of establishing charity in a Christian community is to celebrate a general Eucharistic communion. There is always the danger, of course, that for want of the requisite dispositions, Eucharistic communion may not bring charity with it, and thus be only an empty sign without the reality of which it should have been the cause and which in itself has greater value that the sign. The fact remains that perfection consists in the union of the two.

CHAPTER VIII

On the State of Perfection of the Bishop and of the Priest

IN AN EARLIER EDITION of this book we frankly admitted the anxiety that the problem of the state of perfection can cause a spiritual director. And yet this question may seem so difficult to answer only because it is badly formulated, badly expressed, and because in some cases it is useless. Must we not begin by agreeing with St. Thomas that a Christian may be perfect without being in the state of perfection, and that conversely a sinner may be in a state of perfection without being perfect at all? Besides, the perfection that resides in charity consists in placing oneself in the situation that will permit him to correspond most completely with the intentions that God has for him. That is to say, he must seek to accomplish with his temperament, his heredity, his training, and also with his legitimate tastes, the greatest number of acts of charity of which he is personally capable. This is the way he will respond to his vocation. Clearly, this question goes beyond the matter of one's state in life.

In St. Thomas' day, a person's state of life was defined by the degree of social liberty that he did or did not possess. Today, it would be defined rather by his marital status, as well as by his profession and his means of subsistence. But state of life still remains a bare framework separated by abstraction from its moral content which is represented by duty, and for a Christian therefore, by charity. It is merely a receptacle to be filled, but which remains neutral as long as man's mind and social pressure distinguish and separate it from the obligations that this professional situation brings with it in real life. That is why the words "a good doctor" and "a good shoemaker" can have very different meanings, depending on whether the adjective "good" refers solely to the state, to the qualities of the work it involves, and to its particular end, or whether the adjective refers to the whole man, including not only his state, but also his morality and his last end. The two kinds of "goodness" are not necessarily proportionate or even parallel to one another.

Speaking as Christians and with the Gospel under our eyes, we ought to be less concerned with choosing a state of life than with collaborating in the work of creation, of the Incarnation and Redemption within the exhaustive limit of our aptitudes, our means, and even of our tastes, not to mention the circumstances under which we must struggle. By provisionally abstracting from the professional framework within which a personal and actual vocation is to be realized, this approach tends to pacify souls,—first of all, those that have no control over their future or even over their present, those, too, that cannot find their way amid continual changes, and finally those that hesitate to use extraordinary and very special means, being content to say with Father de Foucauld: *the best place for me is where I can do the most good*. The way to ask the question: where shall I be most perfect? is to ask (God, or one's director, or one's conscience): Where can I best love, serve, and collaborate most efficaciously with the divine plan? This problem is anterior and superior, from the point of view of posing and seeing it, to the problem of the choice of a state of life. And yet the choice of a state of life often uselessly troubles souls eager to be generous, and in cases of hesitation or uncertainty, it may inflict painful inferiority complexes.

Would we not be reviving the aberration of the Scribes and the Pharisees if we imagined that states of life, like sacraments of sorts, could establish us *ipso facto,* if not *ex opere operato,* in perfection? Besides, is not this notion a contradiction in terms? We wayfarers (*viatores,* as was said in the Middle Ages) cannot establish ourselves in perfection here on earth, for our perfection consists in never becoming fixed anywhere, since we have not attained our end, but in seeking always further and higher for the maximum that will make us increasingly resemble our Father who is in heaven, *secundum* Matt. 5:48.

* * *

But after all, when we speak of a state of perfection, we are presupposing a state that is not neutral with relation to charity, but which, because of the generosity that it demands, the mode of life that it implies, the spiritual élan that it assumes, must have a very close relationship with this supreme virtue, a relationship that seeks to attain to the limit of identity.

Are we to understand these words to refer to a state that would oblige us to perfection? Such an interpretation would be awkward, inasmuch as all Christians are obliged to seek perfection, by virtue of the laws and promises of their baptism. At best, we can speak of new obligations added to the original obligation. But what would the moralists think of this formula? Is not the notion of obligation a simple, indivisible idea? All that we can multiply would be its motives, its means, its exigencies, and its performance. Now we are arriving at a clearer view of our problem.

When we speak of states of perfection—and let us not forget that in Christian terms this means states of charity— we think only of states of life in which certain persons professionally practice charity, thanks to the virtues that are means to this end, or better still, thanks to the autogenous soldering of the means to the end,[1] whereby charity is practiced professionally. This last-mentioned state, according to St. Thomas, is the episcopacy, in which the container and the content of action, the material gesture and its spiritual end are one, since both are in the order of charity.

This affirmation calls for a somewhat closer examination.

First of all, what is a state of life? We can take the definition proposed by Suarez, "in whom we see the whole of Scholasticism":[2] *Statum dicunt esse veluti habitum, qui est difficile mobilis, quia est vel consuetudine, vel lege, vel alio modo simili firmatus.*[3] Actually, it is a condensation or an adaptation of St. Thomas' earlier analysis.

Thus, on the one hand, the *state* presupposes a permanent disposition in the subject, a *habitus,* either in his being or in his action. On the other hand, it presupposes a consecration of this *habitus* by law, custom, or in some other way. This might perhaps be adequately expressed in modern terms by saying that the state of life is at once individual and social. It is individual because it affects a subject; and social because it is controlled and maintained by the group to whose organization it contributes.

We find an easy and exact example of this theory in the profession of the artisan, his trade, which in certain French provinces is still called his "state." To be a carpenter or a farmer is not only to possess in one's head and at the tips of

---

[1] We are not using this expression to try to translate the scholastic term "conjoined means to the end."

[2] This is one of Bossuet's expressions, which should be used with discretion.

[3] Fr. Suarez, S.J., *De virtute et statu religionis,* tract. 7, lib. 1, cap. 1. (Paris: Edit. Vives, 1859), Tome 15, p. 3. However, first see St. Thomas, *Quodlibet* III, art. 17, and the *Summa* IIa IIae, qq. 184 ff. We get the impression that from St. Thomas to Suarez the conception of the state of life was strongly influenced by the evolution of social customs from the feudal period to modern times, before the opening of the contemporary period.

one's fingers all the *habitus* necessary for working wood or tilling the soil. It also means belonging to a given class of artisans in society, to a particular organization of workers. The man who is so qualified will spend his life and earn his living in this category. We might mention in passing that it is means of subsistence which on the surface usually distinguish *states*. "Tell me how you earn your living,[4] and I will tell you who you are."

Suarez does not descend to this alimentary definition. On the contrary he rises very high to ask himself if the idea of obligation, that he had found in St. Thomas with reference to this question, is a part of the concept of state of life. He concludes in the affirmative with the author of the *Summa*. To choose a state is also to impose upon oneself a mode of existence, and to renounce more or less complete freedom of action. To have a state is to be restricted to certain ways of being or acting. As we shall see, this remark is of great importance for our subject.

Before discussing the priesthood as a state of perfection, let us first call to mind wherein Christian perfection in general consists. The answer is even easier, although it is often misconstrued in practice. Christian perfection consists in the virtue of charity. This is the essential teaching of our Lord and the puport of the entire Gospel. It is the doctrine of St. Paul and of St. John. Besides, the whole of theological tradition, both ascetical and mystical, is agreed upon this point. St. Thomas' *Summa* completes the ordering of all these truths; and these principles have never been abandoned at least by the Thomists of the strict observance, despite temptations against this doctrine continually brought forward by the proponents of easy holiness. Charity, like perfection with which it is identified, is obligatory, says St. Thomas. Moreover, it exhausts all the Commandments. It is an obligation that has its

---

[4] The Encyclical *Quadragesimo anno* adds "and that of your family" for the benefit of the laity.

root in the sacrament of baptism (and not in the sacrament of Order or in religious perfection). *Estote vos perfecti, sicut et Pater vester caelestis perfectus est.* Charity, precept, perfection—these three ideas are on the same level, and almost equivalent.

"When charity commands it," says St. Francis de Sales, "monks and religious are taken from their cloisters to be made cardinals, prelates, pastors. They are sometimes even reduced to marriage, for the peace of kingdoms, as I have said above. Now, if charity can call out of the cloister those who had bound themselves to it by a solemn vow, there is all the more reason why—and for a lesser reason—one can, through the authority of this same charity, advise certain persons to remain at home, keep their financial resources, marry, indeed even to take up arms and go to war, which is such a dangerous profession.

"Now, when charity leads some to poverty, and withdraws others from it; when it induces some to marry, and others to practice continence; when it imprisons some in the cloister, and causes others to leave it, it needs to make explanations to no one; for charity possesses the fullness of power in Christian law. . . . *That is why we must take from charity the command to exercise the counsels.* For to some, it will command chastity, and not poverty, and so on . . . ; and while it is all of one color which is colorless, yet the flowers that it begets all have their own particular color . . ."[5]

Elsewhere he says: "The perfection of divine love is so supreme that it perfects all the virtues and cannot be perfected by them, not even by obedience, which is the virtue that can best increase perfection in the others."[6]

Therefore, when our Lord spoke the two sentences to the

---

[5] *Treatise on the Love of God,* Book 8, Chapter 6.

[6] *Ibid.,* Book 11, Chapter 9. But there already was the text of St. Thomas, referring precisely to the episcopacy: *quam curam pastoralem negligere non debat episcopus, neque propter divinae contemplationis quietem.* (IIa IIae, q. 185, a. 4.)

rich young man which are at the basis of all elite vocations,
He was not superposing a superior Christianity upon the min-
imum requirements of the first answer. For, with the first
words He had set forth the whole spirit of the New Law and
all the intransigence of the Gospel. But in His second answer
He made explicit the particular demands of charity in a given
case, that of the young man in question.[7] Priests constantly
use the same procedure in their ministry, although they too
often stop midway. They present the whole of Christian
morality in general terms that are less disturbing to their lis-
teners, and wait for more favorable circumstances to dot their
"i's." And yet dotting the "i's" adds nothing to the truth of
the primitive text.

The only question that arises, then, is this: is there a state
of life that is defined by the obligation and the practice of
charity and that is therefore a state of perfection? Now, most
if not all professions permit and even require of a Christian
the practice of charity and the exercise of perfection. And yet
they are neither defined nor constituted, as determined and
named states, by charity in act. A physician is not a man who,
as a physician, practices charity. He is a man who fights ill-
ness. It goes without saying that if he is a Christian he must
cure his patients under the command of charity. The fact remains that if he does it through greed or pride, he is no less a
physician by profession and activity. His profession does not
produce charity in him, as a physician.

Now, there is a state of life, and probably only one, that is
defined and constituted by the exercise of charity. It is the
episcopal state, and *a fortiori* the Sovereign Pontificate. The
bishop is a man whose calling (*sit verbo venia!*) consists in

---

[7] All Thomist theologians (we do not say: all preachers) agree on
this interpretation of the scene with the rich young man. Cf. R. Garrigou-
Lagrange, O.P., *Saint Matthieu,* "in Matth. 19:21," p. 277; also his
Christian Perfection and Contemplation (St. Louis: B. Herder, 1937),
Vol. I. Cf. Father de Guibert, S.J., *Les doublets de saint Thomas d'Aquin*
(Paris, 1926), Chapter 7.

practicing without interruption or measure the loftiest charity, spiritual charity, the charity that consists in saving souls. He exercises charity toward God through his supreme priesthood, and toward the faithful, *his* faithful, through his ministry. He was appointed and even consecrated to this end, if he is, as is the normal procedure, the resident bishop of a real diocese. He is bound forever to this perfect work. If he truly lives up to his responsibility, if he fulfills its functions, then by reason of his state, he will be practicing charity: *servus servorum Dei*. The matter of his professional activity is identified with the very exercise of perfect Christianity.

The creation of this state is one of the marvels of the new religion. Now there are men who exercise the same profession as Christ did, as servant and pastor during His mortal life: *quemadmodum ego feci, ita et vos . . . Non veni ministrai, sed ministrare.* Indeed, we adore in Christ other aspects of His ministry which are reproduced elsewhere in other souls, as for example His poverty. There are poor men in the Church, and in every state of life. But for the moment we are not concerned with this problem. We are simply asking if the sublime and divine social position of Christ has been maintained among us since His visible departure, if there is in the Church a profession which, as such, preserves and incarnates the charity of Christ and is defined by this charity. The facts answer: Yes.

Looking at things in this light, we at once see the distinguishing mark we must attribute to the simple state of the priestly life in the diocese. The priest approaches the state of perfection in the measure in which he participates in the exercise of episcopal charity, within the limits in which he is charged with filling the bishop's place in his religious functions as pontiff, apostle, and pastor. This deputation, this collaboration has a great range of degrees, and none of them will ever equal the professional privilege of the episcopal state. And yet to be a diocesan priest, that is, to be a priest at the disposition of the bishop, already means to benefit by the episcopal state of perfection. The permanent pastor of a parish realizes best and in the greatest possible degree the required conditions, even though he does not fulfill them completely. It is a question of more or less, in which no one except the bishop can aspire to the perfect state of life.[8]

The diocesan priest is at the service of the bishop to help him in all his functions—religious, apostolic, and pastoral. This is the profound, sacramental sense and not merely the canonical sense of: *promittis mihi obedientiam?—Pax tibi.* He is also at the service of the bishop's flock. He must live from this point of view, with this preoccupation, and, one might say, with this anxiety: *sollicitudo omnium ovium ecclesiae.* If the bishop calls upon his help, he may never see the end of the horizons thus opened up. Everything is of concern to him —the works of the past and those of tomorrow. All souls preoccupy him and keep him busy: *ad omne opus bonum paratus.* It is the reason for his existence. This servitude is so far-reaching that the Church counsels and if need be commands the priest not to bind himself too rigorously to a particular asceticism which, in specifying his personal rule of life, might prevent him from fulfilling unforeseen tasks demanded by the needs of the faithful. God and neighbor! Such is the emblem of this servant of charity, this servant of God and of all spiritual needs without exception, this father of all the souls of his little parish, the universal pastor of all who dwell in his bit of hillside or city suburb.

This was the formal doctrine of Cardinal Mercier, as he presented it to his clergy a few years before his death in his great book on the interior life, which is in a sense his testament to them:

---

[8] This question of principle, or rather of law, has no relation to the historical question whether all bishops have always been perfect, and whether priests are in fact the holy priests they should be: *nihil prohibet aliquos esse perfectos, qui non sunt in statu perfectionis, et aliquos esse in statu perfectionis, qui tamen non sunt perfecti. (Summa,* IIa IIae, q. 184, a. 4.)

"The subsidiary means [of perfection] vary from state to state, from individual to individual. It would be erroneous to impose upon or to indiscriminately counsel to clerics, to priests, the means of perfection proper to the special state of the religious; just as it would be wrong to impose upon or counsel to religious all the auxiliaries of charity [that is, of perfection] that ministers of the altar and pastors of souls find in the fulfillment of their ecclesiastical or pastoral functions." [9]

How far we have come from this conception which, in the opinion of a reliable judge,[10] fortunately has never been upheld by any theologian, but floats about like a misty and false vision in the heads of certain of the faithful. It would seem that there are two clergies, one perfect and the other imperfect, the regular clergy and the secular clergy. The former are established in perfection by their vows, their asceticism, and their common life; whereas the latter are the poor relatives or degenerate brothers, who, for lack of courage, have held back from the narrow path and have come to a halt halfway up the mountain of holiness, *respiciens retro* instead of answer-the divine call.

On the contrary, every priest should esteem and love his ecclesiastical state, his *diocesan* state (for we want no more to do with the word *"secular,"* which has a double meaning).[11] How beautiful is this state when seen in the light in which we have been trying to restore it! Born of divine charity, in whose service it was created, it elevates priests above all particular asceticisms, and constitutes them as the fathers and servants of the Christian people. It makes them participate in the life and in the state of the bishop, who is the true

[9] *La Vie Intérieure* (Paris-Brussels, 1919), p. 177.
[10] Father de Guibert, S.J., in the *Revue d'Ascétique et de Mystique,* October-December, 1935, No. 64, pp. 384-385 (footnote).
[11] We accept it only in the sense our Lord used it: *non rogo ut tollas eos de mundo.*

pontiff. Is there any dignity in the world greater than his? It is always service that calls: *ministrare . . . ut fructum afferatis, quemadmodum ego feci . . . sicut pastor . . . operaii in messem.*[12]

The thing that binds a priest to his diocese is his love and desire for complete spiritual fatherhood. Both inwardly and outwardly, it is a love of the divine work that is almost completed: *bonus pastor animam suam dat . . . Charitatem autem non habuero, nihil sum.* In principle and within the limits already indicated, diocesan priests are striving to resemble Christ and His Apostles, and they truly constitute the Church, as her essential, immortal, and irreplaceable hierarchy, under the bishops. They are truly the *fathers,* the *abbots,* the pastors

---

[12] "It is the diocesan clergy that assures the fundamental Christian stability of a country. Every country is composed of dioceses and parishes. It is the parochial clergy who take charge of Christians. They do not devote themselves only to the tasks that are compatible with their capacities. The religious is free to refuse apostolic assignments that his superior does not consider advisable for him. The secular clergy, on the other hand, must take over the entire ministry that comes within their territory.

"We hear the terms *'obligated'* priesthood and apostolate *'incarnate in an environment'!* Who better than parish priests fulfill these formulas, and above all the priests of rural parishes. . . . The communitarian sense of Christianity is maintained through the parochial clergy.

"It is not my intention at all to say that there must be no more religious. . . . We are more than happy that there are specialists in prayer and in preaching. . . . I do not even say that the regular clergy have only a subsidiary role, for this, too, would be incorrect.

"And yet I declare that given the religious situation of France it is time to understand that except for exclusive aspirations to contemplation and except for compelling reasons for living in community, there is every reason to orientate vocations toward what is most urgent, most indispensable, and most pertinent for maintaining the spiritual framework of the country, that is, toward the diocesan clergy. . . ." (His Excellency, P.-Marie Richaud, Bishop of Laval, in his Christmas allocution for 1946, *Semaine Religieuse du diocèse de Laval,* January 5, 1947.)

of the Church, and at the same time her humble folk, her little ones, her rank and file.[13]

---

[13] When I speak in this way I am of course thinking of Rostand and Flambeau, but I am also thinking of rural pastors, and I remember Father Rousselot's words in *Christus:* "Jesus gathers together, strengthens, and exalts in His person the distinctive traits of these meek and these poor whose laments fill the Bible, and who sing in the Psalms of their persevering hope. The French word that best fits this throng is *'les humbles,'* or perhaps *'les endurants. Bienheureux les endurants, car ils posséderont la terre'* [Blessed are the meek, for they shall possess the land]. This is the way an ancient French writer renders the Fourth Beatitude." (1912 edition, p. 702.)

In *Le Figaro* for December 27-30, 1946, François Mauriac presents a picture of Midnight Mass in a Paris parish. After describing the movement of the Christian throng at the Offertory, he adds: "Before the Consecration, the faithful who wish to receive Holy Communion place a host in the ciborium themselves. During this very long procession, the Mass had to be interrupted, and I watched the exhausted face of the young priest who was immobilized before the altar. He had probably spent the day a prisoner of the confessional, slapped for hours on end by the same little tide of mediocre impurities.

"I remembered all the investigations published in Catholic periodicals on 'the agony of Christianity.' How ungrateful we are for the great effort toward renewal of which our young clergy gives us the example! Actually, there is no grave peril for the Church today (and for that matter for the University, elementary education, and for all branches of human activity) except the decline in vocations. It is not that fewer are called than formerly. But how can those who are called help preferring the orderly apostolate of the monasteries to the ministry of large city parishes, consumed by material worries, administrative labors, or to the solitude and dreariness of the rectories of a de-Christianized countryside?

"And yet it is this young priest whom I observed on his platform, pressed by the trampling and recollected crowd, and who, with slightly bowed head, seemed to be carrying his Infant-God in his arms—it is this living host that the Church needs to accomplish her mission in this world. His sufferings, his sacrifices, his entire exhausting apostolate will make 'the agony of the Church' endure until the end of the world (as Pascal said of Christ's agony), the agony that precedes not death but resurrection in the light."

These considerations lead us to conceive of the priestly state as being capable by itself of furnishing its members with means of perfection through and in the exercise of the duties which it imposes upon them, for these duties are acts of charity, and therefore acts of perfection. A diocesan priest who has a true understanding of his state, that is, of its relations with the state of life of his bishop, and who acts accordingly, is perpetually training himself in charity, and therefore training himself in holiness.

It will be noticed, moreover, that this conception of the priestly life is very exacting. Instead of limiting the requirements of the priestly state to a certain number of ascetic exercises that are necessarily restricted in their definition and regulations, the sacrament of Order, as the diocesan priest receives it, not only from a bishop but for a bishop and for a diocese, requires of the priest apostolic self-sacrifice and activity that are limited only by the trust his prelate has in him, the needs of souls, and the priest's own availability. Indeed, the first two coefficients may be limitless.

The diocesan priest will certainly look to asceticism for the protective barriers that his weakness needs, being careful to eliminate any practice that might be contrary to the normal exercise of his apostolic duties. In the second part of this little book we shall consider the great laws of diocesan spirituality.[14]

---

[14] Now, while St. Thomas professes great respect for the episcopal state of perfection (and we have borrowed our theology on this state from him), he is somewhat reserved with regard to simple priests. He has not extended his doctrine in favor of the latter, as we have sought to do. A Dominican recently tried to console me about this by stating that St. Thomas was perhaps judging the priestly state solely from the experiences of his own time. In Suarez' day, the state of the clergy— after the Counter-Reformation and the Catholic renaissance—was doubtless in a better condition. In any case, Suarez goes beyond St. Thomas' thought, and he gives us a fitting introduction to the theology we are now proposing. I owe the following text to the competence of Father Gustav Thils: "censeo sacerdotes ex vi sui ordinis habere statum altiorem et sanctiorem qui ab eis nonnulla perfectionis opera requirit, ratione

cujus obligationis merito dici possunt aliquo modo, inchoactive saltem, in statu perfectionis." (Suarez, *De virtute et statu religionis,* Book 1, chapter 17, in *Opera,* Tome 15, quoted in Thils, *Nature et spiritualité du clergé diocésain,* p. 396.) And the above-mentioned Dominican has been willing to conclude, no doubt with the twentieth century clergy in mind: "Notwithstanding St. Thomas' contrary view, we think that priests are constituted in a state of participated charity. The consequence of this is that they are in a state of perfection which derives from that of the bishop. It seems to us that the great present-day need for a priestly spirituality is to be sought in this direction. It is particularly clear that the priest must sanctify himself by his spiritual and apostolic ministry, and that this approach offers vistas of comprehension and technique that have not as yet been explored, at least not systematically and fruitfully."

CHAPTER IX

The Priest and Catholic Action

To ENCOURAGE the laity to participate in the hierarchical apostolate, the beautiful verses of I *Petri* have been applied to them: "You, however, are a chosen race, a royal priesthood, a holy nation, a purchased people; that you may proclaim the perfections of Him who has called you out of darkness into His marvellous light. You who in times past were not a people, but are now the people of God." [1] The clergy thus explains to the faithful that, solely because of their baptism, they are clothed with a certain priesthood that ordains them to the salvation of their brothers, to the extension of the kingdom of God, and to the growth of the Church. It is to the faithful that the most unanswerable papal documents seem to reserve the specialized evangelization of various social spheres. How often have we reread and commented upon the classical sentence in *Quadragesimo Anno:* "Undoubtedly, the first and immediate apostles of the industrial and commercial world should themselves be employers and merchants." [2]

As a prolongation of the Encyclical, rather than as a translation, it is also shown that only the laity really belong to

---

[1] I Pet. 2:9-10.

[2] English translation in the collection *Five Great Encyclicals* (New York: The Paulist Press, 1939), Paragraph 141, p. 166.

social groups, they alone are genuinely received by these groups, and consequently they alone can exert an influence on them. Moreover, it is pointed out, in order to act it is necessary to know; and to know, one must be able to practice the policy of presence, to have contacts, listen to confidential disclosures, take part in conversations, and be initiated into people's real attitudes. Now, only the layman can penetrate factories, offices, places of recreation and entertainment, worldly or industrial gatherings. The priest remains removed from all this, not only because of his attire which creates around him a zone of silence, suspicion, or simply of respect, but he remains remote also because of his state, his vocation, that makes him a "saint," a separated one, "the man of God." He is no longer of the world because of his consecration and of his purity. Besides he does not belong to any social group, since he belongs to all classes and none of them can claim him as its own nor cares to do so. For all these reasons, it is declared, the apostolate has become almost impossible for him. Fortunately, the laity will replace him in this office. Then they repeat some frightening words of Paul Claudel.[3]

On the other hand, theologians and above all preachers stress for the benefit of priests, in publications and retreat sermons intended for them alone, the ministry of the altar to which they are consecrated and which constitutes their privilege. Priests are seen as men of prayer, both private and public, ministers of sacrifice and of the sacraments, whose true functions are liturgical. These divine offices are presented as

---

[3] *Le Père Humilié,* Act 2, Scene 2. Pope Piux IX speaks: "Orian, my son, what I have not been able to do, you must do, since you do not have this throne to which I am bound in order better to hear the despairing cry of the whole earth; this agony of being tied while the whole earth suffers, knowing that we have salvation within Ourselves,—you must do it, since you do not have this robe before which, through the devil's malice, all hearts draw back and contract. Speak to them, you who know their language, who are not a stranger to any nook and cranny of their nature."

affirming and making the most of the priest's holiness, his separation. And now another traditional text is invoked to bear witness, the one from the *Acts of the Apostles* that deals with the election of the first deacons: "It is not desirable that we should forsake the word of God and serve at tables . . . we will devote ourselves to prayer and to the ministry of the word." [4]

Let us admit it, if a priest were wedged between such a broad definition of the priesthood of the faithful and such a rigid conception of his own priesthood, he would find his life and his activity, his role and his state singularly diminished. He is to console himself, so he is told, by practicing the virtues of counsel of which the religious give him such a beautiful example. As a man of obedience, celibacy, and poverty, as a man of community and discipline, he is to consume his life in the practice of a superior ascesis; and he, too, is to try to convert the world, in some way from the outside, by the admirable example of the holiness of his life.

This necessarily oversimplified view would soon discourage young men, who would prefer to remain among the laity so as to practice the engrossing apostolate of Catholic Action, rather than accept priestly functions and an ecclesiastical state that would make this work of evangelization impossible. But we can no longer reconcile this conclusion with the urgent exhortations of the Encyclical *Ad catholici sacerdotii fastigium* [5] on the discernment and fostering of priestly vocations.

Indeed, such unforseen consequences can only come from erroneous premises, whose exaggerations we must discover and exorcise. The preceding pages of this little book may have helped to right some of these ideas with the help of the principles whose conclusions we shall now marshal forth.

* * *

---

[4] Acts 6:2, 4.
[5] A.A.S. XXVIII, 1936 (Pope Pius XI).

There can be no question of priests abandoning, for the benefit of Catholic Action or the laity, the responsibilities of an apostolate that belongs to them by virtue of their priesthood. Now, this priesthood constitutes them the immediate collaborators of the bishops; and among the essential episcopal functions, themselves sprung from Christ's mediatory and redemptive charity, is the evangelization of the world, that is, the apostolate. In fact, it was the name "Apostle" that Christ chose to designate His successors in the work of saving the world. The twelve Galileans, from whom the episcopacy stems, are called neither pontiffs nor bishops in the Gospels, but Apostles. When they had grown old or were on the eve of martyrdom, they gave their parting instructions to their heirs; or more probably, after their death, their churches elected a single successor to replace each of them from the group of *presbyteri-episcopi* they had named. Great care was taken, at any rate, to retain for the apostolic function, which had become the episcopal function, all of its primitive richness, which included, together with prayer and the breaking of the bread, the ministry of the word in the fullest sense.

But to be a priest, as we have seen, is to participate immediately in the duties as well as the responsibilities of the bishop, under his direction, at his discretion. It therefore means to take part in his apostolic works, in his action, in his priestly action, which is superior to the Catholic Action that is its prolongation, that seeks to imitate it from afar, and that is dependent upon it.

Perhaps the purpose of placing action and the priesthood in opposition was simply to show (and rightly so) that the clergy, in France and in all highly evolved modern countries, has been limited, fortunately, to purer and more spiritualized apostolic interventions. In saying this we do not intend to return to the quasi-Jansenistic heresy of the *pure supernatural,* that is, of an empty, disembodied supernatural in the periphery of real life. But we do mean to say that the insertion of spiritual authority in the world of the living will be more powerful in the measure that it is discreet, less cumbersome and less encumbered.

The days are over for prince-bishops, minister-cardinals, and perhaps even for priest-secretaries of organizations. In the Gospel there is a principle of disinterestedness, a spirit of modesty and respect, that oblige God's representatives to practice humility or discretion. But their reserve increases their authority to the extent that the latter is less compromised by material details, contingencies of application, and questionable corollaries. In the Church there are projects that only a layman can undertake, as well as moral authority that only a priest can have. In this sense, obviously the action of laymen and even their Catholic Action is much more temporal, more visible than that of the clergy, who specialize in the higher levels of purified action, in order to impress all things with the spirit of the Church, which is the spirit of the Gospel.[6]

---

[6] I snatched this idea from the reception discourse of Count Molé at the Académie Française, when he succeeded His Excellency de Quélen, the Archbishop of Paris, in 1840. The latter had once delivered in the *Chambre des Paris* a famous speech against the proposed conversion of government stocks then recommended by M. de Villèle. And Molé says emphatically: "The orator had a great influence on his audience. From that moment on, and perhaps without his wishing it, his reputation was no longer limited to the pulpit. The political world began to judge him. This is surely no place to examine what role our institutions permit a bishop to play in public affairs. I shall however say this: that if among the three orders of the State, the clergy was once first in learning and wealth, today, under the influence of our institutions and above all under the influence of time—that is, of world opjnion and public morality— things have changed. The power of the clergy is still great, and it is perhaps even greater than before, but on condition of being sought and exercised solely in the moral order."

In his answer, the acting director, Monsieur Dupin, remarked: "When the proposal was made to reduce government stock, Archbishop de Quélen fought this dangerous measure not from the political angle, nor for financial reasons, nor with the excuse of its untimeliness. He did it from the point of view that rightly belonged to him, that of pity for the weak whom he believed were being threatened. He defended the small stockholders as he would have defended the poor, and he received their gratitude."

There is still another concession to be made to Catholic Action, but it does not diminish priestly dignity. Quite the contrary! Rightly or wrongly, the priest of today is often obliged to exercise his evangelistic ministry through the laity, and to a certain extent at second hand. He evangelizes by painstakingly training a chosen group of the faithful, who in their turn evangelize their social milieu.[7] But in this way the priest is an apostle twice over, by acting himself upon others who also act. We are familiar with the Pseudo-Denys' enthusiastic description—chiefly from the liturgical point of view—of this action by the pontiff and his clerics upon their inferiors whom they permeate with their own holiness.[8] We can take these

---

[7] There is a subtle reason for this of historical origin, that is perhaps too often unnoticed. The priest, as the auxiliary and representative of the bishop, exercises authority over the faithful and also evangelizes unbelievers. In Catholic countries he has long worn in public the clothing that accredits him to the faithful, and what is more important for the subject under discussion, he has taken the habit of exercising the acknowledged authority that he enjoys among them. But for that very reason, the unbelievers who do not yet accept this authority mistrust and avoid him. And the priest, for that matter, finds it hard to belie his age and his habits and to divide himself in two, practicing successively or simultaneously attitudes of authority and of invitation, the pastorate on the one hand and evangelization on the other. It is a striking fact that preaching has become for us exclusively a ministry of authority, whereas the Apostles exercised it first of all as a missionary and apostolic ministry.

[8] "Every initiator is first of all sanctified by the knowledge of the sacred ministries, and, so to speak, deified by reason of his nature, his aptitude, and his dignity; then he transmits to his inferiors, to the extent that they are capable of receiving it, the divine likeness that he himself has received from above. The latter follow their leader and likewise attract their subordinates, who in turn first obey and then command others. In consequence of these divine and harmonious relations, each one, in the degree that is proper to him, enters into communion with essential beauty, wisdom, and goodness. . . ." (Denys, *De la Hiérarchie ecclésiastique,* chapter 1. French translation by Darboy.)

"Thus the order of the pontiffs is full of power to communicate perfection. It alone possesses the privilege of celebrating the most sublime mysteries of our hierarchy. A capable interpreter, the pontiff reveals to men the science of sacred things, and teaches them to what virtues and to what holiness they are called. The priestly order gives illumination,

generous and optimistic visions and apply them to the ministry of evangelization. Then, nothing human and living is
foreign to the priestly activity of the priest, who is the vivifier
of Catholic Action. Through the laymen that he trains and
instructs, and from whom he receives information and support, he reaches into and even knows all social groupings.
Perhaps it is merely because, being on a higher level, he sees
men with a purer vision, and yet without ignoring any of
their needs, their troubles, or their resources. He perceives
them from a broader and in a sense less impassioned point of
view, because of his perspective.[9]

As for the leaders of Catholic Action, he speaks to them
and touches them directly. He is their immediate father. He
begets them perpetually to life, as St. Paul did his first disciples. And it is truly a renewing of St. Paul's story. St. Paul
had spent his whole life training militants who themselves
stirred synagogues and discovered proselytes. Meanwhile, the
great Apostle was informed of their works, suffered when his
sons suffered, rejoiced when they rejoiced, and took a profound interest in their successes and difficulties. *"Quis infirma-
tur, et ego non infirmor?"* [10]

At a time when the Sovereign Pontiff is so insistently
recommending Catholic Action to the laity, we must not min-
imize the priestly action of priests. This action has never been
more necessary, since without it the action of the laity would
not exist. The hour has come for priests to realize the inward
law of their institution, which is the evangelization of the
world under the dependence of the bishops, chiefly through

---

prepares and leads the initiates to the spectacle of the holy mysteries and
performs the functions of its office in the society of and in dependence
upon the divine pontiffs. . . . The order of deacons has as its mission
to purify, and to discern between good and evil, before invoking the
ministry of the priests, . . ." (*Ibid.,* chapter 4.)

[9] Cf. the following notation from *Etudes* for March 20, 1936, p. 820:
". . . a genuinely priestly soul, capable of bending over these miseries,
without any pharasaical revolt and also without any suspicious delight."

[10] II Cor. 11:29. Cf. Canon Glorieux' *Paul* (Paris: JOC, 1936).

the exercise of influence upon militant Christians. It can even be said that if the burden or the exaggeration of liturgical and sacramental functions were to prevent the clergy from fulfilling their strictly apostolic duties for lack of time, it would be better to renounce the pomp and length of ritual ceremonies than to abandon pastoral action. In St. Paul's own words: *Vae mihi si non evangelizavero*.[11] When we cite St. Peter's words on the day of the institution of the deacons, far from placing the life of prayer in opposition to the life of action, we should remember that this *ministerium verbi* is simply the permanent testament of the things seen and heard in Judea and in Galilee "from the baptism of John to the day of the Ascension." That is to say, it is the preaching of Christianity, the apostolic action which was carried on, then as it is today, in the small gatherings connected with the meetings of the synagogues—analogous to our present-day specialized study groups.

Why do certain masters of pastoral retreats and also certain spiritual publications for the use of the clergy make such severe criticisms of the activity of priests, of their works and the movements they direct? Have those who speak thus of priestly action ever really practiced it themselves? Do they know from personal experience how hard, thankless, and therefore—from their own point of view—sanctifying, is the apostolate of the world? Do they not confuse it with noise and agitation? The fact is that we must distinguish between the apostolate and the backwash of activity. Above all, there

---

[11] I Cor. 9:16. But here we touch upon another problem, as urgent as it is delicate. It is the problem of the adaptation of the liturgy to the Christian life of the common people. In its original institution, the liturgy has been a wonderful pedagogy of the Church, but one that has too often become a dead letter in our hands, a mute symbolism. The day we bring the liturgy back to life, when its value as a sign, as a means of teaching, as a mode of common life and common prayer—the day when its value as action will have attained its full efficacy through our efforts, there will no longer be any conflict between the "ministry" of prayer and the "ministry" of the word.

is need to rediscover and to preach again a spirituality of action and of the content (or matter) of action. For too many centuries now, since the days of Jansenism perhaps, since the "retreat of the mystics," since the decline of the "French School," the chief effort of ascetics has been focussed upon the formality of action, the personal faults of the one who acts, and the ever-present possibility of impurity in his intentions. And yet within this form is the action itself, which is not necessarily evil, and which is sanctifying even if it is only materially good. A successful inquiry group has every chance of being directed by a good priest, for an inquiry group—in order to succeed and because it succeeds—requires sound ideas, painstaking care, intelligent perseverance, and a pure zeal. Then, according to scholastic terminology, from the potency of matter there emerges a good form.

The tendency of moralists to stress the faults of the man who labors, without ever explaining what the content of the work should be, has ended by discouraging priestly good will, especially among the younger priests. This purely negative, purely critical attitude, which imagines it is painting a picture when it is merely providing a frame for it, this mania for considering in human activity and in Christian life only the form and never the matter, gives to certain types of particular and general examens a power of exasperation that defeats their purpose: *et propter vitam, vivendi perdere causas.*[12]

---

[12] "Man always tends to underestimate what the philosophers call material causality," says Gustave Thibon in *Médecine et Marriage* (Lyon, 1937), p. 224. In short, between these two great schools of spirituality to which Brémond sought to reduce all French traditions, and whose beginning he saw in a sentence from Lallamant: "The shortest and surest path to perfection is to study ourselves through pure hearts rather than through the practice of the virtues," there is room for a *via media* between pure form and separated matter. (Cited in Brémond, *Histoire littéraire du sentiment religieux en France* [Paris: Bloud et Gay, 1920], Tome 5, p. 42.) True, it is the intention and therefore the purity of our hearts that primarily constitutes the spiritual value of our actions. Even so, this form requires matter, and this matter when it is well chosen, composed of acts of charity and not only of ascetic exercises cultivated and analyzed for their own sake, in its turn begets purity of form.

It is time to retrieve all our fundamental values, which, though they have never been lost, no longer hold the primary place in preaching and in ascesis that they have a right to. Under the pretense that the administration of the sacraments and even the celebration of Mass do not suffice to sanctify the minister who empties them spiritually of their content, we have for several centuries yielded to the temptation of seeking the principles and means of holiness for the priest outside of his priestly service. We have even sought them in practices foreign to his state, and sometimes incompatible with his duties. Members of religious orders and congregations, whose spiritual life, contrary to that of the diocesan priest, is centered upon their ascetic rule, have generously offered their riches. These they have offered as useful methods, and sometimes as irreplaceable means. It was praiseworthy of them. And yet in giving such counsel, they may have confused two states of life, the state of the diocesan priest and that of the religious. Or rather it was the diocesan priests who forgot their own first principle of sanctification, their pastoral and apostolic office, and the *sollicitudo Ecclesiae,* the will for the extension of the kingdom of God, which St. Paul pointed out as one of the reasons for the priest's existence, his interior force, his goal, and often if not always his cross.

As for the priest's sacramental functions, they are but the symbol—and an efficacious one—of his duty and of his power to perform religious and apostolic action. And the Mass itself is, in the ancient and universal sense of the word, the sacrament, the sensible sign of his profound ministry. It is in the very heart of his state, in its soul, in its end, that he must seek the ultimate solution of his problem. It is in sanctifying others that the priest must in part learn to sanctify himself. This has already been said in a remarkable and courageous article in *La Vie Spirituelle:* "The anxieties of the day's work, the preoccupations of one's state, the difficulties to be overcome in order to live and to do good, are banished from prayer as being distractions. God must not be brought into these trivialities. And so a complicated and artificial spiritual life is contrived. . . . Men who are crushed by their concern for the kingdom of God think it is almost a sin to drag their worries and their burdens everywhere with them . . . as if thinking of all things for God's sake were not also thinking of God. . . . We may consider as false spiritualities all those . . . that would claim to lead us toward God by making us indifferent to our brothers." [13]

The author of these excellent lines seems to have placed his finger on a delicate and painful, but inescapable point: when means and not the end are in question, we should never exceed moderation. Doubtless the priestly ministry is a danger for the priest, but it is first of all, when it is rightly understood and practiced, an essential source of strength for him. Organizations and "movements" should never be denounced as occasions of sin or of dissipation by preachers who have not themselves experienced the sweat and the anguish that real works of *action* cost. On the other hand, the warnings of dangers to be incurred are not altogether false. But is it not better first to teach the priest how to use these delicate and powerful instruments, since they are the very tools of his good work, the means placed at his disposal to fulfill the duties of his state, and since they constitute half of the definition of Christ's own priesthood?

When will someone follow the example of the author we have just cited and tell us, in order to encourage us in our own particular vocation, that priestly action—in the profound sense of the two words: priestly and action—is good and sanctifying in itself. For it is hard and beneficial to make the Gospel penetrate the world and men's lives, to communicate its message and transmit its spirit, by dint of projects, conversations, meetings, inquiries and contacts. It is in this very apostolate, that is part of the definition of the priesthood and that is not outside of the priest's duty, that the priest must seek

---

[13] Article signed "Sacerdos," in *La Vie Spirituelle* for April, 1936. The author, unfortunately for us, has chosen to remain anonymous.

some of his surest means of sanctification. He may of course add to this essence, *ad cautelam,* means drawn from other states of life, and therefore often accidental and replaceable. All these questions will be taken up again in the second part of this book.

The diocesan priest has no reason to envy the action of the Catholic laity. On the contrary, *Catholic Action* groups should normally become centers of priestly vocations, on condition that once these have been expressed and orientated, they find houses of ecclesiastical training where they will grow through educational methods that prolong and accentuate the Christian apostolate in which they were conceived.[14]

Conclusion To Part One

The Christian priesthood, sprung from Christ's, was instituted by Him and recorded in the Gospel. The collation of the power to celebrate the Eucharist is the efficacious sign of this participation in the priestly functions of the Saviour. On these essential points there is unanimous agreement in the Catholic Church.

But there are at least two ways of constructing the evangelical and theological proof of these truths. One method seems to start from a somewhat restricted conception of Christ's priestly functions, which it limits principally if not exclusively

---

[14] "The atmosphere of a seminary is as morally sane as that of a factory is vitiated. Why, then, do some vocations wither in the seminary whereas very beautiful ones sometimes blossom in the factories? Is it not for the following reason: there are fewer occasions to do evil in the seminary, but in the factory there are more occasions to do good? A young seminarian may renounce the priesthood because he has not been completely possessed by an impassioned apostolate; while a Jocist will enter the seminary and become an excellent priest because he has already acquired a love for the apostolate. The ardor of his charity, having increased with each day's action until it has become irresistible, will lead him to the foot of the altar, where his life will complete its immolation for the salvation of his brothers." (Canon Thellier de Poncheville, *Tout l'Évangile dans toute la vie* [Paris: Spes, 1934], p. 102.)

to the offering of the sacrifice of the Cross and the celebration of the Eucharist at the Last Supper. According to this view, when the Saviour gave His Apostles the command and the faculty to renew the Last Supper, He not only ordained priests, but he determined the limits of their priesthood, which consists essentially in this power. Therefore this power properly defines the Apostles' priesthood, to which Jesus added supplementary functions in order *afterwards* to constitute the episcopate. Episcopal powers are distinct from those of the priesthood, and come from other intentions of the Saviour and other passages of the Gospel to be studied later. It should be noted that if this rather narrow theory were to triumph, it would still not succeed in definitively establishing an individualistic conception of the Christian priesthood. After all, it was to a community, that of the Apostles, that our Lord said: *hoc facite*. And it was a community in which there was already a hierarchy, even if it were only because of Peter's privileges, a community which would soon distinguish itself from the faithful and become a clergy.

But there are probably much better things to say, and we can construct a far more substantial proof for the thesis of the priesthood of Christ and of His Apostles. Instead of starting from the simple priesthood and from the sacrifice of the Mass, this proof starts from the episcopacy and from the apostolic and pastoral functions of the bishop.

The sacrifice of Jesus is an act, both on Calvary and at the Last Supper. His priesthood, however, is a state, since it springs from His nature, from His twofold nature in the unity of His Person. Christ is still a Priest, and He always will be. As Mediator, He never ceases acting to reconcile and unite His Father and men. Never during His mortal life did He interrupt the exercise of His functions as an intermediary, required for the glory of His Father and for the spiritual needs of men. As the Collect of the Votive Mass of our Lord Jesus Christ, the Eternal High Priest, says: *Ad majestatis tuae gloriam et generis humani salutem, Unigenitum tuum sum-*

mum atque aeternum constituisti sacerdotem. As Priest, Jesus forgave sins and instituted the sacraments; He prayed for us and taught us to pray; He was the great religious of His Father. Then, turning toward us, He took care of our souls; He revealed God's mysteries to us; He announced the good news to us, the Gospel. Finally, as He loved to repeat, He is the Shepherd of the flock, and we are His sheep, His disciples, His sons, His children.

Head, shepherd, teacher, saviour, king—all these titles, and others mentioned in the Gospels now have their own distinct theology. But they all derive from the dogma of the Son of God made man to save us. And if this great mystery, according to the *Epistle to the Hebrews,* is precisely translated by the title of High Priest of the New Alliance, it is certainly the proof that from this thesis of Christ's priesthood we can deduce—together with the dogma of the Incarnation—the entire content of the Christian mystery and all the spiritual riches that St. Paul saw hidden in God from the beginning and later revealed by and in His only-begotten Son.

Now, during Jesus' mortal life, the Apostles were initiated, trained and authorized by Him to exercise—both then and later—the functions of intermediaries, functions that were both religious and pastoral, directed toward God and toward men so as to unite Him with them, functions that were mediatory and therefore essentially sacerdotal. True, it was in the name of and in dependence upon their master, author, and founder, starting from Him as principle and cause, through His grace and therefore by participation in His mystery of religion, that the Apostles exercised these powers and duties, sanctified souls, spread the kingdom, introduced believers into it, and maintained peace, order, service, and, if you will, exercised authority. They were pastors in place of and by delegation of the Good Shepherd. They were priests not of their own priesthood, but the substitutes and deputies of the one Priest. And this almost undefinable position in which they were nothing of themselves, and yet great because of another, was to find its symbol, its sign, as well as its principle and supreme expression in the sublime institution which is itself the sign and the sacrament of another reality without which it would be nothing, but because of which it contains this mystery. This institution is the Eucharist. How can this be?

The priesthood of Christ had found its expression, its supreme expression, act, and fruitfulness at the moment when Jesus from the Cross offered up and immolated to His Father His body, His soul, His blood, and His life. Calvary had been the sacrifice of this new and eternal religion, of this definitive alliance. This was the culminating point of the Redemption, and the perfect act of the religion of Jesus.

The Eucharist is the sacrament of this religion and of this Redemption. It contains them both, one in the other. It is not a principle, for the Cross is the principle. And yet the Eucharist benefits from all the spiritual riches of the Cross, without which it would be nothing and thanks to which it is Christianity in perfect act.

This is exactly the position of the Apostles and of their priesthood in relation to Christ and to His pontificate: nothing without Him, everything through Him. Is it surprising, therefore, that the collation of the power to celebrate the Eucharist on Holy Thursday should have been the efficacious sign of this dependent priesthood, which is the priesthood of the Apostles? But since the grace of a sacrament is anterior to the sacrament and is not defined by it, similarly the priesthood of the Apostles is not defined solely by the power to celebrate the Eucharist, but by all the powers and all the graces of which the power to celebrate is the visible, necessary, and efficacious sign.

It follows that to understand the limits of the Apostles' priesthood or rather of their episcopacy, we must read the entire Gospel, we must look to Christ in His daily and prolonged relations with His Twelve. How and under what conditions did He put them in His place, at the head of His

Church, so that they might continue in His name, dependent upon Him and through His grace, to serve as intermediaries between God and men?

This would require a review of almost the entire apologetic treatise of the Church, looking down from above, from the angle of the religious and apostolic duties of the Pastors. And the successors of the Apostles were to be called bishops, in Greek *episcopi,* those who see men from above, from God's point of view, because they must take Christ's place in His function as supervising Pastor.

When the Apostles imposed hands to confer the priesthood or the diaconate upon their first collaborators, they conferred all or part of their own powers, so that these presbyters and deacons might exercise them under their authority. The primacy and the superiority of the Apostles and therefore of bishops over their priests is not exterior to this ordination. Rather it is the ordination itself that is subordinate, since the priests accomplish their priestly functions only in dependence upon the priesthood of their bishop. Thus, even if the *presbyteri-episcopi* of the first days had had the same powers of Order as the Apostles, they would still not have had them in the same manner nor under the same sacramental conditions. The current canonical idea of jurisdiction does not take sufficient account of the dominion of the priesthood of some over the priesthood of others.

When the Apostles gave these powers to their subordinates, they simultaneously sanctified their subordinates. Once again, let us not be the dupes of our more recent trends of thought. Even though we have long ago succeeded in distinguishing the character and the grace produced by the sacraments, it is no less true that these two effects are conferred upon us, one for the sake of the other, and that their separation is a sacrilege.

The ancients understood better than we do the idea that to give sacred powers is to sanctify. This doctrine was strongly emphasized in the works of the Pseudo-Areopagiticus, which inspired the spirituality of the entire Scholastic period.

Whence the twofold conclusion that when the bishop ordains his priests he brings them forth to a new grace, which is his own grace, and that they exercise their powers in dependence upon him. It is exactly the situation of a father in relation to his sons, to whom he not only gives life, but also education and training, by initiating them into his own profession.

There is no cause to be upset by the objection concerning ordinations conferred by a strange bishop upon clerics who do not belong to his diocese. For, under pain of personal excommunication, this bishop can confer these ordinations only if he has dimissory letters that prove that he is only the acting procurator for another to whom alone belongs the right to decide, the authority, and the responsibility.

Apostle, bishop, pastor—these words tell to what degree the heads of the Church, by reason of their priesthood which was total at that primitive period, were men of the community. And just as God, who is one, sees us all together at one time and unites us in His love, so the apostle of Christ—in the primitive sense of the word applicable almost exclusively to the Twelve—brings together under his supervision, as *episcopus,* under his crosier, as *pastor,* and *sub alas,* like Christ, this community whose spiritual father he is. He has begotten it, he keeps it alive, provides its nourishment, and leads it to supernatural pastures.

One word sums up this entire demonstration, and it is also the conclusion we were hoping to reach. The Apostles were not ordained separately or granted powers to be used solely on individuals. They were trained and ordained in community to be the heads of a church and to sanctify the souls under their spiritual direction, and this direction was to be both paternal and pastoral. In governing the group they sanctified souls, and conversely, in sanctifying souls they built up the group. And from both points of view they were spiritual leaders and fathers.

As for the Eucharist, it is at once the sacred meal of a community, the principle of the charity that consolidates unity, and the sacrifice of a Church assembled and presided over. For, to celebrate the Eucharist is to offer sacrifice, but it is also to preside over the Church.

And so the textbook treatise on the sacrament of Order, which just yesterday freely spoke of the bishop and the priest in the singular and in an abstract style, is now obliged to explain the problem of the diocesan community, and to show how the priesthood is a function and a grace exercised in collaboration and in society.

PART TWO

———————————

PRIESTLY SPIRITUALITY

CHAPTER I

Spirituality and Spiritualities

CHRISTIANITY inherited from the Greek language and civilization a certain number of words of noble origin that it baptized and filled with new riches. *Mysteries* and *mysticism* belonged to the vocabulary of religious anxiety; *ascetics* and *asceticism* have come down to us from the stadia and the gymnasiums. In recent times a few of these names, too beautiful not to arouse envy, have been borrowed from us in turn, to be used in all sorts of unexpected ways. The words "mysticism," for example, and "spiritual values" have been injected into the most profane views and used to designate a great variety of conceptions of life and of the universe. However the word "spirituality" remains the property of faithful and fervent Christians, until further notice. Let us take advantage of this fact to specify the definition of this word in the singular and in the plural. Its etymology is the holiest of them all, both in Greek and in Latin. Its corresponding adjective, exorcised by St. Paul, had been thrust upon the Apostle by the very name of the Author of every grace, the Holy Spirit of the Father and of the Son. The substantive continues, in its pure syllables, to evoke—together with the perfection of Christian life—the means of intensity and of organization that must introduce this spirituality into our temporal lives. It is a family possession, but one that multiplies itself by being interchanged among the different spiritual families that share the Church of Christ. Indeed, every one of us is in search of a spirituality and hopes to find the most generous one possible, the one most perfectly adapted to our needs—modern, of course! but tied to the most solid and most highly recommended traditions.

"What is a spirituality?" This is a question Bishop Calvet asks somewhere. And he answers: "It is a way of standing before God." [1] We have tried to be even more specific, and the most recent authors almost all agree with the definitions we shall give below.

Spirituality in general, which unites asceticism and mysticism, is the science of the Christian life insofar as it is perfect, the science of the perfection of the Christian life.[2] This science very quickly becomes an art, since it tends by definition to become a practice.

A particular spirituality chooses from among all Christian exigencies deriving from the Gospel and Tradition, a few of the more important ones, in order to emphasize them and thoroughly exploit them, to relate them to an ascetic and if possible a communitarian organization of life, which in its turn would incarnate these chosen doctrines and virtues, surrounding them if necessary with devotions conforming to these preferences. It is because of these accents, of these specializations, that the Church has a number of different spiritualities, which correspond in general—together with their literatures and their teachers—to as many theological schools. Almost all the great religious families have their own spiritualities, which partly explain their inception and the character of their constitutions.

---

[1] Cited without any precise reference in the *Bulletin salésien* for August-September, 1941.

[2] We are not saying: the science of the perfect Christian life, for this unduly exclusive way of speaking would seem to imply that there exists a Christian life that is not perfect.

Father Martimort has given us a very excellent analysis of the concept of the particular spirituality: "Take the expression 'Benedictine spirituality.' What are we to understand by that? An orientation of the soul, a preference for meditating upon a few of the themes of Christian dogma, and for cultivating this or that virtue. . . . All spirituality, therefore, seems to consist in: 1) The deepening of a doctrinal point of view toward which one is drawn by the Holy Ghost; 2) the effort to achieve in one's life a certain unity around this or that virtue, considered as the most characteristic virtue of the particular doctrine to be realized; 3) (since man's earthly life is under the sign of the 'incarnation,' a spirituality cannot remain general) a tendency to concretize the spirituality in observances and practices that constantly call the soul back to its particular vocation through the humble details of its life; 4) a certain communitarian organization which permits those who are brought together by reason of their common spiritual physiognomy, to help one another in their effort and in their search." [3]

All in all, the existence of many spiritualities within a single religion is the consequence of the richness of this religion, and in the present case, of the richness of Christianity. True, there is but one faith and one baptism, and to remain in the state of grace we must adhere without exception to all the truths that have been revealed to us, and receive all the sacraments necessary for salvation. But human life is too short, generations succeed and jostle one another too quickly and impetuously, for one man or one historical period to completely exhaust all the values born of the Gospel. Through the centuries, emphasis has not always been on the same aspect of our institutions nor *a fortiori* on the same crossroads of our forms of piety. Besides, when the last end is in question, the particular means to attain it are different. The Spouse of

---

[3] *Bulletin de l'Union Apostolique,* for September-October, 1945.

Christ is *circumdata varietate,* without forgetting the human element, historic contingence, and divine fulfillments. The rational animal introduces into his supernatural life his peculiarities of the moment, precisely in order to sanctify them by submitting them to the Spirit. It follows that the presence of this Spirit has been manifested through the ages in different ways, and these are as many varied aspects of a single irresistible presence. The history of these successions can be written. It is possible to discover the internal logic of these inheritances and of their consequences.

What an admirable spectacle for psychology, what joy for the believer, what treasures for the faithful! We shall return later to the virile beauty of these vistas.

Which of these human elements that characterize the various spiritualities contribute most of the distinctions between them? First of all, the epoch in which they were born, when, in a given culture and in the presence of a particular humanism, these spiritualities encountered aspirations, needs, historical and social ways of being to which they necessarily responded by borrowing from their spirit, using them as a framework, a support and as the matter of their subtle and organized forms. Then too, the state of life of the Christians to whom they addressed themselves and for whom they were constructed. There have always been interpenetrations of these two factors. Different states of life coexist at the same historical epoch and permit diverse spiritualities to live as contemporaries. These permanent states of life provide the spiritualities with a principle of continuity and duration. But at the same time, this duration, by being prolonged, continues its shifting work of erosion and deposit. That is how new systems are called upon to combine with the old ones, to bring forth new spiritual attitudes. That is how modifications are introduced into states that were considered changeless, bringing with them other initiatives. Such is the history, on the one hand continuous and constant and on the other changing and unforeseen, of this immense surge of life and thought that is called Christian spirituality. Side by side with variations, there is stability. Above stability there is a life that is more powerful than changelessness. It is this life which, one day or another, demands transformations, provokes changes, perhaps even revolutions, and carries along with it, in the ebb and flow of human history, the spiritual values born of the Gospel.

Diocesan spirituality consists precisely in the conjoining of the demands of a permanent state of life that is very particular and well known, the priestly state, with the religious needs, the mystical aspirations, the ascetic organizations of a given historical period. Thus, the spirituality of the diocesan clergy is a spirituality of state, of a state of life whose members, while they are obligated to tend toward the same perfection as all other Christians—the perfection of charity, nonetheless incarnate this charity under different conditions from those of the simple faithful. For the priesthood is a subordinate participation in the religious and pastoral functions of the bishop, and these call for a charity that is not only fraternal but above all paternal.

Diocesan spirituality will of course be colored in each century by the dominant preoccupations as well as the ascetical and mystical methods of the epoch, which are in general excellently represented by the spirituality of the religious orders founded during the epoch in question. Thus, diocesan spirituality has its history, its variations, its development, and its outstanding aspects, which would make it possible to speak in the plural even of clerical spiritualities.

In this way it combines a stable and permanent element, that comes from the state of life, with singularities that derive from the centuries through which it passes.

For all these reasons, there exists a distinct and reasonable diocesan spirituality. It has its masters and its schools, as well as its literature, which begins with the pastoral Epistles of St. Paul. It never ceases posing problems of adaptation and progress. The spectacle it offers is a great historical drama, and the result of God's mercies, as He bends over His Church and over His clergy. And this clergy, as its name indicates, does not constitute the whole Church, but only a part of the Church, the chosen and elect part: κληρος.

CHAPTER II

The Spirituality of the Diocesan Priest:
Its Existence

WE BELIEVE we have established that the priesthood is not primarily nor solely defined by the exercise of the liturgical and sacrificial functions, the Mass and the sacraments, for which it possesses the necessary powers. The priesthood, as we see it, is defined by the general and subordinate cooperation of its members in the religious and apostolic duties of the bishop, who is the successor to the Apostles, the father of churches, the missionary to souls, the bearer and agent of the highest charity, the paternal and redemptive charity of God.

In the beginning, the role of the presbyters may have seemed to be only a communitarian function. But this function had from the first shown itself to be so important, so lofty, and so holy that it had immediately become a profession. In any case, it was soon transformed into a state of life. Saul, who had been a weaver of tents by trade, was soon defined as *the Apostle,* the Apostle by state and a weaver *per accidens.* All allowances being made, the ancients or *presbyteri-episcopi,* who presided over the breaking of the bread in Paul's absence, had in turn become—as a subordinate college and under the authority of the Apostle-founder—the fathers or responsible pastors of the community and even of evangelization.

This conception was already affirmed in the first ecclesiastical document which inaugurates the literature of diocesan spirituality, namely, St. Paul's discourse to the *presbyteri-episcopi* of Ephesus, in the *Acts of the Apostles:* "... the Holy Spirit has placed you as bishops, to rule the Church of God." [1] This is the way the Apostle looked upon his auxiliaries: as spiritual pastors. Momentarily, as is still the case today in certain Eastern lands or even in certain poor dioceses of the West, the priest could in case of necessity unite two states of life, the priesthood and a remunerative profession. However in the organized churches, in accordance with the vital urging of the Gospel, one of these states has long since killed the other. The priesthood has become all-embracing for the one who exercises it, for it takes complete hold of him, so great is its power to fill a life, to satisfy a soul, to unify and direct a man's entire existence.

Despite the powerful constitution of this priestly state of life, certain authors have denied that the diocesan clergy can have its own particular spirituality. They declare that the priesthood is outside the particularisms which by definition set one spirituality apart from another, by reason of the divinity of its institution, its permanence, and its identity with the hierarchy of the Church. According to this view, priests would be the prisoners of their own greatness and of their glorious servitude. Particularities would not be tolerated in those who are of the Church, κλῆρος: *Dominus pars hereditatis meae,* in those who are the Church.

By showing that diocesan spirituality is addressed to a special state of life, distinct from that of the simple faithful, we believe we have already weakened this curious objection. It is an objection that might perhaps be expressed by having the diocesan clergy parody the Rohans' motto: *"Evêque ne*

---

[1] Acts 20:28.

puis; moine ne daigne; prêtre suis—A bishop I cannot be; a monk I may not be; and so I am a priest."

There is a portion of truth in this *videtur quod non,* but it merely emphasizes the dignity of the diocesan state. Indeed, the diocesan priest belongs so completely to the very constitution of the Church, and his office is so totally identified with the essential life of the institution founded by Christ, that he is obliged to set aside certain details and recommendations in the ideas and exercises of the successive spiritualities to which he may turn. The reason for this is that these particular forms of spirituality, because of their very originality, their excessive newness or archaism, or their extreme adaptation to a given transitory situation in the history of the Church, would be incompatible with the diocesan priest's great, burdensome and permanent task: collaboration in the religious and apostolic activities of the bishop.

We have spoken of successive borrowings from various spiritualities. We have spoken also of secondary or contingent aspects born of historical circumstances which give to the spirituality of a state both its physiognomy and its structure. That is how the particular forms of asceticism incarnated in Christian institutions and particularly in the religious congregations of a given period come into contact with the priestly and ecclesiastical state as it pursues its course through the great history of the Church which is in its care.

The clergy of dioceses have been so absorbed in their apostolic tasks in periods of fervor, and so engulfed in temporal institutions and affairs in hours of decadence, that they have not often found the time to construct or to think through their own spirituality. In short, they have not been able to surround the permanent laws of their state with the spiritual contingencies needed by particular eras. In consequence, they have sought to borrow this support or this incarnation from the asceticisms of the regular, monastic, or religious institutions of their time. These monastic orders had often been founded for laymen. The first companions of St. Benedict and St.

Francis of Assisi, the founders of the first spiritual schools that have been most widespread in Christianity and in history, were laymen.[2] This fact needs to be emphasized, because it brought up, long before the advent of *Catholic Action,* the problem of the relations of lay spirituality with priestly spirituality.

But there are not only laymen in religious congregations of men. Today these congregations are almost all composed of priests.[3] We must therefore judge their value from a much higher plane. Their psychological and spiritual history is magnificent in its continuity and therefore in its unity, in its progress and therefore in its internal logic. Century after century, reform after reform, foundation after foundation, we have seen mysticism—and first of all ascesis—obeying a supernatural dialectic and developing according to regular laws.

We are reminded of the cloister in the Pontifical Pavilion at the 1937 Paris Exposition of Arts and Technics, with its picturesque little rooms representing the furnishings of the cells of the principal congregations of men and women. To the extent that sensible daily objects can incarnate the lofty spirituality that guided these foundations, one might have reconstructed a genuine comparative and progressive history of successive asceticisms. One might even have shown the filiation, or if we prefer, the evolution of this development and of these transformations, the past preparing the way for the future without knowing it, and the future leaning upon the past without always admitting it. Then, too, using the simple title "History of pilgrimages through the Christian centuries," we might have unfurled the magnificent panorama, on a

---

[2] Cf. in the *Codex juris,* Canon 487: Status religiosus seu stabilis in communi vivendi modus, quo fideles, praeter communia praecepta, evangelica quoque consilia servanda per vota. . . .

[3] According to a report of the National Catholic Welfare Conference, published in *The Register* (Denver, Colorado), for September 5, 1954, "Of the 271,500 members of religious communities of men, some 113,000 are priests." (Translator's note.)

lower level of values than that of the religious congregations, of ascesis through journeys and through the call of the holy places. Such an overview would have taken us from the medieval *romieu* (pilgrim to Rome) to the modern Boyscout hiker, from the scattered monastic hostelries on the roads to Compostella to the recently invented youth hostels, passing by way of the Lourdes trainloads and the Franciscan cruises.

At any rate, upon the heights where the study of the constitutions of the great Orders keeps us, we can discern veritable laws of progress. From the Fathers of the Desert or the rule of St. Columban to the rule of St. Benedict, from the spirituality of the Greek Fathers to that of St. Augustine, from the mendicant friars of the thirteenth century, the Franciscans and Dominicans, to the foundation of the Society of Jesus in the sixteenth, from the French School of the seventeenth century to contemporary attempts at practicing the religious life in the world, we believe we can say that Christian asceticism has progressed:

—toward an ever greater spiritualization which makes use of results attained to serve increasingly psychological ends. We see that corporeal mortifications have gradually diminished in extent and importance. Less stress is complacently being placed on these means of touching the recesses of the soul. The three virtues of counsel—chastity, poverty, obedience—which have always been cultivated, have nonetheless been successively stressed in the above-mentioned order, in which the body tends to yield first place to the spirit.

—But if this virtue of obedience, which as the supreme means of asceticism draws everything to itself, becomes increasingly narrow and exacting, it also becomes more flexible and lovable. Relationships between superiors and inferiors become less solemn and formal because the spirit of obedience has tended to become the spirit of charity itself.

—Finally, there develops a more and more intimate union between the apostolic life and the ascetic life. In becoming deeper, the ascetic life acquires a greater capacity for boldness and for taking greater liberties. Indeed, it would be possible to write a history of the human geography of ascesis. It starts out in the absolute desert, in Syria or in Egypt, and later seeks remote but fertilizable locations; then it builds towns around abbeys, and finally enters the cities to complete its course if need be in an apartment or even in a family residence. Architecture follows this movement, for it is human and institutional too. The hermitage, the abbey, the priory, the convent, the residence, the seminary—what a magnificent history! It is still inscribed in the monuments that subsist on French soil, monuments that are often disaffected but always evocative. When ancient stones are rightly understood, they are in their own way witnesses to successive asceticisms and psychologies; for they have been superposed and distributed in the service of a given mode of life, of a given kind of rule. St. Thomas tells us that God has given man his reason and his hands: *natura non deficit homini in necessariis . . . quia dedit ei [Deus] rationem et manus quibus possit haec sibi acquirere.*[4] Because asceticism is human, we find in it both reason and the hand.

What is true of the general forms of asceticism is also true of individual lives. Father Penido tells us: "In the course of the life of the same ascetic, and without any change in the final goal, there will be variations of asceticism corresponding to the moral level attained at diverse moments. We know that certain saints allow themselves certain pleasures toward the end of their careers which they have severely denied themselves in the beginning. These delights no longer present any dangers. When virtue is sufficiently strengthened, it no longer fears certain pitfalls. Thus, the year of her death, Thérèse of Lisieux thanked her prioress for not having 'spoiled' her in countless ways during her religious life. But the Mother

---

[4] Ia IIae, q. 5, a. 5, ad 1. ". . . nature does not fail man in necessaries, although it has not provided him with weapons and clothing, . . . because it gave him reason and hands with which he is able to get these things for himself."

Prioress had changed her attitude in the preceding months. Thérèse thanked her again: 'I am deeply touched by this, but I feel that I have nothing to fear. I can now enjoy it as much as I want to.' These words lay bare the fundamental relativity of asceticism. Far from having the rigid homogeneity that Pierre Janet attributes to them, these practices present a variety of forms and presuppose flexibility in their application, which prove their essentially subordinate condition. They are no more than means. Their unity derives only from the moral goal in view and from the effort that their use requires." [5]

Unfortunately, in the long history of asceticism, crises have not always been cleared up as easily as at the Carmel of Lisieux, where for that matter there were sometimes misunderstandings. The reason is that the very development of asceticism provokes scandal in the minds of the representatives of the old methods. A venerable rule had once been imposed, forbidding a given object, or practice, or setting up a certain obligation, so as to mortify evil nature. They had been told that they would save their souls by this means. They have interpreted this to mean that they would save their souls on this condition. The new spirit supervenes, claiming to distinguish further by continuing to combat evil in order to destroy it more completely, but also authorizing the good which, thanks to progress achieved, can now be more thoroughly exploited. This movement forward appears to the elders as a concession to the perverse spirit of the world, and stirs them to protest. It is notable that almost all the great founders of new religious congregations—despite the im-

---

[5] M. T. L. Penido, *La Conscience religieuse*, p. 139. Cf. P. Rousselot and J. Huby, S.J., in *Christus, La Religion chrétienne* (Paris: Beauchesne, 1921), p. 861: "St. Thomas was intimately convinced that since union with God is the sole end of the spiritual life, the evangelical counsels are not perfection itself but only the means for observing the precepts more perfectly, and above all the precept of love of God. . . . One may be tempted at first to judge this spirit to be less Christian, less evangelical. But it is the spirit of St. Paul telling the faithful: *I would have you free from care* (I Cor. 7:32, with regard to virginity)."

mense step forward they were making for asceticism by setting up more absolute requirements—were at first suspected of conceding too much to slothful nature, relaxing discipline, and exposing souls to the proximate danger of sin because of the barriers they were destroying, because of the formerly forbidden acts that they permitted, and in general because of the more intimate contact with the world which they authorized. No one was willing to see that the reason they could allow these new liberties was because they actually held the souls of their disciples much more firmly in hand by more powerful, more perfect, and more psychological means; and since they now demanded more useful sacrifices, they could suppress from their rules without ill effect the abstinences that had become useless, too rigid to be adapted, too uncouth to attract the new generations.

This law is verified of the thirteenth century, when the monks of the Benedictine tradition opposed the foundation of the mendicant orders; of the sixteenth century when the ancient orders, bound to recite their office in choir, were opposed to the foundation of the clerks regular, and in particular to the Jesuits; of the seventeenth century, when the cloistered orders of women opposed the foundations of St. Francis de Sales, St. Vincent de Paul, and others. Should this surprise us? Does not the Gospel show us the original instance of these difficulties: *quare discipuli tui non jejunant?* And so, the divine doctor of total renunciation, the author of the *abneget semetipsum* and of the *tollat crucem suam* was the first to be accused of ruining asceticism, because by giving it delicate gradations He made it more severe. The disciple who best grasped this turning point in the history of asceticism was St. Paul. There were doubtless all sorts of motives and reasons behind the Apostle's relentless war against all the works of the Law, but was not the personal motive uppermost? Saul of Tarsus had suffered too much from being subjected to an uncouth regime that did nothing for his fine and delicate soul. The Cross of Jesus had appeared to him as a rule infinitely

better suited to his needs. He has often insisted upon the sentiment of deliverance, on the enjoyment of freedom that he
found in the newborn Christianity.

And so in the unfolding of the Church's interior life
through the centuries we witness a perpetual and fortunate
mutual interaction of means and end. In metaphysical value,
both divine and human, charity is superior to asceticism,
the end is above the means. In psychology and history, ascesis
comes first, the means precede the end, in accordance with
the scholastic adage: *quod prius est in intentione, ulterius est
in executione.* We have just seen how the priesthood, in order
to establish itself in the perfection of its state, has borrowed
from organized ascetic institutions both means and methods;
or even, going further along the same path, it has organized
itself in religious, monastic, teaching, or missionary congregations. At the other extreme, when the Church is sufficiently
established in a region, when the Christian spirit is already
deeply rooted in the inheritance of families and of traditions,
the priesthood can abandon congregational forms and put
greater trust in its own law, which is the law of apostolic
and pastoral charity with all its exigencies. Then the Church
substitutes the diocesan hierarchy with its clergy and its seminaries for the regime of propaganda and missions, until then
assured by religious. The same emancipations can be seen in
the history of personal vocations. The Church, which is always holy, is not holy everywhere in the same way.

When we have enjoyed this spectacle, or this pilgrimage,
passing from the desert and the hermitage to the cloister and
the abbey, from the abbey to the collegiate church, from the
collegiate church to the convent, to the residence and to the
missionary center;—when we have seen the anchoretic, ceno-
bitic, monastic, canonical, and mendicant lives emerge one
from the other, and, after the great Ignatian revolution of the
Catholic Renaissance of the sixteenth century, the clerks regular combine and exceed all these values, then in their turn

inspire societies of priests and in the nineteenth century inspire missionary congregations;

—when we have seen the ascetic and mystical torch glow for a great while in the desert and in solitude, then illuminate the hills and the country side, enter the cities and finally enkindle far-away missions;

—when we have considered how asceticism first addressed itself to the body through continence, then to the body and soul together through poverty, and finally to the mind through obedience, thus progressively and intelligently conquering the whole man;

—when we have trod the spiritual path that goes from stability to mobility and availability, from the solemnity of hieratic social forms to the simplicity of communitarian gestures, from absolute separation from the world toward an ever more penetrating apostolate;

—when, during this time, the ascetical day was progressively liberated from its fetters so as to allow more time for the ministry, the apostolate, teaching, the education of children, even while the exercises of the interior life were constantly deepened;

—when we contemplate all these things, we cannot help asking ourselves what grand institution in the history of morality and of civilization could ever be compared with the development of organized and communitarian asceticism within Christianity. And what progressive logic! what a dialectic, as we say nowadays, there is in this development!

A great turning point occurred in the sixteenth century, that is of the highest importance for us. When St. Ignatius instituted a congregation in which corporeal mortifications, while not suppressed, were given second rank and were transferred from the order of precepts to the category of counsels; when he eliminated the recitation of the office in choir and made mental prayer, examination of conscience, and the annual retreat part of the rule, in other words when he rendered obligatory what had only been recommended and made optional what had been obligatory, thus reversing the whole existing organization without destroying any of it,—by this bold act of genius, he changed the whole emphasis of asceticism. Mortification of the will now became the most important means, and corporeal mortification was brought down to second place. At the same time, obligatory daily meditation laid stress on the increasing importance of the psychological and interior life.

This is the type of asceticism that has inspired most of the founders of congregations since that time. It is the asceticism that has made possible the spiritual organization of the great seminaries of the following century. Without denying any of her past, the Church in modern times has adopted, with the necessary variations, this flexible, profound, and powerful discipline for the religious and moral education of her priests, whose souls are filled with anxiety and yet tenderly human.

Today the Holy Spirit is asking of diocesan priests an adaptation that is probably bolder still, and that may even be called a revolution.

At each powerful impulse which the Church receives under the action of the Spirit, we see the diocesan clergy morally obliged—and its more generous and intelligent representatives find themselves inwardly drawn—to follow the example, to profit by the experiences, and to accept the lessons or the methods that are offered to it. How could the clergy, which is the hierarchy, fail to be as ascetic as fervent laymen, as heroic monks, as admirable religious and intrepid missionaries? The law of emulation thus explains in great part the interior life of the Church.

Even though we have been speaking in generalities, we can add up our spiritual debts in detail. We have borrowed:

religious celibacy from the Fathers of the Desert and from the institution of monasticism;

the *lectio divina,* the divine office under the form of the breviary, from the monks and from the mendicant friars;

the Rosary from the Dominicans;

methodical meditation, the examination of conscience, spiritual retreats from the clerks regular;

spiritual reading under its present form from modern devotion; and later still, the evening visit to the Blessed Sacrament from St. Alphonsus Liguori perhaps.

We must note, however, that this eminently living reality, which is called the diocesan priestly state, in order to obey the principles of life, has absorbed all the ascetic and mystical substance which came to it from the outside only by subjecting it to its own laws—eliminating, correcting, and adapting the things it borrowed, just as the corporeal organism does with the food that it takes in. The spectator or the fortunate beneficiary of these transpositions can thus grasp the originality and the power that properly belong to diocesan spirituality in the very instances where it seems on the surface to be identified with the institutions of the monks and of the clerks regular. It is in the name of and by the light of apostolic and pastoral charity, which is the judge and ruler of all his decisions, that the diocesan priest makes all his choices and gives expression to distinctions and variations. It is this charity that builds with tireless energy the structures of the state in which it finds its preferred incarnation, and—in the case of the bishop—in which it resides perfectly and exclusively. Thus, certain virtues, in passing from one clergy to another, in changing their immediate end, also modify their exercises and their methods. Their significance is no longer quite the same, since their relationship with charity has followed different paths. For example, obedience, which is first of all an exercise of personal asceticism for the novice and even for the professed religious, is the very condition of unity for the clergy subject to its bishop and also the condition of the apostolic progress of the diocese. Since the primary motives are not the same, the spirituality involved takes on different aspects. With respect to poverty, the most multiform of the virtues, distinctions and, one might almost say, divergencies are still more noticeable.

Besides, when we examine these spiritual borrowings to which so much value has been attached, we see that the diocesan priest, even if he does practice the same exercises as do the religious, does so in a slightly different spirit because he is pursuing a different end—his own particular end, which is the service of God and of the souls entrusted to the bishop.

On the points on which the diocesan and the religious states seem to be materially identified, they continue formally to obey the laws of their respective origins. For the religious, the celebration of Mass is first of all an exercise of the rule; for the diocesan priest it is first of all a parochial service. It goes without saying that for both, it is an act of religion. The obedience that the diocesan priest promises the bishop on the day of his ordination does not have as its primary aim his training in abnegation, but is intended to assure the unity of the diocese. It is a service, rather than an act of personal asceticism. As for ecclesiastical celibacy, there are certainly not two ways of practicing it. And yet, for the religious it is the supreme act of personal renunciation, whereas for the diocesan priest it is the efficacious and ultimate sign of the gift of himself for the sake of others. Seen through a magnifying glass, the motives behind the engagement are not exactly the same for the religious as for the diocesan clergy. For the religious it is an act of asceticism and liberation, a means of practicing charity. For the diocesan priest, it is a gesture of service and collaboration, a necessary condition for the practice of charity. There are delicate gradations in this matter which are perceived in the confidential disclosures made at the moment when the choice of vocation is made.

In the search for the means of perfection, there is an ever-present danger. It is the danger of identifying two states of life whose principles are very different, and of forgetting that the true inward law of the diocesan priesthood is apostolic charity, that this charity is in principle sanctifying of its very self, that it is identified with perfection, and that in the exercise or even in the acquiring of the strictly priestly virtues, and of pastoral and missionary virtues in particular, lies a seed of holiness that no ascesis will ever completely replace.

In any case, to fail to distinguish between two vocations and two states of life is to risk doing injustice to both. In the strict sense of the terms, a seminary is not a noviciate. It is a training center for the diocesan priestly life.

It is not paradoxical to hold that the spirituality of the diocesan clergy is perhaps closer to the spirituality of the laymen in Catholic Action than to the over-specialized asceticism of the religious separated from the world and outside the ordinary conditions of daily life. This remark would even be an argument in favor of priestly third orders, that is, of the application to diocesan priests of constitutions originally established for the laity. Unfortunately, these third orders are all of rather ancient date and too completely subordinated to the historical goal and to the particular spirit of their respective religious institutes to be able at the present time easily to encompass the general and current aspirations of a diocesan clergy in full development. Besides, we are striving to construct a strictly priestly spirituality, not merely in the name of the ascetic exigencies of baptism, but to satisfy the conditions of the sacrament of Order and of the priestly life. In case of conflict or of a twofold use as between a particular tradition and the laws of the priestly state, it is the laws of the priestly state that must be decisive.[6]

Moreover, the diocesan clergy as such, makes no vows, because its state of life is defined by its relations with the bishop and by charity, and therefore does not as such involve any

---

[6] "To enter a third order is to become affiliated with an order, to live by its spirituality, within reach of its houses, and under the more or less direct influence of its religious. Now, there is question whether a specialized spirituality like that of a great order is necessarily best suited to a priesthood called to act in accordance with its own line of apostolate, in a very different environment from that of the religious life properly so-called." Louis Soubigou, A.A., in *L'Année théologique,* 7th year, 1946, Parts 2-3, p. 309.

vow whatsoever. And one cannot make the vow of charity. Vows apply only to the counsels. And the diocesan priestly state as such is not defined by the canonical practice of the virtues of counsel. More precisely, it does not of itself demand that the virtues of counsel that are addressed to everyone, and therefore to the diocesan priest, be incarnated by him—with the exception of celibacy—in invariable and contractual canonical forms.

We must not, after all, confuse the indefinite exigencies of a virtue with the promise made to God to exercise this virtue to the limit and therefore within the limits fixed by the constitutions of a religious order. That would amount to putting Canon Law not only in the Gospel, where it has its rightful, well-defined and therefore limited place, but actually above the Gospel, and to this it can make no claim. Finally, it would be putting the letter above the spirit, written law above charity.

Now, the fact remains that the vow is a liberation, because of the problems it solves once and for all. St. Thomas has told us so in excellent terms, following St. Paul. But after all, a psychological and social deliverance does not put an end to invitations of conscience, to ulterior calls from God, nor to the endless requests of charity. To simplify a question is not necessarily to solve it.

Whether we like it or not, the problem of perfection is not absolutely solved by the three vows. In any case, it can be solved otherwise. St. Paul, who was so proud and happy about his celibacy, practiced poverty not according to disciplinary rules fixed in advance, but in accordance with the changing demands of a constantly renewed apostolate.

The priestly state, therefore, appears to be strong and consistent enough to construct its own spirituality under the authority of the bishops who, at its summit, are both the heads and members of this great body, the ones most deeply interested in and obliged to work for the permanent success of this vital and organized movement. Several times during the course of history, the diocesan clergy has been triumphant over itself and over difficulties, taking inspiration from the religious trends of the epoch and attaining an original result. It is in those centuries that it was most fervent. We are reminded in this connection of the canons regular of the Middle Ages; and closer to our own needs, we might mention the masters of the French School of the seventeenth century, who are still exerting influence in France at Saint-Sulpice and elsewhere. These spiritual leaders took their inspiration from the Ignatian and Oratorian spiritualities of the Counter-Reformation, adapting them to the needs of their time. In so doing they laid the foundation for the great spiritual organization of the ecclesiastical state which still vivifies seminaries and dioceses.

The diocesan clergy needs only to seek inspiration from these doctrines and these examples in order to continue the same movement.

The first beneficiaries of this change in interior tone and climate have been pious exercises—what am I saying? its first beneficiary has been the divine office itself. In their origins, most of the exercises of devotion and prayers were simply the methodical and regular organization of the Christian life born of baptism.[7] They were instituted for Christian laymen, for monks, for the first companions—who were laymen, too—of Ignatius of Loyola, both as ascetic gestures for the cultivation of the virtues and as acts of religion for the glory of God. But when they were adopted by the diocesan clergy to serve as the backbone and the armature of their religious day and thus incorporated into the priestly life, they became the means by which priests could offer up to God their gifts and their supplications for the sins of the people and in their name.

---

[7] Cf. St. Thomas: "In vitis Patrum (lib. 6, 1, 9) legitur quod candam gratiam consequuntur religionem ingradientes quam consequuntur baptisati—We read in the *Lives of the Fathers* 6:1 that by entering religion one receives the same grace as by being baptized." IIa IIae, q. 189, a. 3, ad 3.

They have become the private or liturgical expression of the Church's sentiments of adoration and thanksgiving.

The moralism of the last centuries has certainly tried to reduce the goal and the significance of pious exercises to the point of considering them merely ascetic barriers against indifference and negligence. But in reality as far as the breviary is concerned, in the mind of the Church these exercises have become priestly gestures, acts of religion, official or semi-official praises in God's honor. On the lips of the priest they are raised to a superior order of values, in which are affirmed the priest's transcendence with respect to the laity, the autonomy of the priestly state, its privilege, its monopoly, as well as its distinctive mark in the use of the religious practices which it has in common with hermits, monks, and religious laymen, or even with fervent Christians in the world.[8]

Now, this professional spirituality has long since been that of the entire French School. It has never ceased being taught at Saint-Sulpice, where the moralism of pious exercises—their asceticism as Brémond would have said—has never destroyed their significance for religion and adoration. These exercises are performed first of all in imitation of, in conformity to, and in union with Christ praying and adoring His Father during His mortal life, in the desert, in the temple, in the privacy of His chamber—both His public and communitarian prayer and His private or nocturnal prayer: *erat pernoctans in oratione Dei*. Like Christ, the priest is the religious of the Father, not only as a simple monk for the sake of the community, but in the name of the community of which he is the head, the pastor, the father, *ut offerat dona et sacrificia pro peccatis et in laudem Dei*.

Thus, in the solemn, grave, and heroic hour of the Counter-Reformation and of the Catholic Renaissance, the diocesan

---

[8] This properly religious value of pious exercises and of the entire life of the priest has recently been powerfully stressed by Bishop Ancel in a lecture given in Paris and published by the periodical *L'Union* [*des Oeuvres*] for April, 1947.

clergy of the period (in the sixteenth century in Italy and in the seventeenth century in France) had, with the grace of God, succeeded in building a spirituality of its own, in which borrowings had been transformed into a specialized organization.

We have no intention of straying from this glorious and powerful tradition. All we dare hope is that, if God grants it, we may prolong it in the light of the equally traditional theology that we have presented in the first part of this book, a theology that is demanding acceptance almost everywhere at the present time. If the Christian centuries that have just preceded us have necessarily left unexplored certain aspects of human nature, certain possibilities of Christian life, we are trying, in the light of the needs and discoveries of our own time, to add new fields to those that our elders have already cultivated. And to avoid the encumberment that Father Doncoeur feared so much, and of which we shall have to speak later, we are depending on the law of life by virtue of which useless refuse is eliminated and new acquisitions are transformed.

There will, of course, be a difference in principle and in method as between yesterday and today. In the measure that we shall have thought through again the law that is proper and essential to the ecclesiastical state and to the priesthood, we shall be inspired to search further for new choices and solutions. We shall remember that it was upon a Christian, at once a son of Adam and a son of God that the bishop imposed hands. We shall remember that the water of baptism flowed over this fragile flesh before it was consecrated by the presbyteral unction. More than ever, the young priest is held to an asceticism derived from the obligations of baptism, specialized through the centuries and raised to the highest degree of perfection in monastic, regular, congregational, and religious institutions. More than ever, he is obliged to be perfect, and he has a twofold obligation to practice the means of perfection. But this baptismal ascesis is now subject to a higher and more exacting law, the law of service to the bishop and to souls. Far from being dulled by this control, it will be made stronger, more delicate, finer, more penetrating. At the same time, it will undergo certain modifications, as it receives subtle variations from new trends and from more specialized interior movements under the influence of the septiform Spirit who has so many ways of His own of impressing His power and making known His demands.

We believe that with this preamble we can speak seriously, as among serious people, of serious and inescapable problems.

Any solution or approach that would exclude the idea and the presence of the bishop, and likewise the idea and the presence of the total diocesan community, would be a drastic compromise that would not go to the heart of the problem. Nor is there any question of creating a religious congregation of which the bishop would be the superior. The bishop is far more than that. He is the successor to the Apostles, and the head—*caput*—of the presbyterium. Neither is there any question of imposing upon priests ascetical obligations from which their bishop would be exempt. The bishop and his priests constitute a single body, and therefore they must continue to have the same essential rule of spiritual and canonical life. And generally speaking, while the asceticism of religious is an excellent institution, and one that is indispensable to the Church's plenitude of life, and while a well-defined discipline is useful to every Christian life and necessary to every priestly life, the trend of ideas that we are trying to understand and interpret at the moment does not have as its immediate goal the institution of a new rule of life for the diocesan clergy, that would be exterior to its original institution.

The conditions of the clergy's life and apostolate change much more quickly than do religious constitutions, fixed once and for all. If there is need to seek new spiritual values outside the priestly state, it is better to choose them from among more recent modes of life, for the diocesan clergy is by definition fortunately obliged to belong to its own time and to be always on call. And that is why certain courageous young priests of the present time have been tempted to borrow their asceticism from the Scout *Route,* with its three great incarnated virtues: the rugged life, the simple (or poor) life, and the loyal life. This is a modern return to Bishop d'Hulst's confraternity of the *Bois-Blanc,* and to the spirituality of the young leader.[9]

Similarly flexible solutions inspired by the same principles would be called for to solve the problem of poverty, which once again preoccupies many young priests. There are so many ways of conceiving of and practicing the vow of poverty, and that is all the more reason why there are so many ways of practicing the virtue that commands this vow. Here again, apostolic demands will inspire the diocesan priest to a variety of forms of asceticism, shades of application in which he will affirm his detachment from the riches of this world. Formerly, in Christian lands the pastor was the king of his people and had to live to some extent at the level if not of the wealthy

---

[9] Scouting in France, which is really Catholic scouting and which finds expression today in *La Route,* anteceded Catholic Action by ten years. It has had more time to influence spirituality. We ought not to be surprised that young priests seek to borrow from this movement. The hard life, the loyal life, the simplified life: these are modern translations of the eternal virtues of poverty and obedience. To submit to the real in order to obey it, as did the monks to their abbots and the Jesuits to their superiors, to accept the physical life, not to find pleasure but joy, not for enjoyment but to find reality: heat and cold, air, water, sun, and at night the primitive and maternal earth—there is in all this a different approach to nature, not one that would enter man's heart to soften and tempt him, and of which the ancients used to say in the bad Epicurean sense, *sequere naturam.* Here nature demands from without that we bow before her wholesome and powerful laws, and in a different, a heroic sense, that we obey and follow her. There are already priests who are *routiers.* It is the path of borrowings. We know that this path is dependent upon the highroad it must enter, upon the priestly institution itself and the demands of its internal laws. Cf. *Humanisme Routier* by Pierre Goutet (Paris: Scouts de France, 1934), taken from the collection *Témoignages* of La Pierre-qui-vive, consecrated to humanism.

families at least of the middle classes, in order to conform with the consideration of which he was the object. But the curate of working class neighborhoods is now beginning to think, in mission lands, that he must almost descend to the rank of the proletarians if he wants to preach the Sermon on the Mount and the holiness of the Church to the poor and dispossessed of this world. The entire material organization of the priest's life and his whole standard of living have been upset by these revolutions. And thus the spirit of poverty is leading to entirely different consequences from those that it once recommended or inspired.[10]

---

[10] Cf. Joseph Folliet, *Les Chrétiens au carrefour* (1947), p. 38. He goes still further: "We have reached a time when the priesthood is no longer a liberal profession, but a form of proletariat."

The Spirituality of the Diocesan Priest: Its Essential Principles and Their Current Application

WE ALL KNOW St. Thomas' great definition of the priesthood, which we have already cited, and which can rightly be preferred to all others as a definition of the essential priesthood: "The office proper to a priest is to be a mediator between God and the people: to wit, inasmuch as he bestows divine things on the people, . . . and again, forasmuch as he offers up the people's prayers to God, and, in a manner, makes satisfaction to God for their sins." [1] Of this twofold function orientated in two directions, the French School has primarily retained and exploited the first, without, for that matter, excluding the second. The spirituality of adoration of this school is principally organized around the duties of religion to be rendered to God. This school is incomparable in its respect for the divine majesty both in the private and public cult, and in the care it brings to the liturgical ceremonies. Is not Jesus, the supreme Priest, first of all the great religious of His Father?

We must abandon nothing of this noble tradition, nor of the pious exercises that, like so many satellites, gravitate in the

---

[1] IIIa, q. 22, a. 1, c.

course of the priestly day around the celebration of the Holy Sacrifice. Recently some singular and unexpected difficulties have been raised on this subject.

Two important articles dealing with the breviary, one by a noted Jesuit and the other by a courageous young Oratorian, have inquired whether the present day organization of the diocesan priest's religious day could be considered perfect and definitive. Father Doncoeur's article appeared in *Etudes* for May, 1945. Father Bouyer's was published in the third number of *Maison-Dieu*. Independently of each other, the two authors judged that the divine office has not yet been given the place it deserves in the diocesan priest's life, nor the influence to which it has a right. The reason, according to Father Doncoeur, is that the office has not been integrated into the general spirituality of the clergy; and according to Father Bouyer, that it has not been integrated into the daily life of the priest. In the first view, there has not yet been established a fusion between the ancient forms of prayer inherited from the canonical and monastic institution, of which the breviary is the nucleus, and on the other hand the modern methods born of the *Exercises* of St. Ignatius, which govern the personal religious life of the seminarian and of the priest. It would seem that the diocesan priest is, without knowing it, torn asunder in God's eyes. The second critic is more reserved. After having considered various gaps, lacks, and errors in logic, he hesitates to reach a conclusion, proposing remedies rather than reforms. But in both cases, a serious problem of ascetical organization, that we had thought solved, has been posed once again.

We might be less severe than Father Doncoeur on modern spirituality, which has come to us from the sixteenth century. The revolution accomplished by St. Ignatius of Loyola has been so fruitful! It is this revolution that probably made the institution of seminaries possible in the following century. The monastic institution and the recitation of the office in choir would have been too burdensome. They would have cluttered up the day that was intended to be used for intensive study and also, at the beginning, for the first efforts of the ministry. In the Ignatian system, the mental prayer of the morning, the particular examen, the spiritual reading of the evening, leave the middle of the day free for scholastic work and for husbanding physical resources necessary for serving the faithful. In this system, we admit that the breviary may appear to have a twofold use with the rest of the exercises. But in the days when ancient Christianity was supposedly firmly established, in rural parishes, in the *otium cum dignitate* of the old canons, when life was not overloaded with occupations, the breviary took the place of scholastic studies which were supposedly terminated, and it filled hours which would otherwise have been idle. Circumstances have certainly changed since then. Today a young priest is obliged to lessen not the intensity or the depth of his religious life, but the length of time devoted to pious exercises. But even in this overburdened life, the breviary, because of its canonically obligatory character and of its amenability to material control, offers a halting place. Better still, it offers a barrier, a boulevard in the military terminology of sieges. It is the last solid rampart against supreme abandon. Mental prayer and all its derivatives in Ignatian spirituality would have difficulty replacing the breviary in this thankless and indispensable service.

And yet is it true that diocesan priests, by dint of borrowing ascetic riches from the regular clergy, find their day filled with pious exercises born of contrary or at least different spiritualities, out of which it would be hard to make a unified whole? Are the seminarian and the priest really stifled between two conceptions—the monastic conception of asceticism and mysticism, organized around an hourly plan for the canonical office, and the silent, strictly psychological and moral spirituality inaugurated by St. Ignatius and the clerks regular of the sixteenth century?

This would be a grave objection. But does it not spring from a false perspective? It would seem to imply that the diocesan priest has never done anything but borrow from the outside, so as to cover himself with all these successive vestments, just as the bishop dons all the ornaments of the inferior clergy for the pontifical Mass—heaping Pelion upon Ossa, and finally succumbing under these burdens that are too heavy for a twenty-four hour day.

Looking at the problem only from this angle, we forget that the diocesan clergy has its own law, a law that we have tried to clarify; we forget, too, that by virtue of its origins as well as of its end, the diocesan clergy can discern, among the forms of nourishment that come to it from the outside, those that are suitable for it. And our figure of speech is still imperfect, unless we add the figure of digestion that transforms food by means of a vital process, subjecting this food to the new law of the assimilating body.

It is not certain, for example, that the solution of the problem of the breviary is for the diocesan priest to strive for greater fidelity to the solar distribution of the canonical hours. The monk or friar, whose first duty of state is to recite the divine office in community, must organize his day and his occupations so as to assure this horary regularity and the division of the day into successive and spaced periods in choir. But the pastor of a parish, whose great duty is his pastoral responsibility, must organize the recitation of his breviary so as to assure without fail and without delay the spiritual services that he owes to the faithful and the unbelievers entrusted to his care.

There remains the acute problem of the overcrowding of modern priestly life in the large cities, in working-class neighborhoods, in immense parishes, and in over-enrolled colleges. The question would be insoluble if piety and interior life were values of a single dimension, extended in time, breadth, and surface. Happily, they also have depth, inwardness, intensity, qualities that cannot be measured by the quarter hour. It is in this direction that we must seek solutions, it would seem.[2]

With respect to the side of the priesthood that is turned toward God, our antecedent institutions, especially in the French School, have attained such a degree of perfection that it would be impertinent to seek and to build any further. It is with respect to the other side of the priesthood, orientated toward the service of men, that we must seek to complete the existing tradition and spirituality which are already so rich.

We shall inquire further, from the ascetical and mystical point of view, into the second movement of the diocesan priest's day, the movement that goes from heaven toward earth, to bring to men, through evangelization and the pastorate, the graces of God entrusted to the priesthood. This is the second panel of the diptych. It is an answer to the first sacred impact, but in the opposite direction. This program remains to be completed.

Inspiration for this project can be found in the precious little volume that Father Pourrat, one of the most noted authorities in the Society of Saint-Sulpice, recently edited under the title: *Le Sacerdoce, Doctrine de l'École Française.* After having clearly presented, with the help of chosen texts, the teaching of the masters of the French School, in which the priesthood is seen as the religion of Jesus Christ, the adorer of the Father, the author closed by giving a brief description and program of the second aspect of the priest's ministry, orientated toward the faithful for their sanctification.

---

[2] "No one will change my opinion that an hour of meditation suffices for scholastics, provided they practice mortification and abnegation. For they will then profit more from prayer in a quarter of an hour than others who are immortified will profit in two hours." (*Scripta de S. Ignatio,* 1,278, cited by A. Tenneson, S.J., in *Prêtre et Apôtre,* 28th year, No. 332, July 15, 1946, p. 103.)

Starting from the foundations laid by Father Pourrat,[3] we must continue to build, without destroying any of the structure erected earlier, through which the French clergy of the past three centuries has acquired the habit of adoring the Father through the Son in the unity of the Holy Spirit.

To achieve the synthesis of the two attitudes of the two movements, we must seek inspiration from the definition of the presbyteral priesthood, conceived as a participation in episcopal responsibilities, which we discussed in the first part of this volume.

As an anonymous writer, a member of the regular clergy, recently wrote: "It is necessary to restore to the diocesan priest the sense of his plentitude. It is characteristic of him to have charge of everything. His speciality is to be the guardian of the highest sources . . . to be a man of the Church, *the man of the Church*. . . . We have recognized in this program the one Bossuet claimed to be that of the Oratory, and which Saint-Sulpice has for three centuries presented to generations of clerics as the code of priestly perfection. . . . The presbyterate [must be] conceived as the simple diffusion of the episcopacy in its inseparable auxiliaries." [4]

With this definition as a starting point, we can now clarify better than formerly all the elements of a permanent diocesan spirituality, one that is both enduring and up-to-date, in which diocesan priests will quickly recognize the immutable and practical laws of their state. His Excellency Émile Guerry, Coadjutor-Archbishop of Cambrai and Secretary-General of the Assembly of the Cardinals and Arch-

---

[3] "The priest will find, in the inspirations of his zeal, new means adapted to the particular needs of each epoch in the life of the Church, and corresponding to the various transformations of the social state. If we had the zeal of the reformers of the clergy of the seventeenth century, we would discover, as they did for their own time, the methods which are best suited today to win back souls. True zeal is industrious and full of initiative."

[4] *Maison-Dieu*, No. 3 (1944–1945), pp. 88-89.

bishops of France, has pursued this analysis with authority, clarity, and vigor, in a report first published in the periodical *Maison-Dieu,* of the Parochial Liturgical Center, and later published in *L'Union Apostolique* for November-December, 1945 and for January-February, 1946. Archbishop Guerry reduces to three the characteristic marks of clerical spirituality:

1. The bond with the bishop, who is the father of his priests;
2. the community of the diocese;
3. the pastoral mission.

Within this tripartite framework, our research, our meditations, and also our practical applications will probably be encompassed for a long time to come. It is this framework, with a few variations, that will furnish the title of the following chapters.

In several articles that appeared in *La Vie Spirituelle* for 1945-1946, an anonymous author, who chose to hide the very lofty functions he is now exercising in the Church in France, adopted a threefold division that is slightly different from the one above. In his analysis of the possible rebirths to be sought in the major seminaries, he summarized under three headings the institutional reform and the work of spirituality to be accomplished to fill the needs of the rising generation: 1) the value of action in the Christian life; 2) the place of the body in the spiritual life; 3) the sense of community in the Church. He returned to the great Augustinian and Thomistic tradition to find certain aspects of asceticism and mysticism that the classical and Cartesian centuries had put in the background and neglected, in their efforts to answer the intellectual needs of their time.

As it is not our purpose here to study the grave question of the major seminaries and of ecclesiastical education, which is beyond our authority if not beyond our competence, we have adopted chapter headings which are different from those of the eminent churchman referred to above. It was not our purpose to study the necessary incarnations, that is, the place to be given to the presence and activity of the body in the human composite informed by grace. However the reader will see that in speaking of the community and of its principles, we have not hesitated to stress the *carnal* part (in the sense Peguy uses it) of an integral spirituality.

But very emphatically, we shall seek new means of sanctification in the pastoral responsibility deriving from the apostolic function of the bishop. Offices of religion toward God have been organized and in part transformed into pious exercises, in order to assure the interior life of the priest himself. On the other hand, the apostolate, zeal for neighbor, has not yet been sufficiently exploited as a means of perfection. Indeed, activity has often been considered as a danger, and a veritable obstacle to holiness. In other words, the entire spirituality of priestly action is still to be established, as is that of Catholic Action. These are the problems of our time. Already many theoretical and practical efforts have been made in this direction.[5]

But it is not so easy for man in general, and for the man of the Church in particular, to belong to his own time. For one thing, our epoch does not know itself, and finds expression in chaotic tendencies rather than in defined programs and in clear explanations. Besides, the supernatural, because of its

---

[5] Cf. Bishop René de la Serre, Pro-Rector of the Institut Catholique de Paris, in his pamphlet *L'Éducation générale* (Paris: UGSEL, 1942): "Does not the training of the majority of the clergy . . . in the school of high spirituality of the seventeenth century . . . in the footsteps of the Berulles and the Olliers, offer us, together with numerous reasons and advantages that require us to remain faithful to it, incomplete preparation for the task ahead of us? . . . The significant place given to other, more combative spiritualities, the ever-increasing opportunity even in the seminary of acting and controlling one's action, the concern over productivity of work as well as over exactitude in following the rule, indicate some of the variations to be introduced so that the French priesthood may increasingly fashion for itself an elite that is capable of fulfilling its onerous mission."

very transcendence, constantly increases the distance which, since original sin—and in spite of baptism which has not eliminated all the consequences of original sin—continues to separate the solutions given by grace from the problems posed by creation. It is easy for us, after being his spiritual beneficiaries for three centuries, to admire Ignatius of Loyola's stroke of genius, which reversed the order of ascetic values, in order to adapt them, without destroying them, to the needs of the Christians of the Renaissance. But neither he nor his contemporaries grasped this admirable miracle of the Spirit quite so clearly. In the revolution which is now shaking us, we do not see clearly what nature has a right to ask and what the Spirit intends to grant her or to demand of her. Only a few great trends are beginning to be visible. We can already forsee that Catholic Action will modify many spiritual positions, not only among laymen, but by way of reaction, of consequence, of osmosis or parallelism, among priests. Everywhere we begin to hear talk of the spirituality of Catholics of action. By virtue of an historical law that we have recognized as part of the interior and institutional life of the Church, these needs or these generosities of the laity cannot fail to be transformed into exigencies for the clergy.

But human action and Christian action make a vast world. Action is mortifying and it is constructive. It is a promise and it is a refusal. It is an exercise and an application. It sows and it reaps. It is a means, and at its term when it is charity in act, it is almost an end. We shall therefore be obliged to devote two complementary chapters to it, in which we shall try, after we have justified the asceticism of mortification, to construct a positive spirituality of action. Because of its very richness, this spirituality of action can be studied twice, as it applies to the priest himself, under the name of asceticism, then as it applies to neighbor, under the species and the sign of service. Actually, these are two attitudes which constantly influence and beget one another, so as to be more completely intermingled. What is certain is that the spirituality of action must never wrong the ancient spirituality of piety which remains as indispensable as it is intangible. There are many reasons why this should be, the first deriving from one of the most reliable and deepest laws of psychology. Man is an animal who is essentially attuned to two rhythms. Does not the earth, for that matter, live by alternations in its revolutions and its seasons? Work is possible only because of the rest that has preceded or is to follow it. Action aspires to contemplation in order to purify and justify itself. It needs prayer if it is to endure.

Moreover, if we restore to action its entire metaphysical content, which signifies the movement of a being toward its end, then priestly action, orientated at once toward God and toward men to serve as an intermediary between heaven and earth, is an action that is as religious as it is apostolic, and that is filled with charity toward God and with charity toward neighbor. We may speak, if we wish, of readjusting the spirituality of priestly prayer. There can be no question, however, of substituting something else for it.

But this religious life as well as this apostolic existence, one in the other, fit into the framework of a communitarian life. We have certainly stressed this enough in the first part of this book, when we were trying to combat the individualistic conception of the priesthood, and to show that the priesthood has its origin, its reason for being, and its definition in the concession that the bishop makes to it of a part of his functions and of his personal responsibilities. The priest who, through his baptism was already a member of the mystical body of Christ, is now a member of another organism, which is the backbone of the other, and in which he continues to be articulated to a living whole.

This communitarian aspect of the priestly life is now seen in its full light and is constantly giving rise to new discoveries and applications. Without claiming to exhaust this subject which is in full process of fermentation, we shall devote a concluding chapter to it.

CHAPTER IV

The Necessary Asceticism

THE FERMENT of ideas in which the diocesan priest finds himself, the cascade of institutions which he sees crumble before his amazed eyes, the new contacts that Catholic Action demands or suggests with laymen and their families, oblige him to think through again some of the problems that Christianity has always succeeded in solving through the centuries. Among these problems is that of asceticism, whose fine point, or rather heroic gesture, is represented by ecclesiastical celibacy. Formerly, in a firmly established Christendom, this celibacy was the solid, respected, and well-understood foundation of the priest's pastoral authority. Today, in a missionary and challenged Church, it is the object of sceptical, hostile, scornful, or amused, and sometimes of admiring astonishment. The new conditions of the priests's apostolate oblige him to surround it with more precautions than formerly, or in any case with different precautions, since now more than ever the priest must be in the world without being of the world. Celibacy constitutes a value that is all the more vulnerable in that it is so exceptional.

This is not the first time that Christianity is establishing itself in a pagan environment in order to propagate itself. That is how its history began. But this is perhaps the first time that Christianity intends to maintain itself and to grow in such an environment, while preserving the essential institutions of a Christian society that it has, in the interval, succeeded in establishing upon earth. The presbyters, upon whom St. Paul advised Titus or Timothy to lay hands in the newborn Churches, were fathers of families. The diocesan priest has no longer any personal family life. And yet a long progressive evolution of the apostolate, of the regime of the sacrament of penance, of spiritual direction, of psychology and trust, invites or obliges the diocesan priest to penetrate more and more into the secrets of men's souls and to a certain point into the intimacy of the family life of others. The Catholic Action study groups have in any case completely modified and enriched the priest's knowledge of the world as well as his contacts with the faithful. Asceticism emerges from all this more necessary than ever, and together with it, we believe, celibacy is more inevitable, too.

We ask permission, however, not to make too many allusions to this particular situation, and to take up the problem from a higher point of view, in its generality.

* * *

A pure Greek substantive, light, supple, and resistent, the image of strength and beauty, has recently crossed the threshold of Christian language, to remain henceforth a part of of it. This word is ascesis, ἄσκησις, which signifies etymologically *exercise*. Through a misplaced sense of modesty, grammarians of former times dressed it up with heavy suffixes. They authorized the use of the French words: *ascétisme* and *ascétique*. And the English language, which is even more puritanical, speaks of *asceticism*. But ascesis finally escaped from the porticoes and the lawns of the physical culture gymnasiums, and rose to the spiritual level of religious and moral values. This is the capital most recently taken from the temples of the ancient divinities to serve as an ornament in the churches of the true God. We now speak of Christian ascesis, just as we have long spoken of *spiritual exercises*.[1]

When St. Paul, in his First Epistle to the Corinthians, compared the Christian to the athlete of the Hellenic games, he was merely taking up again at a supernatural level the counsels that Plato addressed to the ascetics of his temporal city, in Book III of *The Republic*:

> "We need some more ingenious form of training for our athletes of war, since these must be as it were sleepless hounds, and have the keenest possible perceptions of sight and hearing, and in their campaigns undergo many changes in their drinking water, their food, and in exposure to the heat of the sun and to storms, without disturbance of their health."[2]

We shall draw inspiration from these venerable texts in examining the psychology, and with its help, the metaphysics of ascesis. We shall not hesitate to start from the etymology of

---

[1] I have found the word "ascèse" in Renan's *Avenir de la Science, pensées* [and text, so he tells us] *de 1848,* published at the beginning of the Third Republic. This term may have come to him from his ecclesiastical education. In any case, the word is not to be found in Littré (1876).

The three conjugate terms: asceticism, ascetic, ascesis, really come from the purest and most authentic Greek, from the language of the schools, the proticoes, and the stadia. Ἄσκησις means exercise; ἀσκητής, the one who exercises, the athlete, the gymnast. The civilization of that time placed the exercises of the body and of the mind at about the same level in its thought and esteem: ἀσχεῖν σοφίαν χαι ἀσετὴν (Plato): to train oneself in wisdom and virtue. ἀσχεῖν τὰ δίχαια (Sophocles): to learn justice. ἀσχεῖν την ἱππιχην (Xenophon): to learn to ride horseback.

Almost always add the idea of endurance or of maintenance of vigor: χειμῶνι ἀσχεῖν σῶμα (Euripides): to harden the body against the cold by exercise. (Examples borrowed from the Dictionnaire apologétique (Alès), Volume I, col. 293.)

[2] English translation by Paul Shorey (New York: G. P. Putnam's Sons, 1930), Volume I, p. 267.

the word. Ascesis was from the beginning and has remained exercise. But how are we to define exercise?

We might be tempted to see in exercise only the methodical decomposition of a total act or gesture into its elementary fragments, the art of accomplishing separately, by repeating them several times, the successive parts of a complex movement—a movement that life would then unify and reconstruct anew, once discipline had analyzed it so as to master it. Exercise would be only the application of a famous principle of Machiavelli's, which is quite immoral: *divide ut imperes*. The fastidious rhythms of the soldiers' training school or of the Swedish gymnasium suggest this superficial view of the problem. But a closer consideration leads to more difficult and more illuminating conclusions.

Exercise, and therefore ascesis, involves much more than a simple division of a gesture into its elementary movements. It includes first of all a schematic and therefore geometric or regular construction of provisional and rigid lines which will later disappear in the definitive and real operation. Thus, a sharp-edged will for a while replaces with a rigid framework the flexible and instinctive forms of nature. Rational intelligence has followed this path, and it has placed its mark upon the system. Accustomed to handling solids with straight lines, it has eliminated the sinuous and curving contours of the original gesture or of the gesture to come. In contrast, the pure and simple animal never exercises. His instinct seems to him more infallible than all the scaffoldings of angular movements. But on the other hand, he never makes any progress, and he is always repeating the same monotonous and limited successes.

The intelligence of the rational animal, on the contrary, enables him with each new generation, with each new discovery, to outstrip the earlier stages of a civilization which has gotten further and further away from the original conditions of creation. Is it surprising that this intelligence should impose its methods, which are those of the schematic concept, upon fundamentally instinctive functions, so as to raise them to new levels and attain new results?

Do you remember the way the children of two generations ago were taught to write? Those of us who learned by that method remember it as if it were yesterday, for it marked the entrance of our fragile minds into the millenary current of human cultures. We were given writing notebooks, with horizontal lines, on which we first wrote simple vertical lines, inclined in a north-west south-east direction. Each child was supposed to imitate the model given him by making lines with its own trembling hand, lines that have no place anywhere in the real alphabet, but which are, as it were, the internal scaffolding, the foundation of the real letters. On the next page, we learned to transform our straight lines into down-strokes, and thus to form m's and n's. And so by dint of patient and geometric exercises, our children's pens progressively escaped from the prisons where they were kept for their own good, and one day they began to run over the paper with all the vigor and originality that give to each of us his own distinctive handwriting, which reveal his hand, his psychology, and even his personality.

Thanks to this ascesis, the child who was once able to do no more than scribble formless and meaningless drawings, could now express thoughts, sacramentalize his intelligence, form letters and compose words that everybody could recognize and understand.

The same process could be outlined for elementary gymnastics as well as for swimming, and for riding a bicycle without falling off. Nowadays, it appears, children are so precocious that they can get on a bicycle and hold their balance without having to learn, just as little savages swim without being taught. The milestone has been passed for the group as well as for the individual, because the habit has been formed, or—as in the case of the little primitive swimmers—preserved.

Thus habit, rightly understood, is almost the opposite of exercise. Exercise turns away from instinct, at least provisionally, in order to mortify, discipline, and rationalize it, and thereby to allow the rational animal to exceed his original powers. Habit, on the contrary, brings an action back into the instinctive life from which it has come or which it has surpassed, so as to liberate the reason from concern over an inferior value, and to give it the strength and time for nobler and more useful occupations. It is impossible to understand either exercise or habit if our definitions of them persist in abstracting from their immanent end that explains and constitutes them.

Habit would be a regression, a return to pure animality and instinct if its end were not to permit its possessor the superior, more varied, more refined, and more fruitful use of his attention, of his reflective attention which is one of the marks of reason. Exercise, in turn, would be a tyrannical and odious dictatorship of geometric intelligence, shattering the instinctive flights of a proud and virginal nature, if its end were not —by reason of a provisional and apparent bullying—to teach the rational animal the art of surpassing himself.

The candidate for a driver's permit takes exercises at the wheel of a driving school car, so as to acquire the habit of the instinctive movements of a professional driver. His hand will soon execute the necessary actions without the visible help of reason, though reason will remain available in emergencies for whatever supplementary solutions are needed. By relegating to the shadows of the subconscious classical and elementary movements, the writer, the artisan, and the sportsman preserve the liberty and the attention of their genius for unexpected, decisive and triumphant discoveries.

In short, acquired habit is a gain only because, by taking over inferior tasks, it liberates the intelligence for new, loftier, more difficult, and more advanced work. If this were not so, even though morality and ascesis should recognize it as a good habit, it would make us renounce the noblest privileges of man, who is capable of reflection, consciousness, and decision. But thanks to this quasi-subconscious mechanization of our inferior activities, habit becomes the means of reserving our rational faculties for the tackling of more human tasks. Thanks to habit, our reasonable humanity rests upon a broad base of easy movements that function secretly but infallibly to the profit of our higher faculties. And it is previous exercise that has in great part brought about these precious results.

We have progressed far from the term "ascetic exercise" (a pleonasm in Greek), conceived as the simple fragmentation of the total action into its elements. We are really in the presence of an eminently human method, of a procedure that is essential to the rational animal, of a mark of the intelligence as it takes possession of the world of instinct so as to surpass it in the very act of using it—only to plunge the action back into the subconscious world once the result has been attained, so as to carry effort higher and further. And so, in a fruitful and unending circle, exercises and habits beget and replace one another in writing the history of progress and of civilizations.

Is it surprising that the day the grace of God asked men to cross the supreme threshold, that would lead them from the level of nature to that of supernature—is it surprising that the intelligence, whether solicited or freely desirous of offering its assistance to this superhuman work, should have used its habitual methods and practiced ascesis?

Seen from the outside, ascesis seems to be a mortification, a diminution. After the analysis we have just made, we see to what extent this renunciation is provisional and constructive. But it is more than ever indispensable. And this is probably the reason why.

The expression "the naturally Christian human soul," attributed to Tertullian, has been much spoken about. Supernatural charity is the psychological prolongation (we do not say ontological prolongation) of natural love. And in this sense it seems to be instinctive. Actually, if it were no more than instinctive, it would be the product of freedom and of nature; it would not have begun to be supernatural, redemptive, in the theological, salutary sense. How are we to respect this concordance of direction (we are not saying: concordance of term or of end) between nature and supernature, between natural philanthropy or munificence on the one hand and divine charity on the other? And how can we pass from one level to the other, and yet avoid the illusion of mistaking the former for the latter? After all, service rendered to a passer-by through a display of physical activity, through pure vanity, by virtue of the superiority complex treasured by every Frenchman, does not necessarily equal the renunciation to egoism and the attachment to God and to His love that a genuine act of Christian charity demands.

A few moments ago, we observed the transition from the formless but natural drawings of a child to his initiation into the characters of intelligent and conventional writing. The principle is the same as for the transition from the instinctive and lazy gesture of an adolescent who is stretching his legs or his arms, to the meritorious and lasting endurance of one of Hébert's disciples; or the transition from the improvised actions of an extemporaneous life-saver to the rational and much more efficacious methods of the Red Cross.

In each of the above cases we saw the intelligence, thanks to exercise, move away from instinct provisionally and geometrically, so as to exceed instinct by bathing it in reason, and for that matter only to find it once again under the form of a habit in which it has become a second nature—but much stronger, more fruitful, more apt to succeed and to produce masterpieces, surer of itself for achieving new progress. Exercises in themselves are inferior to nature, just as the straight line of the inert solid or of the currently stylish man's suit is less beautiful than the curve outlined by the flexible and flowing forms of the living body. Exercise for exercise's sake is a monster or a tyrant. But exercise as a method is a wonderful and indispensable instrument, the servant of a cause that is beyond it but which legitimizes and honors it.

The same holds true on the spiritual level. There are virtues that are inferior to charity because they are not materially within the line of man's last end, and because in any case their provisional value condemns them one day to disappear. But precisely because they are not in the line of charity, they are in no danger of producing the illusion of which acts of purely natural benevolence are capable. These are the ascetic virtues, also called the virtues of counsel because they are not always necessarily indicated or obligatory, and because their practice requires at every moment preliminary reflections, the making of decisions, and consequently the asking of counsel. Reason, enlightened by faith, perceives them to be indispensable.[3]

They are often virtues of renunciation, because spiritual exercise, like that of the gymnasiums and of the camps, requires abstinence and mortification. They are means and not an end. As long as a body in motion has not attained its end, it must sacrifice the sweetness of the progress it has just made to attain the end toward which it is tending. The situation of a traveler on a journey is very complex. While he is happy to have reached his present location, and while he has a right to enjoy the scenery about him, still if he is to reach his destination which is his real good, he must not stop on the way. He must learn to renounce the provisional spectacle, and go onward toward the contemplation of the ultimate splendors that are his goal.

Such must be the attitude of the Christian toward created being. He must admire it as the work of a loving God, and go beyond it to a love and knowledge of God that will take him further, higher, closer, until he is finally face to face with God. When he has reached the supreme goal, all values will be telescoped: the end of man will be lost in the glory

---

[3] Cf. Mathieu, Paul, in *Préludes à l'Action catholique* (Aix-en-Provence, June-July, 1946), p. 3: "Under the pretext that charity is the queen of the virtues, have we not neglected subsidiary virtues like humility or mortification, whose precise object is to purify charity? And consequently, what we have taken to be charity has perhaps been only an ersatz."

of God, the triumph of created being will be lost in eternal vision.

All these comparisons bring us back to the intelligence, which we just saw renouncing instinct only to find nature again on a higher level of control and peace. It is clear that from this point of view mortification, which has too often been considered the essential element of ascesis, is really only one of its secondary aspects, just as fatigue and sweat are for the athlete only accidents of a necessary and legitimate exercise.

If our memories are good, we shall remember that such was already the case under the porticoes of Athens and Sparta, when the purpose of ascesis was to furnish young athletes for the protection of the Republic, "good guardians," as Plato expressed it.

And so it is that here on earth, charity, because of its very perfection and because of the imperfection of our state, must often seek outside of itself, under the name of spiritual exercises, for the means that are useful and perhaps necessary to establish it within us. In principle, charity is sufficient to itself, and it is sufficient for all things. In practice, it needs the inferior virtues, which have moral and divine value only if they are informed and vivified by charity. The Christian life maintains its equilibrium only if these two levels perpetually react upon each other. Ascesis without charity is pure formalism, an odious ragging, a permanent hypocrisy, a form of puritanism without soul or loyalty. It falls *ipso facto* under all the condemnations addressed by St. Paul to the works of the law. It is a lie, it revolts souls that are rightly proud, it is repugnant to youth, and it dries up the springs for the recruitment of the Church and of the clergy.

On the other hand, charity without ascesis always runs the danger of being a utopia or an illusion. Precisely because charity is our end, it requires means. In its naked state, without the vesture of the virtues of counsel, it runs the risk of being confused with our natural end which is always directed toward charity but remains insufficient.

In demanding of the will enlightened by faith painful acts that are not materially directed to our end, ascesis obviates the ever-present risk of confusion between nature and supernature. At the same time it makes us practice the millenary method which is the very mark of the human intelligence in all its efforts toward progress. This method, of course, is that by which objects are provisionally made to serve ends which are not their own, in order, thanks to this interlude, to this exercise, to overcome an obstacle, to reach a higher level, and find nature again on higher ground. In the present case, these means are used to go beyond all of nature's potentialities and, through the grace of God, to attain to supernature, to authentic charity, the charity that loves God for Himself and loves neighbor for the love of God, thus realizing our end which is to save ourselves through love.

The authentic Christian position, under the regime of the Redemption, is very complex and can find expression only in successive gradations. On the one hand, it must terminate in a positive construction, in a utilization and triumph of created being, which, through its full development, must sing the glory of the Creator. On the supernatural level to which we are called, charity is responsible for this work. In principle, charity should make the maximum direct use of the resources of nature and thus widely encourage the joy of living and loving.

However sin has supervened, and has made illusions possible. Hence the need for a provisional and constant mortification. But since this mortification is destined to be only a means, it can find expression here or there, it can vary its formulas, choose its matter, and it must never abuse of its method. Since it is not the end of man nor part of the divine plan, it is entirely relative to its purpose and without value in itself. That is why it varies exceedingly according to civilizations, climates, modes of life, to the great astonishment of simple or candid souls, and to the great anger of the pharisees or sectarians who are amazed at the extraordinary freedom of choice that ascesis enjoys within the bosom of Christianity.

The Church, for that matter, has the right to express her preferences, and to set order in her house by transforming her choices into institutions, which become obligatory when she makes them the object of a contract: in baptism, for all the faithful; at the moment of religious profession, for professional ascetics; at the subdiaconate, for the clergy.

Experience proves that this delicate balance between the end and the means is very difficult to maintain in sermons, in education, in spiritual literature and institutions in general. Those systems of ascesis which are actually adopted always tend to solidify, to become rigid, and to set themselves up as absolutes. Familial and ecclesiastical authority as well as social constraints exercise their influence in the same direction. They are always in danger of giving preference to ascesis over charity, interdiction over use. The trouble with this regime— which is meant to be a guarantee against sin—is that we often lack good examples of the legitimate use and blossoming forth of created being. To counterbalance the immense romantic literature on sin, we have far too few works which tell of the grandeurs of a loyal, sincere, total Christian love. The Bourgets and the Mauriacs are legion, and the Malègues are too rare. The reason for this in that Jansenism is easier to expose and to exploit than is genuine Catholicism. This is even truer, alas, of educational methods.

Until now, we have not mentioned by name the three great virtues of counsel that constitute the historical bases of Christian ascesis: virginity (or celibacy), poverty, and obedience. And yet it must be clear that we had them constantly in mind in our meditations on these problems. In the original sense of the word, they constitute the spiritual exercises *par excellence*. The worst disservice that we could render to their cause would be to erect them as a sort of super-Christianity, superior to charity. This is a temptation to which Christian orators and authors often yield when they do not watch the bases of their theology. But it is a lamentable error, which consists in preferring the remedy to the cure, hygiene to good health, or more exactly, the means to the end. The virtues of counsel can make no claim whatever to primacy, because they are only instruments of second rank, as St. Thomas tells us,[4] because they cannot claim to be an absolute and universal obligation, as St. Francis de Sales says,[5] because they do not represent our last end, and while they have become necessary by reason of sin, they would have been useless and even to be condemned if there had been no sin.[6] But sin exists, and we live under the plan of the Redemption, and not under the regime of original justice. That is how and by what right the virtues of counsel are an integral part of the Christian system, until the eternal day when charity, their queen and mother even as of now, will suffice to itself and also for us.

But in our pitiless deductions, which might better be called feelers, there remains one further step to take. We must pass from the sphere of the individual to the social sphere.

The three divine Persons *are* relations. Human persons *have* relations. The divine subsisting Persons are identical to their unique essence. The terms of our relations are not part of our essence, but the fact that we have relations is essential to us. The consequence is that a human person cannot fulfill his humanity alone, without concern for his relations, that is, without cultivating them, and, if the terms of these relations are persons, without willing and doing them good.

The spirit of the spiritual and moral life of Christians is already inscribed in the preceding formulas. We must reconcile respect for and the development of our persons with respect for and the good of our relations. The law of charity

---

[4] *Summa,* Ia Iae, q. 184, a. 3.

[5] *Treatise on the Love of God,* Book VIII, Chapter 6; Book XI, Chapter 11.

[6] *Summa,* Ia, q. 118, a. 2, ad 3 (against certain Greek Fathers).

identifies our good at once with the good of God and with the good of our neighbor.

We were wrong, therefore, to be content until now with considering ascesis in the isolated individual. This narrowness of vision in a way facilitated delicate and subtle analysis. But the Christian does not live alone nor for himself alone. He is part of an immense body, the mystical and spiritual body of Christ. And the one life that all Christians live is lived in community. No one is an ascetic for himself alone. He must be ascetic for others, which is a better way of being an ascetic for himself, too. And since the body of Christ is organized, it includes members specialized in this or that function. In this society there are professionals of this or that ascesis, of poverty, virginity, celibacy. Besides, the social body has demands that the individual body does not feel: it calls for living lessons, lived examples, heroic gestures, all of which are entrusted to elite souls. Ascesis, which was once only a series of acts or gestures, a period of dedicated time, a preliminary and provisory exercise, can and must become in an organized community a social function and even, for certain members of the body, a state of life.

Thus we come for a second time within the Christian system to reserved celibacy, to religious virginity. Celibacy is not necessarily bound to the ecclesiastical state. And yet we can say that beginning with a certain stage in the spiritual development of the Church, it is practically required by the very perfection in which the clergy is established, by the moral and interior influence that the clergy intends to exercise and that the faithful demand of it.

Historically, it seems that the example of the monks, that is, of the ascetics specialized in continence, morally demanded that the clergy—if it was to maintain its primacy and its influence—follow the example of laymen vowed to celibacy. But beneath the surface of history, a deeper law happily required the bishops and priests to give, on this most delicate point, the proof of their practical belief in obligatory perfection, and

thus to spiritualize corporally and psychologically an existence that was already totally dedicated to sacred things, to
the exerting of moral influence, and to the service of God.
And Catholic Action, by obliging the clergy to progressively
deepen its spiritual functions and to assume the roles of directors and chaplains, by inviting laymen to vow themselves personally to celibacy in the world so as to better consecrate
their entire lives to bearing witness and to the apostolate—
Catholic Action, far from lessening the role and the necessity
of ecclesiastical celibacy, was to make it morally more necessary than ever. Continence and virginity are not at the summit of ascesis. Those lofty heights are held by poverty and
obedience, represented today by detachment, the rugged life,
submission to the real and to service. But celibacy is the foundation of ecclesiastical ascesis, the invisible and immovable
rock, the silent and powerful rock on which it quietly rests.
Celibacy, then, is all of this, but no more than this. For, "if I
deliver my body to be burned, yet do not have charity, it
profits me nothing." [7]

The great Apostle of spiritual athletics thus put ascesis in
its place, which is not the most exalted one. And yet he was
the first to practice it: *preceptum Domini non habeo, con-
silium do.*[8]

---

[7] I Cor. 13:3.
[8] I Cor. 7:25.

CHAPTER V

Action [1]

HONORABLE scruples and well founded fears may consider too generous the thesis that would identify perfection, and therefore charity, with its multiple activities, even if they be apostolic like Catholic Action, to which many priests and Christian laymen are devoting themselves. For perfection, it is pointed out, does not reside in action but in contemplation, and it is Mary, not Martha, who chose the better part. Must we then renounce the possibility of reconciling action and charity? And does Thomism, which teaches the primacy of the intelligence over the will, which identifies eternal beatitude with vision, oblige us to make this definitive sacrifice?

This problem is not a vain imagining. It brings suffering to many souls at the hour when they must choose a state of life, in the dark days of exhausting and apparently sterile physical or moral fatigue, when the time for disillusion and for exam-

---

[1] In *Prêtre et Apôtre* (Bonne Presse) 28th year, No. 332, for July 15, 1946, p. 105, there is a reliable bibliography on the spirituality of action. We might also add the work of Father Teilhard de Chardin, S.J., on *Le Milieu divin, essai de vie intérieure,* especially the first two parts: "La divinisation des activités," "la divinisation des passivités." The last three or four words provide a whole program.

ination of conscience arrives. It has given rise to many controversies, and clouded many a vocation.

To speak of an apostolate of prayer does not solve the problem of the value of the apostolate through action. To present the interior life as "the soul of the apostolate" still gives us to understand that the apostolate as such needs to look outside of itself for a life that it does not itself possess.

And yet St. Paul, that eternal itinerant, that tireless founder of far-flung churches, defends us from this objection. There has never been a more fervent believer in missionary activity and apostolic action than the Apostle of the Gentiles. It is erroneous, therefore, to construct only the antithesis which, by opposing action and perfection, would deny action the right of being a spirituality and a school of sanctity. And yet we are told that we need only read spiritual authors, listen to preachers, and prepare the edict of condemnation as they dictate it. A flood of words, swelled with edifying eloquence and learned arguments, has progressively depreciated the concept of action in the Church. Actions in the plural were at first praised, and then action in the singular was held up as something to distrust. From action we turned to activity, and from activity to agitation, and under cover of the latter both action and activity were condemned pellmell. Under the impact of this descending dialectic, action—even apostolic, even priestly action—is in danger of always remaining suspect: *Martha, Martha, sollicita es et turbaris erga plurima.*

On the psychological and moral level, the case can be made quite as easily: action implies the search for and the use of means. Search implies anxiety, hunting, dissipation, and dispersion. Means suggest a position that is inferior to the end and the possibility of forgetting the end. With relation to the end, action is centrifugal; it distributes us in time and space, it tears us apart, it impassions us, diverts us, and is always in danger of making us impure. *O homo, in teipsum redi: in interiore homine habitat veritas.* It was St. Augustine, I think, who voiced this thought. And this great Doctor of the West can certainly never be accused of quietism. After him, the author of the *Imitation of Jesus Christ* took up the same theme, dedicating his four classical books of "internal consolation" to praising the sole way of interior prayer: *qui multum peregrinantur, raro sanctificantur*. The cause of the spiritual value of action thus seems hopeless. Who would undertake the defense of poor Martha, whom our Lord Himself seems to have abandoned to her sad fate?

Perhaps the best way of saving her would be to admit at once that she needs purification and correction. But this would not be pleading her cause thoroughly. There are better things to say. Let us begin to clear the way by throwing light on it. The search for and the use of means in the pursuit of a good end are not necessarily a cause of perdition. In fact, the presumption is in their favor. Beings such as we are, advancing toward perfection, blossom forth by developing their possibilities in the service of their end. In God, of course, being and act are identified. In us, the progress of action can assure development of the being. And ascesis, over which tradition lavishes its praise, is a series of exercises and therefore an action.

Martha's critics always seem to assume that her activity is necessarily the fruit of the selfish tendencies of a nature that delights in dispersion, entertainment, and agitation: a nature that seeks the pleasure of expressing itself outwardly, of being spoken about, of exercising its powers and its means, of practicing evasion to avoid recollection and prayer, and even to avoid God. Yet all these grave and dangerous faults, which occur frequently and are to be condemned, are perhaps only the results of a badly regulated or badly directed energy. It is possible to abuse of the best things and transform them into instruments of damnation, even though these creatures, these forms of life are not irrevocably evil. It is their very goodness perhaps, when ill-used, that is the cause of their evil influence: *corruptio optimi pessima*. It might perhaps suffice to regulate their use: *uti, non abuti*. It is simply a question of degree, unless it be a problem of duration. Everything that lasts abuses of itself and of its success, and in the end no longer maintains its own effort. Many activities are harmful only because they continue too long.

Action, which implies a loss of energy, suffers more than anything else from the effects of duration and time. It was pure at its inception, when it emerged from the verile decision of a generous will, when it applied itself with exactitude to the austere and necessary goal it had set for itself, when it was totally subordinated to its end, informed by this end, and mystically impregnated by the spirit that vivified it. It is during the course of its activity that it began to take pleasure in itself as in a final end, that it delighted in its own movement, and rejoiced in its pleasure without remembering its goal. Then it became heavy with its impurities, and failed to take time to eliminate them. It was a this moment that it was severely judged in the words of the Missal: *pondus propriae actionis gravat.*[2]

Well then, it is purification and redress that it needs, nothing more. It needs first of all to be informed by a pure intention, or—at the start of the work of conversion—by disinterested intentions (in the plural). This is the classical method for training beginners. Intentions are suggested to them, and they choose others themselves: "I will offer my work for the conversion of unbelievers, or for the recovery of a sick person who has asked me to remember him." This is a beginning of purification.

However an upright and pure intention (in the singular) is preferable. This is the *recta piaque mens* of which St. Pius X spoke with reference to frequent and daily Eucharistic Communion, the absolute, total, unified intention. To redress our course, to find the direction that leads to God, to base all our reasons for acting on this line of thought, to impregnate all our gestures, all our endeavors with it, is to practice a heroic

---

[2] Collect for the Common of a Martyr Pontiff.

spirituality of perfection. It is a spirituality from which action is not absent, inasmuch as action constitutes its matter. And so the problem is solved in a single stroke. It is almost too good to be true. It is perhaps better to divide this effort into its parts, to analyze this interior state, and to determine its duration. Let us try to make a few distinctions.

Action can be agreeable or painful, the source of pleasure or the cause of annoyance, the bringer of joyous exaltation or of acute suffering. In the latter case, spirituality has long since taken possession of it to make of it a means of perfection in union with the passion and death of Jesus Christ. Action is then identified with the sacrifices that it demands, and becomes a complement to the merits of the Saviour, in the service of the Redemption: *adimpleo ea quae desunt. . . .*

This is not a thesis, it is the whole spirit of Christianity. It is such a classical doctrine that we shall lay no further stress on it in a work whose intent, and a rather pretentious one it may be, is to delve into unresolved problems.

When action begets pleasure, just as youth brings forth its flower and the year produces spring, it is always more dangerous for purity of intention. There still remains the great solution, which belongs to the eternal kingdom, the solution of the sacrifice of praise. This will be the renewal of the canticle of Daniel's three young men, the rebirth of the Franciscan or the Salesian soul, the singing of God's glory, thanking the Creator for the joy of living and acting that fills our breast, our muscles, our mind, our entire being. Once again, temptation can be conquered when the soul finds its end and its god.

This momentary success will set us on the path to a universal solution of the problem of action. In short, it is a matter of bringing us back to God and making us subject to Him, of finding and taking up the position of the lover before his beloved, to whom he subordinates himself so that he may feel that he has been heard and delivered up, that he has been conquered and yet is himself a conqueror—that he has been conquered by the solution, and yet is the conqueror of the problem, that he has been conquered by another, but by reason of this very abdication is finally master of his own destiny and therefore of his being.

The spiritual enemies and the professional critics of action have not seen that action in this moment of success, Aristotle to the contrary notwithstanding, can be psychologically realized and felt like a passion: a passion in the noble Greek sense of the word, a total submission to a cause, a cause that is at once efficient and final and that gives us being.

True, action can sometimes be the vehement explosion of egoism and of all the centrifugal forces that make us die inwardly by dissolving us. But given other intentions and moving in a different interior direction, action, on the contrary, is submission to the real and obedience to it, it is answering "Yes!" to one's state in life, to the needs of our brothers, and finally to the call of God. This servitude of action to being transforms action into a power that is united to its source and its goal, that unfolds in an orderly manner, that finds its purity and its end once again, if they have been lost. This purity of action, which is possible and even obligatory, must be developed so as to bring forth a spirituality.

Clearly the detractors of action, who are not necessarily true contemplatives, are wrong in supposing that activity in all its forms is necessarily the fruit of an egoism that is not aware of itself or that is seeking its own ends.

But first of all, as we have just pointed out, action is not necessarily agreeable, service to neighbor is not inevitably a pleasure. Do these severe critics suspect all the difficulties a conscientious man can face in carrying out an enterprise, a responsibility, a function, or a mandate? At any rate, action, inasmuch as it is submission to the real, service to neighbor, acceptance of being, is passivity in the mystical sense of the word. Now, does not all mysticism amount to accepting God, submitting to Him lovingly: *pati divina,* sensing and loving this legitimate and real domination? Action is the affirmation of this submission in the realm of fact, of the real, of the actual. When we sense that our action is a service, and live it as such, the state of charity has become conscious within us.

We need not be surprised that a whole spirituality is in process of affirming itself in this direction. We owe this enrichment of our spiritual heritage to two or three principal causes: on the one hand, the development of Catholic Action which almost from the start posed the problem for the militants as well as for the simple members of circles, of an interior life that would vivify the apostolic effort demanded of them. On the other hand, there have been spiritual movements tending to restore the value and the dignity of the essentially active, pastoral, or missionary clergy. On the part of both laity and clergy, the same concerns and the same objects of inquiry have given rise to formulas which are increasingly alike. There is a third reason for the progress that has been made: the intense campaign in favor of large families or simply in honor of the family and of marriage has necessitated the rehabilitation of the labor of married couples, of fathers and mothers. While many of them are not at all available to the contemplative life, they none the less realize, in the monotonous, fastidious details of their daily lives, an admirable and necessary program of Christian life.

These are realities in the face of which certain abstract theories and platitudes must yield. We found a painful admission of this, combined with a respectful reproach, written by a young priest who just yesterday was a *routier* and today is a curate:

"At the end of his years of study, the diocesan priest naturally envisions his priestly life as a continuation of his years in the seminary. He hopes that his ministry will not prevent him from living his interior life, or from maintaining the spirituality of union with God in imitation of Christ, which had been the method and the spirit of his years of training. This training has included personal improvement, combat against faults, renunciation of egoism to resemble Christ more closely, and likewise a regularity of life, obedience to a rule that prevented dispersion and the personal search for unduly varied activities, and above all the contemplation of Christ in prayer and study, in the practice of sacrifice and mortification.

"But the parochial ministry soon upsets this program—apparently or in reality. The apostolic responsibility for others, the service of the cult and numerous obligations and services consume the time of the young priest, absorbing all his energies, changing his habits, and in the end preventing him from doing what he had intended. Periodically, a pastoral retreat tears him away from his occupations and reminds him of the conditions of spiritual life anticipated in the seminary. He then realizes its deficiencies and its impossibilities, and returns to his post without having found a spirituality attuned to his life as a diocesan priest. Couldn't something be changed? There must be a means of unifying this priestly existence through a spirituality adapted to the function of the priest, who is at the service of the faithful and the collaborator with his bishop. It would seem that the apostolate of St. Paul never hindered his interior life: this apostolate orientated his whole life, and his life was to make Christ known. His prayers, activities, sufferings—all were centered upon this ministry. . . ."

The young author went on to show how earlier obedience to rule, patterned on that of the religious, now became obedience to the real, with all the flexibility that the real demands, all the adaptations that are required in the service of the first comer, all the continual initiatives that are indispensable to anyone who would make the kingdom of God reign everywhere, and finally the constant availability for apostolic service to the bishop, with all the renunciations that such a heavy program presupposes.

Such frank admissions of interior dismemberment give to those who receive these disclosures the right and the duty to ask certain questions.

When action and contemplation are juxtaposed as being

the possible principles of two different states of life, is sufficient attention given to the fact that they are not necessarily in opposition on the spiritual level?

Has it been realized that human action, the human act of the moral theologians—and by extension all our activity—, is sufficiently complex to be at the root of a twofold movement of the soul, one that might be called centrifugal and the other centripetal, the former dissipating and dissolving, the latter unifying and gathering together?

On the one hand, human activity, the daughter of concepts and of reason applied to material things and to changing values, is essentially the search for influence and for means. From this point of view, it is the principle of pride and of dissipation when it is badly directed. It disperses us and tears us to shreds, and it drives us away from the one necessary good, which is God. It is from this point of view that it is so severely judged by the exclusive partisans of the contemplative life, who forget that the contemplative life is founded upon ascesis or encompassed by it, and that ascesis, by definition, is also exercise and therefore action.

On the other hand, human action, when it is inwardly directed to its last end, is nothing else but the acceptance of the will of God and the very fulfillment of this will. In this sense, it is the principle of interior unity, it is in act the tendency toward God which is at once our definition and our duty; it is submission to order, subordination to our end. We even dare say, without being paradoxical, that it is a "passion" in the mystical and Aristotelian sense of the word: *pati divina,* by which we accept God and accomplish His holy will.

Is this not the way to find the very principle of all mystical life? And on this ground, would not action and contemplation succeed in coming together, at least on this earth which is the provisory field of our pilgrimage?

Have we not neglected this aspect of the spiritual problem, or rather of its solution, under the influence of unilateral preaching and literature, composed by specialists in the contemplative life and not for laymen and diocesan priests?

Would there not be some interest in exploiting more thoroughly, of delving deeper into the sense in which action manfests itself as a submission to order, to the end, to God, and therefore the sense in which, on the supernatural level, it is charity, or in any case one of the incarnations of charity? Would not such an effort be desirable even if it were only to reassure Christians who are in love with perfection and with the apostolate?

We should not forget the regrettable and dangerous bifurcation which we pointed out in the beginning and which is still possible, by virtue of which action can drive us away from our end. This danger must be eliminated by a spirituality of meditation and by the traditional spiritual exercises. In this way mysticism will counterbalance activity, just as for the professional contemplative meditation is placed in a framework of asceticism.

Once these principles are accepted, we still have to examine how and under what conditions action in itself, and apostolic action in particular—which is the most perfect action of all—generates union with God and likewise generates charity and perfection. The formula is generally accepted when there is question of mortifying action. We say that suffering, trials, or even actions that are painful to nature conform us to the passion of Christ and bring us closer to God. But this way of thinking, exact as it may be, is already a concession to the thesis that we have been combating, in the sense that this view restricts to one type of action what may be true of any action whatsoever.

Must we not show that agreeable and lovable action, dangerous as it may be for a nature given to selfish and sensible pleasure, is not evil in principle? That it must be referred to God as well as the painful action, even if only to make it the object of uninterrupted thanksgivings? At any rate, when pleasurable action represents the performance of duty and therefore the will of God, it bears within it this submission, this subordination, this "passivity," in which we have recognized perfection as well as the very essence of the mystical life.

And so we always come back to the idea that action, insofar as it is theocentric, can and must be a principle of holiness.

A spirituality could be constructed with this orientation, particularly for the use of all who are dedicated to Catholic or priestly action. We dream, for example, of a particular examen, in the style of Tronson, that would ask:

Have we recognized in action not only the legitimate expansion of our nature but the expression of the will of God, the incarnation of our duty, and in this sense, the realization of our end?

Have we willingly abstracted from the agreeable or painful character of a proposed action, so as to see in it only our submission to a divine call, our subordination to God?

And yet, have we begun by examining the manner of life and therefore the obligations that would be best suited to our potentialities, so that our action might be more successful? For after all, is this not one of the ways of knowing and following our vocation?

But once this vocation was known and determined upon, have we embraced it with all its exigencies, and have we devoted ourselves to all the activities that it demands of us?

Within this framework, are we concerned with knowing and constantly accomplishing the most useful works for the glory of God and for the sanctification of our neighbor?

Have we taken care, in our preparatory examens or in our examinations of conscience, to consider the matter of our acts less than the form by virtue of which they represent God's will for us?

Have we found delight in this adorable will, submitting to it with all our strength and all our love, so as to have in our very action the filial passivity toward God our Father which is almost a complete definition of the mystical life of the Christian?

Have we sometimes been happy to feel exhausted, crushed, even physically so, under the weight of this lovable will, so that we might better feel that we do not belong to ourselves but to God? And that it is not only our goods, our thoughts, or our prayers that are being returned to Him, but the material tissue of our whole lives? [3]

The only thing, perhaps, that is lacking to this spirituality of action is that it has not been sufficiently studied, explained, and practiced. We possess innumerable treatises, that are both true and useful, on the necessity and value of mortification and abstinence. In fact, the word "asceticism" has come to have a negative and privative sense in the minds of many people, whereas its exact signification is "exercise," without reference to its direction.

We have relatively fewer works on the way of making use of action to sanctify ourselves. It would seem that the mother of a large family, the needy father, the priest who is crushed and "consumed," and the apostolic bishop deserve that someone should bend over their lives to help them to see and to feel—mystically—how their servitudes are forms of greatness, since they are acts of charity and expressions of love.

As for ascesis in general, it has been conceived and detailed for the most part on the periphery of real life, as an exterior

---

[3] Much fun is poked at Tronson's Particular Examens, because of their archaic character and their mania for outworn details. The Fathers of Saint-Sulpice are doing their best to rejuvenate them by successive adaptations, at the risk of being one edition behind with regard to customs and vocabulary.

And yet is the tripartite principle of the *Examens* open to so much criticism? The analysis, in the first and third points, of action referred to God as being an incarnation of one of Christ's mysteries has great mystical value that should be preserved. In practice, the ascetic tendency, which was also very visible in the *Examens,* has been the stronger. This is perhaps regrettable. (Father Louis Tronson, 1622–1700, was the third Superior-General of the Society of Saint-Sulpice. Translator's note.)

means by which real life can sanctify itself. And yet it should have been noticed that the word *exercise* which is the etymological and exact translation of the beautiful Greek word "ascesis," today has two meanings (at least in French) which must be distinguished when they are applied to the spiritual life.

Ascesis first of all designates the methodical practice of activities by which a man prepares himself for and becomes accustomed to fulfilling his functions. Exercise is therefore a means, it is the fruit of the conception of an organizing mind. That is why it often begins by the decomposition of the elementary movements of the action, so that it can afterwards bring them together through a progressive coordination. It is with such a purpose that soldiers do gymnastic exercises. They are neither gymnasts nor athletes by profession, but in order to exercise their military profession they need a strong and flexible musculature and excellent general health. The reason they take exercise is because they are not exercising their profession. By means of this comparison between the passive form of the verb and its intransitive form,[4] we can see that the activity of these men is immediately directed toward themselves, and only indirectly toward their end.

In the second place, the word exercise designates the activity of a function pursuing and attaining its end. Thus we speak of a judge in the exercise of his responsibility, of a mayor who exercises his functions in the community, of a member of the Society of St. Vincent de Paul devoting himself to the exercise of charity.

In practice and in language, the two conceptions tend to approximate one another. Conjoint means to the end do exist. Methodical exercises often end by becoming the exercise of a final act. For instance when a child learns to read or to write, a reading lesson and the composition of an anniversary letter

---

[4] This refers to the French for the preceding sentence: "Voilà pourquoi ils s'exercent; ils n'exercent pas."

to his parents are at once means and ends. Exercises of piety almost all belong to this composite type. They attain to the very practice of the obligatory virtue of religion at the same time that they constitute a methodical and formative ascesis.

Charity alone, which is strictly an end, can never be a pure exercise of means. When we are training ourselves to practice it, we are already practicing it, we are already exercising it. The father who is a member of the Society of St. Vincent de Paul and who takes his son with him to bring help to the poor, is exercising charity, and he is making his son exercise charity at the very moment he is teaching him to exercise it. In this sense, we cannot take exercises in charity, although we can perform acts of poverty or obedience that are exercises done for the sake of charity. But it is the privilege of charity to be incapable of being a means, and therefore to coincide with its own ascesis.

This is a coincidence which students of spirituality should consider in detail, by analyzing all the acts of the duty of the apostolic state and of apostolic activity. In so doing, they will flood the apostolate with mystical light.

In any case, with regard to priestly action which has been the concern of the masters of the spiritual life, we believe it can be said that the traditional direction has been maintained, and that this tradition is being continued in the proposal of a diocesan spirituality intimately bound to pastoral, apostolic, and missionary activity.

Was this not the intention of the masters of the French School, who are fortunately still with us today in the persons of their successors at Saint-Sulpice, Saint-Lazare, the Oratory, and elsewhere? What had the founders of seminaries dared and willed, if not to create a spirituality proper to the diocesan clergy—a spirituality that would exist by the side of the monastic and regular traditions and also utilize them in part, but a spirituality that would have its origins in the diocesan priesthood as such? They had taken from the priesthood itself all the duties that concern the cult of God, and they had set out to sanctify the priest by means of his Mass, his breviary, the exercise of his ecclesiastical functions. In the proper exercise of the priesthood itself, they had found the means of sanctifying the priest and of leading him to perfection.

"We can always recognize a former student of Saint-Sulpice," a Dominican was telling us recently, "by the way he speaks of the ecclesiastical state, by the particular respect with which he surrounds the liturgical functions, by the professional esteem he shows for the Mass, the breviary, and the divine service at the altar and in the church."

That is excellent. But there are in the priesthood, by definition, two series of functions, two orientations of activity—one turned toward God, of which we have just spoken, and one turned toward men. For the priest, in his quality as minister of religion, is the one who unites men to God, and also brings God to men. And in this quality he exercises his priesthood over the neighbor who is in his care. Let us repeat with St. Thomas: "The office proper to a priest is to be a mediator between God and the people: to wit, inasmuch as He bestows divine things on the people, . . . and again, forasmuch as he offers up the people's prayers to God." [5]

This being so, we need only prolong the theses of the French School in the direction of the faithful. In fact the French School has already begun to do this by speaking of the duties of the pastorate. Today we would add to these the missionary duties of the diocesan priest. Let us conceive of both sets of activities not only as duties but as means of perfection, inasmuch as they are incarnations of charity toward neighbor. If we do this, we shall remain within the great line of tradition and at the same time reach out to the extreme outposts of the most recent thought and of the most urgent reforms. We shall then recognize a good priest by the way he exercises his activity, his apostolate. A spirituality of action will then exist for the diocesan priest.

---

[5] *Summa*, IIIa, q. 22, a. 1, c.

In one of his articles full of shock and lightning, which we have mentioned before, in which he handles explosives without assuming the responsibility for setting them off, Father Doncoeur evaluates the superposition of the trends born of St. Benedict and St. Ignatius as they have been incorporated into the French School. He seems to think that it is hard for diocesan priests to bear the weight of so many riches. And to lighten their burden, he writes: "What harmony there is in the life of a priest who sanctifies himself *by* his preaching, *by* the baptism, penance, matrimony, etc. that he administers, by the sacrifice that he performs, *by* the charity that he exercises, . . ."[6]

The power of this proposition, that seems so simple and yet is so daring, resides entirely in the preposition *by* which we have taken the liberty of underlining, without, we believe, distorting the thought of the author. A few years ago, an anonymous author, writing in the Dominican publication *La Vie Spirituelle,* was content to attack the problem and to solve it from the other end, by proposing the integration of the preoccupations of action into the life of prayer.[7] But in both cases there is question of conjoining contemplation and action, so as to sustain the one by the other, and of rehabilitating action by associating it to the dignity and purity of contemplation. This approach is a sign of our times.

The spirituality of the members of Catholic Action must probably be sought at the level of the laity, but in the same direction as that of the diocesan priesthood. When shall we teach one another to see God's call and presence in the irksome problem to be settled, the importunate visit, the fastidious task, in necessary delays, enforced patience, in all the servitudes that make up the day of a man of action, who is above all a man of acceptance? If we sensed God's presence in all this, we would be mystics. Then the mystical state or its

[6] Paul Doncoeur, S.J., in *Études,* for May, 1945, p. 264.
[7] Cf. *La Vie Spirituelle,* April 1, 1936, article signed "Sacerdos."

ascetic equivalent in the life of a Catholic of action would *be* this very action.

However, a serious difficulty remains. We have alluded to it at the start of this chapter and several times afterwards. We must now come back to it in concluding. The difficulty is this:

Basically, this spirituality asks us to put contemplation into our action, since it is a question of seeing and sensing God's presence in elements in which we have not until now been accustomed to find Him. Let us admit that this restitution is not easy, and that centrifugal action constantly obscures the vision of God. Exercises of contemplation will always be necessary to remedy the loss of energy and the wear and tear caused by time and duration.

Here we come back to the pious exercises of the ancient methods of spirituality. There is no question of abandoning them. They are well known, and too diverse in accordance with the various schools of spirituality to permit restatement here. And yet they are not outside the scope of our subject, even if they have sometimes been in danger of remaining outside the scope of real life. Please God, the thoughts which we have so far expressed will not result in the elimination of exercises of piety and religion, but in their greater integration into the apostolate. These exercises will perhaps not become the soul of the apostolate, but they will at least be its nourishment and its bulwark, the assurance of its life.

If action is to be charity, if it is to be equal to and identical with charity, it must be inwardly informed by contemplation, at least under the secret form of the latter, which is pure intention. But neither supernatural charity nor Christian contemplation are natural to man, since they are divine gifts. In any case, action, at its birth and in the course of its expansion, is much too weak—since it is burdened with its own weight— to assure by itself our union to God through contemplation.

Contemplation must be cultivated separately, in itself, and even outside of action, in special exercises which are proper to it alone. These are the exercises of piety, the special acts of religion, of which the most important is mental prayer.[8]

Following this path, we come to habitual spirituality, which we may have learned by now to understand and use better, and perhaps to make less burdensome inasmuch as light purifies all that it touches. Perhaps too, this spirituality will have become richer and more complete for us, and justified by the respectful criticisms to which we have taken the liberty of subjecting it.

Our search for a spirituality of action has not led us to any definitive conclusions. We are still in a period of experiments and gropings, when souls filled with good will and anxiety must communicate their results to one another without ex-

---

[8] Mr. Daniel-Rops has recently enumerated and analyzed the diseases of the feelings, that become debased as they grow older because they have not defended themselves against their unconscious perversion. A complete treatise on the spirituality of action would include a bulky chapter on the diseases of action. These diseases would find their place at the two extremes of the psychological regime, whose middle sphere is occupied by sound health. In the first case, that of the *propriae actionis gravat,* a man allows himself to be driven by his successive activities so as no longer to be obliged to think, to reflect, or even to will, and thus becomes the perpetual slave of every invitation from the outside that dispenses him from deciding and taking sides. Action becomes the great entertainment, and in the end, as in the case of forced labor, the great degradation, absolute passivity, total servitude. We would not dare say that the priestly life is an example of this temptation and of this abuse, in which prayer disappears before reflexes and alibis.

On the other hand, man can suppress action under the pretext of dominating it more perfectly by setting it aside, in order supposedly to devote himself to meditation, study, and to personal culture. He will then mistake his whims or his dreams for authentic contemplation. This is the victory of dilettantism, snobbishness, laziness, and of the ivory tower. This state is dangerous, too.

Between the two extremes there is the contact of resistance and submission to the real, in which man, in which the Christian actively lives this mystical passivity, this subordination to the true, which is perfect equilibrium, life in conformity with order, action in accordance with charity.

pecting to impose them on their neighbor. It is a time, too, when we must admit our defeats and yet not abandon patient effort.

Moreover, the preliminary inquiries are far from completed. It would seem best first of all to consult the spiritual tradition of the past centuries, to discover the roots and principles of the solutions that are necessary today. The problem of action is as ancient as Christianity and humanity. While it has not always been in the forefront of ascetic and mystical theologies, it has never been absent from the thoughts of the masters of the perfect life.

The Fathers of the Greek Church, those last heirs of Hellenic humanism, never sought to escape either from their epoch or from their civilizations. They solved in their own way the problem of the relationship of religion to life. In the West, Augustinianism for a long time occupied the theological scene by itself. Despite its apparent pessimism and combativeness, it was really a great school of optimism and enthusiasm. And no one could ever accuse its successor, Scholasticism, of having turned its back on the culture of its epoch, captivated as it was by order, synthesis, and rational constructions.

Starting with the Counter-Reformation and with our Catholic Renaissance, all spiritual writers, all the founders of orders and congregations were haunted by the desire to introduce Christianity into the concrete life of their readers and disciples. What enterprising men were those giants of mysticism named Ignatius of Loyola, John of the Cross, Francis de Sales, Jean-Jacques Olier, and others! To repeat, this entire tradition should be consulted and thoroughly understood.

Coming from the opposite direction would be the daily experience of the Christians of today, the members and militants of Catholic Action, the priests of the diocesan clergy, religious missionaries and apostles, pioneers in the communitarian movement. Their testimony would dominate all these debates and bring them to a close more effectively than all our poor deductions. Besides, these deductions lend themselves to very diverse applications. Some may prefer to analyze in detail the daily life and the professional occupations of their state, so as to pour into them drop by drop the intention of charity, which, we believe, is the solution to the problem of pastoral action, missionary action, as well as ordinary lay Christian action. Those who would follow the gradual approach might be called the ascetics of charity. Others, whose mystical tendencies are more pronounced, will reach the total solution in one leap. With God's grace they will try to establish themselves once and for all in a state of interior availability that will make them at every moment servants of the real. They will always readily say "Yes!" to the real, because they will recognize in it at every moment the call of God. This will be another way, one that is more synthetic and unified, of cultivating a spirituality of action.

In conclusion, the proportion between action and silent contemplation, without which there can be no interior life, will not always be the same for all the servants and patrons of the method. We shall inevitably come back to the two great categories, the ascetics and the mystics, respectively stressing their own dominant faculty and vocation. There will be a corresponding variation in the distribution, the plan and the duration of exercises of piety. There will be souls, and they are perhaps the most privileged ones, who will be able alternately to lead the strictly secluded, contemplative life, and the life of the ministry. This should not surprise us if, as the Scholastics teach us, it is true that contemplation represents the perfect end in whose service charity asks us to use the means of action for the good of our neighbor.

We are contemplatives traveling on the road that leads from Jerusalem to Jericho, on which we have brothers to save. We must interrupt our journey, without if possible ceasing to meditate, and take the time to guide them to the inn. On the road, with our patient on our shoulders or on our mount, we shall not all have the same reactions of attention and distraction. This is inevitable, given the fact that our individual psy-

chologies, our heredities, our climates, our races, and our interior dispositions are so different. The important thing is
not to arrive alone at the inn, like the priest and the Levite,
declaring to the innkeeper that we had seen no one on the
way. The men of the circumcision and of the law may have
thought they were perfect because they recited their psalms
and praised the name of Yahveh on their journey. And yet
they were not real contemplatives because, in their travel, they
had not *seen* God under the form of their wounded and naked
brother.

Definitively, the problem of action and of its relationship
to contemplation is a problem of humanism. To repeat, it consists in reconciling our last end with the conditions of our
provisional state. We must not confuse the term with the
path that leads to it. And yet we must take this path, not for
itself but for the goal to which it leads us. While we must
not value it for its own sake, we must still esteem and love it,
and go forward on it, our eyes filled with the distant rays of
the beatific vision, like St. Francis of Assisi at the plow.

And now, we ask the reader kindly to combine the results
of this chapter with the conclusion we reached at the end of
Part One, devoted to the state of perfection of the bishop
and of the priest. There we considered the matter of priestly
action, which is the professional exercise of charity, insofar
as it is identical with the duty of the priestly state. Here, we
have studied the form of this action, and shown why action,
understood as submission to the will of God, can and must
become a mystical attitude.

By these two parallel paths, subordinated to one another,
we reach the Christian perfection whose summits we were
seeking at the beginning of this book. Consequently if the
priest, whose profession is to exercise charity and therefore to
exercise perfection, fulfills his task with the help of God in
the spirit that we have tried to analyze, then his whole existence, in its matter and in its form, in its content and by
reason of its direction, all of his actions, considered at once
as means and as ends, will help him more each day to estab-

lish himself in the interior and exterior state which will be
the state of perfection.

NOTE 1

In the IIa IIae of the *Summa,* there is a famous article in
which St. Thomas, in the evening of his life, gave expression
to the fervor which had once led him to enter an heroic order
that had just been born in the Church with an entirely new
spirit. The Friars Preachers have always seen in these lines
the definition of their ideal of life, and perhaps of all human
life: *contemplari, et contemplata aliis tradere* (IIa IIae, q.
188, a. 6). And perhaps they are not wrong. We might trans-
pose this motto to fit our present subject by calling it the
alternation between the internal and the external, provided
we understand these words in their most exalted sense as referring to the interior life and the life of the apostolate,
thought and action.[9] Now, modern psychology has taught us
that many human temperaments are unable, because of the
noble animality in them, to prolong their contemplation for
very long—that is to say, to prolong their thought, their meditation, their planning, their cerebration in the broadest sense—
without resuming contact at intervals with an action, an environment, a concrete reality in which their contemplation
proves itself by becoming incarnate, and from which it starts
out again with new leaps forward. This is perhaps the most
poignant aspect of the great problem of psychological duration
of which Bergson speaks. But it is interesting for theologians
to realize that St. Thomas had already remarked it in the
vocabulary and the frames of reference of his own time, as
well as in the writings of St. Gregory.[10]

It is easy for us to add that because of the accelerated

---

[9] *"Summum gradum in religionibus tenent quae ordinantur ad
docendum et praedicandum, quae et propinquissimae sunt perfectioni
episcoporum*—"Accordingly the highest place in religious orders is held
by those which are directed to teaching and preaching, which, moreover,
are nearest to the episcopal perfection." (IIa IIae, q. 188, a. 6, c.)

[10] IIa IIae, q. 182, a. 4, ad 3.

rhythm of modern life, these contacts with the real must be much more frequent than formerly. Contemplation and study must be constantly verified, used, and nourished even in the most generous and intense souls by a constantly renewed experience of life and of men. After all, we are not pure spirits. The prolongation of a meditative or introspective life soon exhausts us. Again, it is St. Thomas who calls this to our attention.[11] Except for the rare cases of an exclusively contemplative vocation, total inaction and solitude create obsessions, together with their consequence: maladjustment.

Now, the *presbyteri-episcopi* were born of the exigencies of the apostolic life, and therefore of an invitation to action, and that is at least half of the definition of their state. It is the sign, too, of the majority of the best "diocesan" vocations, those for which the seminaries exist.[12]

---

[11] IIa IIae, q. 180, a. 8, ad 2.

[12] There are very courageous testimonials that give pause for thought in the report by Father G. Guérin, chaplain-in-chief of the Y.C.W., given before the Thirteenth National Congress for the Recruitment of Priests, at Bourges (October 20-24, 1937), and published in *Le Recrutement sacerdotal* for January-February-March, 1938 (38th year, No. 47 of the new series):

"Let us not be too harsh in our condemnation of the organization and mentality of our seminaries. But let us realize that there are vocations from difficult environments, that have known the exuberant activity of the apostolate, tasted the joys of conquest, and communed intimately with the sufferings and distress of the souls about them. Such men find themselves deeply and sometimes invincibly disorientated by their new environment. The following words, for instance, expressed by one of these seminarians, show to what depth we must penetrate this problem if we are to think it through again correctly: 'The Y.C.W. still helps me here in the seminary. In my moments of dryness, of spiritual laziness or lassitude, I strive to think of past action, of my comrades who are still fighting at the present time, of all who are still to be won over. And I assure you that this fills me again with the Jocist fever, with enthusiasm, and helps me to pray for a few instants. My first days at the seminary were painful because of that: my action had been so completely united to prayer, that prayer was disorganized when action disappeared.' "

The reasons behind this partial failure pointed out by an authorized witness are very complex. They are incomprehensible to certain temperaments that have not gone through the same experience at all. The vocation of the diocesan priest is to give God to every soul. We do not intend this formula to apply only to a visible ministry, for the apostolate can exist without any physical contact with men, in which case it would consist in prayer, sacrifice, personal sanctification, etc. . . . We do not say, therefore, that a concrete ministry is absolutely necessary to prepare a future apostolate, for the good reason that tomorrow's apostolate will very often have a different form from today's. But pressing the analysis deeper, we see that as between love of souls and love of God, the latter does not always have priority in the psychological order. Moreover, these two forms of the same charity sustain one another, not only in their inception but also in their development. And this is in part the reason why the two great commandments are really only one. Doubtless, the perception of our neighbor, that is, of human existences around us, does not suffice to inspire us to generosity and self-sacrifice; but in certain souls it may be indispensable for arousing and nourishing a love of God that transfigures all these preliminary attitudes into charity.

Now, this perception may require a contact, an association with individual, concrete men, men that are not symbolical of reality like our colleagues, but men that are real the way historic reality is real, made up of unexpected quirks, discoveries, sufferings to be relieved, problems to be solved, responsibilities and collaboration.

The proximity of our neighbor can indeed make even greater demands: it may demand action, because certain temperaments perceive only in action the reality of an object and its exigencies, which are the exigencies of charity.

To repeat, not every character, not every temperament has the need for this association or for this activity. Those whose vocation, and therefore whose nature is personally ascetic, and for that reason strictly contemplative, will not experience this need. For the problem to exist, it suffices for the need to make itself strongly felt in a few who cannot experience, judge, or realize their vocation to give themselves except at the moment of giving. For such persons, consequently, a pure preparation somewhat in a vacuum makes no sense. On the contrary, it generates childishness, fixed ideas, selfish introspection, indifference, or neurasthenia. Such temperaments will not find their spiritual life enriched by the years of internship. Any preparation that is not at the same time a beginning, a departure, a gospel, will always risk being sterile.

The spirituality of action is liberating, because of its respect for the human personality. In this sense it is "personalistic." Its partner asceticism, which is given to organizing, must on the contrary remain pure, and constantly strive not to replace the spirit by the letter.

NOTE 2

The earlier publication of this chapter on action in one of the editions of *Amor* brought me a very useful letter, from which I shall quote the following page:

"It seems to me that action, understood in the sense you give it, is compatible with union to God—I am speaking of conscious union to a certain degree. We must not let ourselves be hypnotized by the idea that prolonged and regular mental prayer is the only or the best means of union and of contemplation. But we must also hold that mental power is one of the great means of union with God, and silence will always be one of the most intense needs of the most active souls. However, there is a form of mental prayer that may be adapted to the active life, the prayer of life: it comprises first of all the supernatural and conscious intention of the act, an intention that is not simply an offering, but also a 'vigilance' of every moment so that the action may correspond in its perfection and in its efficacy to the intention of love that bears it. . . . It is easy to write this, but it is the slow work of the Holy Ghost that gives the disposition to do it. The prayer of life also involves great vigilance in taking advantage of every free moment for thinking through again the great motives of action: the salvation of the world, the glorification of the Father, etc.; profiting by every meeting to see God in our brothers; making every thought turn toward God. The prayer of life presupposes an harmonious combination of human qualities that are perhaps not required in the same way by other forms of mental prayer. There is need of great psychological equilibrium so as to maintain mastery of self; control of activities so that they will not get the better of us. This calls for a full-fledged ascesis. . . . At this moment, I am even astonished at the depth of this form of prayer which, at first sight, might evoke no more than well-said traditional ejaculatory prayers.

"Compared to the prayer of life, the active life (and I am

speaking of the very active life of our epoch) seems to me to call for a certain 'style' of Christian virtues that consists in reconciling virtues that are apparently contradictory. I shall explain myself by using a few examples: the use of wealth in such a way as to affirm the dignity of man and his taste for beauty, combined with a real and effective poverty consisting in a denudation of self that is invisible to others; the development of energy, conjoined with trust in God; true inward humility finding external expression in what others call audacity; supernatural prudence that gives the appearance of temerity; availability to neighbor, and yet striving inwardly to be totally united in the desire to love God even when sharing the rather futile worries of neighbor. The active life requires a secret life with God, secret not only because it dwells in the solitude of the heart in the presence of God, as the life of faith and charity must always do, but secret also because it hides under appearances that often seem to be an obstacle to its development. This opposition to be overcome deepens the soul; it gives the soul an awareness of its solitude with God and of the need for persevering in the love of God. . . ."

CHAPTER VI

The Community

THE TIME has not yet come to write a history of the communitarian movement among the clergy of France, nor to outline its possible developments in the immediate future. We are still much too close to events to appraise, describe, or predict them, for we do not yet know how far the Holy Spirit can lead us in this direction. What we do glimpse is a great interior drive within the general framework of contemporary trends, urging the diocesan priesthood on, under the pressure of the vital need to survive, toward new forms of organization for the priestly life—and away from the individualism and aloofness that had characterized the Concordat era, when the century of the *"desservants"* succeeded the epoch of the *"benefices."* [1]

---

[1] The bibliography on the subject is vast. It consists in part of pamphlets written for certain occasions or for propaganda purposes, which have succeeded one another with varying emphasis, but which it would be useless to try to find in any bookstore. There are also hastily-written works by persons whose intentions were better than their information, that have distorted the history of the diocesan clergy in the past both in their praise and in their criticism.

At the end of Canon Collin's pamphlet, *Vie communautaire et sanctification du clergé diocésain* (Paris: Bonne Presse, 1944) in the Collection *Pastor bonus,* there is a preliminary list of fundamental and historical works which the author entitles "Abridged bibliography."

And yet let us not be unjust toward the nineteenth century, which has truly been the century of the diocesan priest's rebirth in France. Those who have tried to point out and write the history of the attempts of all kinds that were then made to bring priests together and to coordinate their efforts, have been amazed at the large number of projects, acts of generosity, and labors that mark the progress of the Church in France in the communitarian direction. Many endeavors were abortive or changed their course after a short time. It was very difficult to hold a middle course between the state of annihilation in which the government of the Concordat wanted to keep the dioceses, and the temptation generous souls experienced to found one more religious congregation by obtaining episcopal exemption from Rome, or by simply creating a clergy within the clergy in the diocese—a very difficult position to maintain.

The true forerunners of the present movement are those who persisted in remaining faithful to their bishop, to their diocese, to their colleagues, to their ministry, and at the same time wove a fraternal fabric of common bonds so as to assure not only their personal perseverance but also the success of the collective and organized ministry.

However we are approaching the subject less as a historian than as a philosopher or a theologian.

We propose to study first of all the psychology of this movement that is currently attracting youth, youth in all walks of life, and that makes their elders dream with admiration and regret, because they have not experienced this enthusiasm or at least not under the same form.

We are obliged from the start to compare different generations because there is something new in this communitarian movement, even if it is only in the deeper and more extensive meaning given to these words.

Of course, there have always been communities in the Church, and the Church herself is a community. And yet there are different ways of grasping this idea and of incarnating it in real life.

To help us grasp these shades of meaning, it is proposed that we henceforth distinguish between society and community. Now the two ideas, and therefore the two words, are not contradictory, any more than are nature and person, justice and charity, law and grace. But one of these terms means more than the other, for it penetrates more deeply the reality that the other tries to translate. In the measure that human action springs from one or the other of these two visions of the world, it is correspondingly rich in psychological and religious values.

Society is an organization with a specific goal, defined by regulations and contracts that have been clearly delimited by man's intelligence. It is the daughter of abstract reason, because it understands itself perfectly; it knows where it is going because ordinarily it is born of the deliberate will of its members.

The community, which does not necessarily exclude this logical structure, springs directly from the deep instinct that impels man to live with his fellows, to speak to them, to mingle his labors with theirs, if for no other reason than to enjoy the happiness of admiring himself in others and of rediscovering himself in them.

In society, action comes after the engagement has been entered into, as one of the consequences of the contract; and since this has been decided upon once and for all it is not necessary to speak of it at length or often. Conversation is limited to expediting the business at hand. Souls and minds reveal only a part of themselves, and this is one of the conditions for their harmonious relations.

In the community, action comes first. Inasmuch as action is natural to man, it is under the form of an *élan vital* that it in great part brings about the existence of the group and afterwards assures its continuance. And souls have given themselves to this action completely (together with their bodies, for in communities men think with their hands, according to a famous dictum). In consequence, the action which is undertaken in common is the object of uninterrupted and total conversation. The group lives by words as much as by concerted action: the one creates the other, and vice versa.

Society, born of concepts, is always in danger of sharing some of their coldness. It has no absolute need of symbols, nor of games, laughter, corporeal rhythms, harmonious movements. It does not necessarily arouse in its members common emotions or participated joys. It is alien to the true, corporeal, common life, eating from the same platter, sleeping under the same tent, joining in sports elbow to elbow. Society is a daughter of Descartes, and so the Scout Movement and Hébertism mean little to it. Even the liturgy has become, for society, a respect for rubrics; and when ritual has been reduced to its proper concept, it is no longer a spiritual impact or an evocation.

The community sets out to regain possession of these abandoned riches, even while subjecting them to the wisdom of reason. It is determined to allow none of the substructures of the human composite to be lost. It senses and it knows that all these values, including muscular gestures and the sufferings of hunger and thirst, are meant to collaborate—at least as symbols—with the spirit, to unite men through what they possess most deeply in common—their flesh, born of Adam, born of dust, and in another sense born of God. To conclude, the community cannot conceive of itself without a collection of songs and even of dances, without a real liturgy, even if it be no more than the liturgy of the *Marseillaise,* bellowed in common on a day of defeat or of victory.

We refer to the constitution of a state, but to the traits of a race or of a nation; we refer to the statutes of a trade union, but to the aspirations of the working class; we refer to the minutes of a meeting, but to the mood of a gathering; to the rules of a religious institute, but to the spirit of a congregation. In each of these cases, a provisional opposition is affirmed on the one hand between the visible, logical, and conceptual structure of a group, and on the other hand the interior life that vivifies and completes its definition, even though this life is itself very difficult to define. And as for the group, it will have a very different aspect and history in the measure that its members give first place, in their interrelationships, to the written and juridical demands of their social contract, or on the contrary allow themselves to be carried along by the vital and communitarian upsurge that impelled, accompanied, or facilitated their coming together.

A human association can survive for a long time, sustained only by its social regulations, just as a living animal can stand on its feet, supported only by its skeleton. However, it is the interplay of flexible muscles, the freshness of a healthy flesh that assure the movement and vitality of an organism. The same is true of the community: it is its spirit that assures its robust functioning. Finally, society and the community, one within the other, respectively condition their common existence in their own way, and successively express their needs to one another. The community, with its unforeseen impulsive movements, surrounds the somewhat rigid solidity of society, upon which it depends. The community must respect the constitution of society, but also vivify it so as to allow it to flourish. Society must humbly recognize that without the throbbings of love, friendship, or solidarity which are the endowment of its companion, it would soon be nothing but the empty and formalistic framework of a convention, powerful perhaps but still arid and tiresome.

In short, society and the community are to each other somewhat the same as technics and mysticism. Society tries to reduce the essence of the real to simple and precise terms, so as to extract from it the maximum in clear ideas and useful applications; the community gathers up all that lies outside these evident concepts and linear conclusions, so that nothing may be lost of the total, concrete, personal, existential being.

Mysticism, too, is both below and above the rational. It is below the rational, because it turns back to gather together all the primitive and carnal components from which the clear idea has sprung forth, and which it has been momentarily obliged to neglect or abandon so as to go further or higher, in a clean, straight line. Mysticism may also be said to be beyond the rational because the intelligible is vaster than the rational; therefore it is within the province of intelligence to strive to exceed the abstract and general definition of a thing, in order to grasp its reality by eminently human procedures that are beyond reason but that reason does not disown. Mysticism is all-embracing, in its subject as well as in its object, in its subject which surrenders wholly to the total object so as to possess it integrally.

Undoubtedly, once the rational frontier has been crossed, discoveries become ineffable, and in any case untransmittable by clear and analytic language. But it is still possible to induce one's neighbor to surmise them or even to discover them himself by means of impelling incantations, or by an appeal to some personal experience or vision.

Let us not be too quick to label this sentimentality. No, this is reality, and by that token it is intelligible. It is something perceived, and yet irreducible to the rational. It is a superb commingling of all the constituent powers of being, in which the whole man grasps his entire object:

—the whole man, with all his fleshly powers attuned to his reasoning powers, the former under the dominion of the latter, and the latter nourished by the former and leaning upon them, permeated with their warmth, with their science of channeling power and of establishing contact, and with their capacity for incarnation and incantation;

—the whole man, with his indefinite prolongations, the spirit beyond the idea and beyond the letter that translates the idea, the *anima* beyond the *animus,* intelligence beyond reason; and as the result of all this, another channeling of being mingled with or superposed to the flesh, and fused with it in a pure and ethereal atmosphere of spirituality and of life-giving breath. We might compare this action to that of a cool, moderate, and yet powerful breath of air penetrating our lungs, and dilating, purifying, and nourishing them in some way with light and purity.

In the fervent hours of the beginnings of the Church, the Christian priesthood was born in a community and for the purpose of serving it. Jesus had called His disciples individually to the perfect life only with the intention of grouping them into a society all of whose members would love one another in the unity of a single spiritual exultation. The kingdom of God, existing within the soul of each one of the elect, was also a fraternity, an institution, a visible body with its leaders, its traditions, its doctrine. The first witnesses of Jesus were charged by Him to extend indefinitely the propaganda of the initial movement which they themselves had seen. They were to act in concert, and under the presidency and primacy of Peter they were to form a college, a team, the first *presbyterium*. As the disciples were accepted, they would continue to form a spiritual family. The Spirit of the Church, which is the Spirit of God Himself, was and remains a Spirit of community.

We reach the same conclusions when we start from the charity that Christ bequeathed to His disciples, as the interior soul of His institution, as the very definition of His grace, as the summing-up of His whole religion and of the moral and spiritual life identified with it. "You are all brothers, and you have but one master, Christ, just as you have but one Father in heaven." We would be abolishing Christianity and we would be denying the very principle of the Church if we renounced the communitarian idea and the communitarian institution.

The Church, the great Church of Christ, is therefore both a society and a community. She is a society because Christ, her founder, has given her a precise constitution and based her upon a determinate hierarchy, with at least three or four degrees—the bishops, the priests, the inferior ministers, and the faithful.[2] Her purpose is well defined. She has her rules of government and her methods of action, her dogmas, her code of morality, her sacraments. She knows what she has come into the world to do, and she can explain all this to those outside her fold.

She began by respecting the hierarchic laws of her institution. The collaborative and subordinate union of the priests to their bishop is the very charter of all priestly spirituality. Nothing without the bishop, nothing without the presbyterium. This rule had already been formulated by the most ancient of our ecclesiastical writers, St. Ignatius of Antioch.[3] The principle has not changed, any more than has the constitution of the Church.

But the Church is also a community, and it is even more of a community than it is a society. The vital instinct and biological drives are replaced in the Church by a spirit, which is the Spirit of God. And this Spirit, poured out upon the world, implants in the hearts of Christians the charity of Christ whose demands, and whose applications as well, are unlimited. The life of Jesus which animates the members of the Church is communicated to them to unite them in a single body, in a single soul. It is a body all of whose members are brothers, animated with the same sentiments, sharing the same ideas and emotions, because a single breath of divine life determines the rhythms of the movements of this vast organism.

Why must human nature, when it is left to itself, to its indolence, its routines, its politics of the least effort, always run the risk of restricting the Church to its framework as a society? As we have defined the Church earlier, she is an institution predestined to embrace the whole man, and to demand of him not only concepts, but his soul, not only his can-

[2] Council of Trent, Session XXIII, Canon 6.
[3] *Ad Trallianos*, 3:1; *ad Romanos*, 3:2; *ad Smyrnios*, 8:1.

onical obedience but his love, not only the constitutional min-imum but the total gift of himself, in which he will pledge his whole soul and his whole body.

The underlying purpose of the current team movement which captivates youth is precisely to re-establish perpetually this absolute gift and bond, and to pursue to the utmost limit these demands of our nature and of our supernature.

Before considering in some detail the marks of this move-ment, we want to lay great stress on the fact that we have no intention of discrediting or of abolishing the admirable cur-rent of personal and interior spirituality which—since the six-teenth and seventeenth centuries, since the thirteenth, in fact since the beginning—has uplifted Western and Latin Chris-tianity. Truly, this current has made it more than ever pos-sible for recollected, silent, and, if you will, solitary souls to find God. We believe that the setting up of mental prayer as distinct from prayer in choir has been a progressive step and a gain, that low and private Masses are on certain days indispensable to our modern souls. The same would apply to a number of other developments.

But we must repeat that Descartes has crossed our horizon. He had no idea of the human composite. He called upon each individual human reason to construct its certitudes by itself alone. He brought order and clearness everywhere, but he lowered man's temperature, he isolated what his disciple Leib-nitz called the "monad," the solipsism. Under his influence, society has ceased being a community, because, according to his philosophy, man is no longer a rational animal but an in-telligence served by organs.

We do believe, of course, that on the intellectual plane, when a certain level of thought and research is reached, the personal method and solitary work are preferable to work in common. Whenever there is question of reason, we can follow Descartes if we see the need of it, and live in a compartment-alized society rather than in an intermingled community.

However man does not derive his nourishment solely from

ideas and concepts. He is far more complex than the thinking reed of which Pascal used to speak, unless we see in this reed all the vegetative and animal life that is part of his being.

The mysticism of the team movement restores to man and to the Christian all these substrata, all these foundations of nature and of supernature. We have only to look about us at the endeavors of small Christian communities which, under the name of colonies, vacation camps, days of recollection, YCW or YCS Study Weeks, Scout camps, and finally under the name of teams, are striving to incarnate social bonds through gestures, words, works, organizations, in which all the participating souls are corporally involved. To give expression to these holy innovations—which are probably providential reversions—our youths have had to create their own vocabulary by giving an unknown ring to ancient words. They speak of crossroads, of chapters (deriving from the monastic or canonical sense of the word), of vigils, exchanges, and so on. The A.C.J.F.* study group that we used to know has completely changed its structure. The famous report, which was a masterly monologue but still extraneous to real life, has given place to guided discussions, to re-evaluations of influence, to hunting scenes, and to countless other innovations.

These movements are filled with a joyous optimism, which was lacking to our austere Gallican and Concordat institutions. Singing has attained an importance in these movements that we would not have thought possible. Whereas it was formerly forbidden in religious houses except in the chapel and in singing classes, it is now present everywhere, as the catechism hymns of Saint-Sulpice once were. It is song which translates this magnetic current that unites souls through the harmony of voices, gestures, attitudes, shouts. All this would formerly have been considered out of place and offensive to "modesty," but now it is seen to be the very expression of the

---

* Association Catholique de la Jeunesse Française (National Catholic Youth Association of France).

good will and trust that binds all these individuals to their masters, their directors, and to the Church. In consequence, the relationships between superiors and inferiors have been modified. A verse from Racine will sum it all up superbly:

Un peu moins de respect et plus de confiance.[4]

A final and inevitable aspect of this transformation is the re-establishment of manual labor in common in our houses of education or at least in our vacation and outdoor organizations. To think with one's hands is to learn to think, to live, to speak in common, and at last to have a subject of conversation that is neither conventional, nor artificial, nor superficial. This eternal problem is eliminated thanks to the real exchanges of ideas required by work undertaken in unison. The theme of talks is carved from life, it is natural and by that very token has many chances of becoming supernatural and conformable to charity. The ancients used to say, "To speak with men is to be truly Greek." Is it not also truly Christian, apostolic, and priestly?

For the most beautiful of works to be seen, judged, and undertaken in common is the apostolate. The priestly team can assure its life and its duration only by means of apostolic work pursued in collaboration. Once again, action will save the community.

Finally, the noblest of Christian works, the *opus Dei* par excellence is the liturgy, if we are to believe authorized etymology. The communitarian movement is closely bound to the liturgical renaissance which began earlier and which is continuing before our eyes. The two have joined forces. This concordance is significant, and above all it is perfectly normal. To restore to our society its communitarian dynamism, with all due respect for the profound laws of nature, is unquestionably to assure, through God's grace, the victory of supernature and of the Spirit.

---

[4] "A little less respect and more trust."

We now know the goal to be attained: we must recognize the hierarchical constitution of the Church as a society; we must then restore to this organic skeleton all the communitarian life for which it provides a solid and unshakable foundation. This is the whole program to be realized. We have already seen, in the light of contemporary developments, to what extent the priestly generation of today is drawn in this direction, to what extent it yearns, within this Catholic Church whose entire structure it respects and obeys with exactitude, to live the communitarian mysticism which can and must animate this organized body.

There is nothing altogether new in all this. It is the eternal functioning of an institution willed by Christ. It is a return to origins. And what may be less—or more—than that, it is taking cognizance of an ever-present reality. Because our hierarchies are so well known and so clearly defined, because they are changeless, they are always in danger of being reduced to their institutional schema, to their social lines, under whose protection our orthodoxy rests assured. And yet this is a dry schema, this bony structure is hard, these definitions are very abstract. We must restore to them the life that Christ gave them, a life that is warm-blooded, filled with holy passion. Then, thanks to the spirit of community, we shall be restoring to this solid skeleton the living flesh that must be joined to it to constitute a living body.

The divine constitution of the Church is not necessarily used always in the same places. According to the needs of the time, it is possible to put greater strain on this or that articulation, without for that reason denying the value and necessity of the others.

Now, it is certain that in the epoch that preceded ours the community of the pastor with his obedient parishioners was much better established than now, and it sufficed to create for the priest a milieu, at once human and supernatural, within which his happy and well-surrounded life followed its peaceful course. And the seminary of that time could be content to prepare for such situations that were at once isolated and yet without solitude.

Today, however, in the majority of the rural dioceses and in the dioceses of the large industrial cities of France the parish has been disaggregated and as it were volatilized. The pastor would not only be separated but alone throughout his life if he did not depend upon other aspects of the Christian community, those that unite him at once to his confreres and to his bishop. This is perhaps the reason behind the ferment directed toward the common life, toward collaboration, toward the bonds of teamwork which can be noticed everywhere and which will necessarily lead to profound changes in the accidental structure of our dioceses and seminaries. We are in the presence of a clear and certain gain.

And so, in the use of the constitution of the Church as a society, there will perhaps be a greater tendency than before to seek the support from above of the father—the bishop—and of his representatives, the superiors and directors, and also to seek help from fellow-priests who will have become more than ever brothers, friends, and comrades in the good sense of the word. This trend will be enhanced by the fact that below, among the laymen—whom we no longer call simply the faithful—supports have become less real, and because among the members of Catholic Action (which is a sign and a hope of rebirth), increased demands have become a heavier burden for the shoulders of the priest to bear.

However, we already know that the communitarian inspiration in the Church is composed of two trends. First of all, there are all the resources of animal and spiritual nature on the level of created being, with its social instinct, its needs for contacts and exchanges, all its potentialities for relationships, expression and behavior, all its forms of civilization and culture. All these elements, which God has left to the preferences and choices of men, are variables and contingents. Moreover, they are not the most important elements in the synthesis to which they contribute their dynamism; but they are the most visible, the most open to criticism, and the most criticized. At the same time, we must admit that a past generation has no right to impose them absolutely upon its successors. Man is not obliged always to exploit in the same way the riches that are offered to him by his own nature and by created beings in general.

On this inferior level, the spirit of community can, through the ages, be translated or incarnated in different ways. We know, for example, all that the youth movements have rediscovered since the start of the century in seeking to escape the parching dryness of the earlier cerebral and individualistic civilization. The conception of recreation, which is now called leisure, has been almost completely renewed. In France, walks are now called *"routes."* In the change of names lies hidden one of those small revolutions to which youth attaches so much importance. The spirit of community has found other terms by which to express itself. All around us there are many organizations in the prime of life or at the height of transformation that are realizing this renaissance before our eyes. The diocesan clergy has only to borrow their means, their techniques, their methods, which can be those of the clergy, too, since they are human. Through its shouts, its songs, its rhythms, the body is collaborating more than formerly with the works of the soul. And what if it does! These explosions of joy, desire, friendship are simply following once again the program that the liturgy, in the thriving days of its beginnings, had sought to realize for the glory of God.

Side by side with these contingencies, however, there are in the Christian spirit of community and in the spirit of priestly teamwork eternal values that never change. And these are the charity and the grace of Christ. They come to us from the Father, from whom descends every perfect gift, from Him who is the author and the real head of all our spiritual and earthly families. They have come to us through the Son, and they are communicated to us by the Spirit. They have passed and are still passing through the canal of the Blessed Virgin. All our great dogmas are communitarian.

Indeed, all our dogmas are interrelated so as to form an indissoluble chain. So true is this that to grasp and make the fullest use of one of them is at the same time to attract each of the others in turn. For example, the seminaries that have created Marian teams can rest assured. By collaborating with the Blessed Virgin, they have not narrowed their horizon or their program. Christianity is in all that adheres to it, like Jerusalem, *cujus participatio ejus in idipsum.* To accept it at one point is to accept it in its entirety. Mary is our Mother: a mother is the head of her family; therefore there is a family, the family of the sons of God.

So it seems we have not invented anything. So much the better! At most, we have restored more movement to certain vital functions that were slightly dormant. Our successors may be led to the conclusion that we have neglected certain others which they will take up in their turn. But the Holy Spirit does not sleep; or rather He breathes where He will. Today the team is our source of inspiration.

Appendix to Chapter Six

Reflections on a Vacation Camp

The other day one of my lanky students came to me with a beaming countenance and a joyful heart. He was just back from what the YCW calls a "camp," that is, a study week of vacation in the company of young men brought together by the same interests, the same ideal, and the same activities. It was a group of seminarians who had spent a preparatory week at a summer camp where they were to be counselors and directors.

When I asked my young visitor the reasons for his happiness he said: "I have just discovered my colleagues. A week of life in common in the open air amid nature has made me know them better, and appreciate and love them better than have nine months of the school year. And yet we belonged to the same group at the seminary. The difference was that at the seminary our lips were sealed and our souls were closed. The camp revealed us to one another."

I have thought a great deal about these words, which merely confirmed earlier experiences and disclosures. Here is the result of my meditations. I have tried to understand, I have sought out the causes: *vere scire est per causas scire.*

The seminary is more of a society, and the camp is more of a community, in the precise sense we have given these words as different from or complementary to each other. The seminary pursues a certain number of precise and specific ends which are not directly ordered to the common life of its members, even though life in common is one of the means it utilizes to attain its ends. Among these ends might be mentioned, for example: the recruitment of the clergy for the diocese, the spiritual, interior, and apostolic training of future priests, the teaching of the theological sciences necessary to the ecclesiastical ministry, the acquisition by the young clerics of habits of moral discipline that are indispensable to their state, etc. These goals to be attained are not merely pretexts. They represent the very reason for the seminary's existence. To reach them, means and methods will be used, exercises will be practiced, the totality of which—inspired by reason informed by grace—will constitute a system of education, a program of life, in short an ascesis, with its rules and hourly schedule.

This whole structure can be discussed in detail. But in principle, it is a rational construction, a societal regime which is imposed upon all who are pursuing the same end. The rational animal passes through a civilizing or spiritual stage only by using means, only by following a method ordained to the proximate and particular end in view. If he does not do this, he is merely treading in space, he is delaying and immobilizing himself in his purely instinctive reflexes, in his outworn and sterile attitudes. And so, pursuing many confused goals at once, he attains none. In any case, he cannot in this way make any progress whatever.

This societal structure, inspired by reason, participates in all the power and all the weaknesses of the precise and specific concept that begot it. The clear idea, the rigorous proposition, and with them the ordering of the means to the end, resemble drill presses that fray the way for workers in dark tunnels and ultimately lead up toward daylight. Reason leads the way, beyond acquired results, beyond contracted habits, beyond reflexes and inherited instincts. Reason is the author and the instrument of progress. If man renounced his right to use it, he would abdicate his primacy over all other animals.

To attain these results, however, human intelligence uses its own methods, which are abstraction, generalization, and deduction. It starts out by carving out of reality the object of its vision and the goal of its action. It reduces this object to simple and schematic lines, around which it will organize the no less geometrical scaffolding of its methods. Thus, it is doubly abstract. It is abstract in its object, which it has denuded of all its concrete and individual particularities in order to reduce it to its essence. It is abstract, too, in its subject, in the man who momentarily renounces all his primitive, animal, carnal, sensible, and imaginative powers, and obeys only the orders of that terrible, superior, invincible faculty: reason.

At this price, man attains levels that are superior to his earlier positions. He opens up for himself new paths on which he will venture forth as explorer and conqueror, only to take up again later all the individual and personal riches which he had at first renounced. It is much like a capable artisan who sets aside his concern for his family, even though it is for this family that he is working, and thinks only of his work. Or perhaps it is like a father who is the first to emigrate to a distant land as a prospector, so as to send for his wife and children later and enable them to profit by his success.

Rational intelligence, the pure idea, methods ordered to a

particular end, stripping of self, renunciation, exercises, ascesis—all these values are interrelated on the same level of existence, that of reason, the level of means, the level of society. If society abandons itself to the system which begets it, it is doomed to become cerebral. Society possesses all the power of abstraction, from which it is born; but it is also subject to all its limitations, and it shares in all its absuses. Society becomes cold and rigid by dint of being penetrating and self-reliant.

I can remember visiting and living in houses of spiritual retreat that were inspired by a certain conception of the *Exercises* of St. Ignatius. Everything was so well organized to this particular end in these houses that one got the impression, in this methodical, organized, specialized atmosphere, of actually being in a bath of abstractions. If the retreatant abstracted from his unruly passions, then this may have been an excellent place for him to make the required decision at the end of the four famous Ignatian weeks. However, if he abstracted from reality, then it was dangerous. For certain temperaments, this environment was a torture that made them shudder. The unfortunate thing about this system was that one could never know how the retreatant would react to it, whether he was going to profit by a fruitful stripping of self, or suffer the ill-effects of desiccating cerebration. In any case, these houses were ascesis incarnate both in their structure and in their furnishings, and quite the opposite of vacation camps.

Most of the large buildings in which modern man organizes his life or earns his living are conceived in the same way. The office, the factory, the barracks, the high school and the university are all buildings born of an abstract idea. To be admitted to them, the provisional prisoner must strip himself of a part of his being, often the most intimate, the most personal, in any case the most concrete and the most ineffable. The institution does not know what to do with the individual. Many of our secrets are of no interest to it, and so it reduces us to a common type, whether we will or no; and this is accomplished by amputating those of our peculiarities that are not amenable to its end. The institution is on its guard against unforseen and passionate explosions of nature, against those mysterious substrata of our vague sensibilities that could thwart the general plan as anticipated, and frankly do not fit into the social contract. I have allowed myself to say, without believing it, that the rule of a novitiate forbids young postulants from speaking among themselves of their reading, their families, their earlier life. Obviously if this were true, they would be permitted to speak only of the interests of the community—of the community as an institution, that is, of the interests of the society. But how could living souls, thus repressed, learn to know and to love one another?

Happily, God, who created societies, has also laid within us the foundations of communities in the modern sense of the word. We must now reflect on these communities. This will bring us back to the vacation camps and to our lively students who started us off on these reflections.

It is difficult to realize simultaneously the aims of society and the aims of the community. In general men have preferred to pursue them alternatively, under diverse names which sometimes blur the differences between them. However, we readily juxtapose the duty of our state in life and leisure-time organizations, the cares of a profession and the joys of the family, the factory and the neighborhood, the weekdays and Sunday, technics and mysticism, the state and the nation. Each of these fragments of the same existence has its attitudes, its morality and its customs, even its mode of dress, which are proper to it. The first group is always abstract, cold, courageous but mortifying: it is societal. The second group is supposed to nourish and to sing of the joy of living: it is communitarian.

It is possible to abuse of one of these systems, to the point of denying, atrophying, or asphyxiating the other. Let us admit that the educational methods born of the Renaissance and of Cartesianism have on the whole sacrificed communitarian aspirations in favor of societal concerns. We have already cited some of the courageous and wise articles, recently published in *La Vie Spirituelle,* which set out to analyze the Cartesian, anti-Thomistic, anti-Augustinian causes of this deviation, one that is perhaps common in our present-day seminaries.[1]

It is beyond doubt that we are witnessing a communitarian renaissance, which is the converse of the cerebral education of the Classical period. Youth—from among whom our seminaries will fortunately always be obliged to find their recruits—has been swept along by a vast movement in which song, the liturgy, the life of manual labor, and sports are continually restoring to their rightful place in life all the deep and common powers that cerebral education had silenced. Modern civilization has restored to these powers their flesh, their marrow, and their rhythm. And in these young bodies which are again permitted to act in common, the brain is beginning once more to sense that its arteries throb under the command of the heart and of the blood.

Now, the vacation camp is a community in the contemporary sense of the word. While the program of studies is not merely a pretext, it takes second place. What interests these young people and the basic reason for their presence in wheat fields and in the open air is the joy of living together, of performing harmonious movements in a group. It is their desire to exploit, to manifest, to explode this instinctive and primitively carnal foundation of the happiness of being young, of being human, and,—since we are speaking of Christians—of being sons of God together, simultaneously, shoulder to shoulder, in a team. Any particular ends in view in the present case, such as preparation for the role of director in a vacation camp, pale before the much more general and much deeper—we were about to write more human—end, which consists in living and acting together.

---

[1] Cf. *La Vie Spirituelle,* Nos. 302-303, December, 1945, and January, 1946, in which the value of action, the role of the body, and the sense of community are re-established in the spiritual life.

We know that the current expression *"faire quelquechose à deux"* [2] really admits of two very different meanings. First of all, we can pair off to do a piece of work because it would be too hard or too vast for a single person. In such a case, each one will perform half of the work. There will be an addition and collaboration, following a discussion, an agreement, a contract, and the tasks will be shared, in order afterwards to be brought back to unity.

Working in pairs has another, and much more affective meaning, which relates not to the goal but to the actors, to the pleasure they experience in *being* together rather than in *working* together. The task to be accomplished is but a pretext or a material cause for their reunion and their understanding, as well as their joy. So much the worse for methods and techniques, since the important thing is not to achieve a determined result, a completed *thing,* but to remain and to live together. Or rather, if there are methods, they will be of another kind. Since this is a matter of fusing souls rather than of producing a piece of work, the members of the community will give themselves to one another just as they are, with all their personal and intimate resources, without holding anything back. And so, in order to sustain their enthusiasm and nourish their thought, they will call upon those great human forces, those great fundamental instincts in which our reflective consciousness is plunged: gestures, words, calls, songs, movements, all the bodily signs through which the soul can express and give itself, everything that gives man corporeal standing and action in the presence of his fellows. All these mysterious and mystical powers will be thrown into the treasury of the community, so that each one may commune with his neighbor, with the joy or the illusion of contacting him in his depths, so that all of them together may express and sense that they are men and children of God.

We have just used the word "mystical." That word is very

---

[2] The English equivalent is: "Doing things in pairs."

much in style. It is eminently pertinent to our subject. We
unhesitatingly say that mysticism is *beyond* reason: "The
heart has its reasons, that reason cannot know." This is true
of mysticism in the strict sense of the word, the mysticism of
supernatural prayer, of the contemplation of God, inspired
and sustained by the grace of the Holy Spirit. It then belongs
to another order, as Pascal also tells us, the order of charity
that begets and vivifies it. But when we deal with psychological and natural mysticism, the one we are trying to describe here in order to understand the community whose soul
it is, we can apply reason to this area *beyond reason* within
which mystical life or behavior are supposed to reside.

As we have seen in the beginning, it is the very real role
and function of abstract reason to proceed alone, with the help
of a rigorous ascesis and of a courageous technique, beyond
the results of humanism already attained by the rational animal, and to lead him on further than he has yet gone. And
here Pascal gives us another inspiration when he rightly
claims, as do all true philosophers, that "all bodies, the firmament, the stars, the earth and its kingdoms are not worth
as much as the least of the spirits." But when reason and the
societies that it has founded to help and sustain it, have attained their results, made their discoveries, by means of this
mortifying ascesis that has for a while eliminated the confused
collaboration of the obscure, inferior, and carnal powers, then
victorious intelligence must—under pain of becoming desic-
cated in a deadly cerebralism—call back these forces of sensibility that have remained behind and are now worthy, thanks
to their abstinence, to take part in the royal banquet of victory. That is the moment when societies must become communities, and when the abstract idea, in a living liturgy, must
resume flesh and consistency so as to vivify the rational animal in all his mysterious crypts.

Through the centuries, these two positions have alternated.
There are classical generations and romantic reactions, just as
there are glacial periods and periods of intense solar heat. The

literary romanticism of the last century violently ushered in an era of sensibility which was then only on the surface, but which has found a triumphant and incoercible continuation in the symbolism of the present day.

It might be better to say that everything is complex. Within the same century, movements deriving from different inspirations can coexist, complementing each other in their very opposition. Our secular and industrial culture has so gravely abused reason and is now abusing technics so badly, that our young men seek refuge from it, so that it may not destroy them, by turning to what they call "the life of nature," that is, a human existence that prefers to use the resources offered by created things in their primitive state rather than the artifices of civilization. Thus, camping corrects the influence of the cinema, the *"route"* hiking cures us of the smoking lounge, walking takes its revenge on card games, sports dethrone cocktail parties, and the methods of Muller or Hébert abolish Swedish gymnastics which are still too geometric.

This is the revenge of the total life upon the abstract idea. In the medical field, this is the principle of the Vittoz method. In the theater, we see the victory of gestures over words, and the exit of the *Chancerel* theater. In the religious sphere, it is the triumph of the liturgy, of the true and living liturgy, which is nothing but the collective expression, by means of gestures, words, singing, and movements, of the community's sentiments of prayer in the presence of its Christ and of its God. The last glows of the Christian camp fire beneath the firmament of the moon and stars are accompanied by the melancholy and yet assured chant of Compline:

In manus tuas commendo spiritum meum.

NOTE

It is much too soon to give even the broad outlines of the ascesis of the communitarian movement, for it is still seeking its direction and its laws. The first pioneers of the idea, at the beginning of this century, had naturally borrowed a part of their regulations from methods which they rightly or wrongly called "Ignatian," those that had dominated the spirituality of the preceding century and still commanded the obedience of all men of good will. We now realize that the most powerful bonds of the priestly community must be sought less from pious exercises in common (leaving aside the problem of the morning or evening hours of the breviary) than from apostolic collaboration in the Christian or missionary pastorate: from parishes, works, movements, Catholic Action. Efforts are now being made to exploit these broad and generous areas of service that are properly professional and sacerdotal, that derive from the very state of life of the diocesan priest, and constitute the reason for his existence.

We could make analogous observations concerning the attitudes currently demanded of the diocesan priest in the name of the virtue of poverty. Under the same spiritual influences, an attempt was made to exercise control over expenses and leisure time, to set up a budgetary and personal bookkeeping system. But the apostolic exigencies of the present epoch are of another sort and far more powerful. The working-class laity is in the process of inviting the diocesan clergy to accept profound changes in its style and standard of living. I should like to insert here, by way of documentation, the following remarks taken from an anonymous article in *Témoignage Chrétien* for June 27, 1947: "To close the gap that separates the Church from the people, the Christian laity has already buried many of its prejudices under shovels of earth; but this is a rough and exhausting task, and it cannot do it alone. Bound as it is to the working class, the Christian laity yearns, desires, expects that priests—all priests and not only a few of them—, at last liberated from all compromise with money and all that it represents, will come and join it. It foresees, it sees these priests stripped, simple and poor, just as Christ was."

CONCLUSION TO PART TWO

The Apostolic or Episcopal Spirit

It is impossible at this time to give any very precise technical conclusions to this second part of our work. First of all, such practical applications would normally depend upon the authority and the action of the bishops. Besides, the period of transition and change through which we are now passing would make any attempt at concrete prophecy meaningless. After a long period of trials and hesitations, the communitarian idea has just begun to flourish on a large scale at Lisieux [now Limoges—reference to Seminary of the Mission de France] on the specifically diocesan level. However, it seems best to wait a little while longer before making a statement on the direction that the Holy Spirit will definitely impress upon it. As for apostolic action, it is in the process of completely renovating its methods and its means. In the past few years, the images conjured up by the words "mission" and "missionary" have been profoundly changed from what they were during the last century.

For all these reasons, and so as not to exceed our rights or our competence, we shall now do no more than try to express once again the principles or the mysticism of these great spiritual movements.

Our analyses and our reflections have brought us to an understanding of the institution of the diocesan priesthood. We have seen that this priesthood must be defined by its relationship to the episcopacy, which represents the state of perfection in the Church. The priesthood of simple priests derives from the episcopacy as from its principle, without however possessing all of its richness. The priesthood is an imperfect participation in a perfect state, to which it is subordinate, without which it would not exist, but through which it is conceived and defined. In short, it is in the episcopacy that the priesthood has its origin, the reason for its existence, its essential direction, and consequently all its causes. Let the diocesan priest be content with this guiding idea, and let him not push it to extremes since he has neither the right nor the duty to do so. His honor consists in being content with the glory of another, profiting by it without laying any claim to it; it consists in finding in a perfect superior a reason for existing, namely, the service of this master, and in imitating him without ever being his equal.

If the episcopacy, according to Bossuet's famous dictum, is a servitude that charity imposes on prelates to save men's souls, then the priesthood consists in helping the bishop in this service of God and man.

In this position with its subtle nuances, in this movement toward a goal that is never attained but which furnishes a direction and an explanation, lies all the charm of the diocesan priesthood, activated by the perfection of the episcopal priesthood which it obeys as a member obeys the head. In this dependence and in the acceptance of these limitations, the diocesan priest discovers the joy of doubting his own strength and yet believing in it, of being at once humble and proud.

Obviously, the organization of a state of life with so many delicate gradations, with such blurred contours, has always presented serious difficulties. The *Pastoral Epistles* are the first witnesses to this anxiety which explains the whole canonical and institutional history, the whole interior and supernatural life of the diocesan clergy.

It would be an error, or in any case an omission, to try to organize this state solely on the basis of baptism and its demands for perfection, and as a logical consequence, on the basis only of ascetic institutions which, through the centuries, have canonized the means and methods of the Christian life of the simple faithful.

True, the diocesan priest is a man, born of Adam like all other men, a baptized Christian, and a son of God. He would therefore be guilty of the most culpable imprudence if he did not profit by all the resources that are offered him by the his-

tory of the regular institutions that have canonized the great
ascetic and mystical tradition of the Church in spiritual exercises. But after all, the priest's state of life is no longer to be
defined on the basis of baptism alone. The explanation and
the supreme requirements of the position he occupies in the
Church must be sought elsewhere.

It follows that the diocesan priest must choose from among
specialized forms of asceticism only the rules that are compatible with his state, those that can and will help him in the
fulfillment of his very specific duties. Seizing his advantage
wherever he finds it, he will follow the advice of St. Paul by
carefully discerning and selecting what is suitable for him.
His personal spirituality used to stem from baptism, and in a
sense it still does, with all that this implies: belief in original
sin and in its consequences, trust in the grace of Christ, a
spirit of faith, respect for the counsels and the practice of the
virtues of counsel. But the fact remains that the spirituality of
his state has its roots in another sacrament. It belongs to
Christian prudence to avoid any confusion between different
methods and goals in a state of life which is simple, unique,
sufficient unto itself, and original in the most inclusive sense
of the word.

It is to the honor of the Society of Saint-Sulpice, and thanks
to it and to the masters of the French School, it is to the honor
also of our major seminaries that they have resisted appeals to
compromise and have maintained what might be called in
philosophy the consistence of the ecclesiastical diocesan state.
And yet diocesan priests are constantly in danger of leaving
this safe terrain, and threatened with confusion. They may
find themselves in this predicament through their own fault,
through a kind of perpetual surrender of their dignity, through
an ideological evasion of their state, through renunciation of
their origins, their history, and their end. Many diocesan
priests entrust the care of their consciences to religious, who
in turn think they can help them best by communicating to
them their own spiritual treasures, the only ones they possess,

those of their congregation. The majority of pastoral retreats, monthly retreats, deanery conferences, and even many clerical publications are entrusted by their Excellencies the Bishops to eminent or simply conscientious members of religious congregations. Quite naturally, they bring to the diocesan priests the spirituality of their holy founders, which they have learned in the novitiate and practiced all their lives.

By all these different paths, the vigor of the diocesan priest slips away and is lost. In the end, he tries unsuccessfully to surrender his interior life to spiritualities that are not intended for him, and that apply only imperfectly to his duties and to his state.

Now, all the spiritual methods, observances, and attitudes in these great trends that are compatible with the law of the diocesan state can certainly be retained: *a fortiori* this is true of all forms of spirituality that can help in the fulfillment of the diocesan priest's essential duty. And yet in these adaptations, we surmise that all kinds of historical or personal contingencies have intervened to authorize the greatest freedom of initiative and to permit solutions that are very relative, fluid, and left to the free interpretation of each century, each country, and even of each individual. After all, is there anything more multiform than devotion, piety, and the interior life?

Conversely, the essential and institutional law of the diocesan clergy and of its state of life remains very stable. Around this unchanging nucleus, spiritualities peculiar to this state can be organized through the centuries. They may be made up in part of borrowings, if you will, but they will have been tested, sifted, classified, organized, adapted, and coordinated. The diocesan clergy is capable of constituting a spirituality proper to itself.

Not too far from our own time, we have seen this happen in seventeenth century France, when the seminaries were established. The masters of the French School lived in a Church that seemed to be solidly established, under the protection of a very stable and totalitarian temporal royalty, but in the midst of a clergy that was either too worldly or too rustic. Under the circumstances, greatest emphasis was placed on the functions of worship and the liturgy, the duties of ecclesiastics toward God. We would neither deny nor retrench any of this glorious heritage.[1] However, we can prolong and complete this great movement by conjoining it to the consideration of the priestly functions orientated toward the faithful, toward their service, the apostolate, action, missionary work. In these preoccupations with man, the diocesan priest can find not only reasons for living, but also the principle or the necessity of new graces, the enriching of his diocesan spirituality, the reverse side of his spiritual exercises. Here again, religious, particularly the active and missionary orders, can share their treasures with the diocesan priest, but always under

---

[1] At the same time, in order to assure the cementing of the past and the present, we might suggest a few adjustments.

These spiritualities were originally constructed for a clergy well established in the society in which it had its roots, within a kingdom of which it constituted one of the great classes, the first of the orders of the Estates-General. Among the purposes of these spiritualities was the protection of priests against wealth, idleness, indolence, and self-satisfaction. All of these problems have been completely reversed or eliminated, at least in the majority of the cities and provinces of France. The system was able to maintain itself in the nineteenth century to the extent that the Concordat gave the illusion of a restoration of the old order. It was particularly the rural pastors who found in the classical organization of their priestly day a remedy for their solitude, an occupation for their leisure hours; for the system is far better adapted to filling unoccupied hours than to facilitating burdensome labors, such as those of the curates of our city neighborhoods, of our pastors of five or six parishes, of our college professors, and of our Catholic Action chaplains. It might be possible, for example, to establish for priests of action the weekly day or half-day of rest (which would not, of course, be Sunday), and which would be exclusively devoted to silence, prayer, intellectual non-servile work (that is, etymologically speaking, not spent directly in the service of neighbor). It would be the equivalent of the Christian Sunday of former days, or rather of the monastic life: *to live with oneself under the eye of God.*

the same conditions, namely, authorizing him to make his choice, allowing him to adapt their methods to the exigencies of his own state, whose own law of existence must not be modified or impaired.

We have dared to contemplate this state in the light of the episcopal state that dominates it and vivifies it with its grace, that ties it to the Apostles and to Christ directly, without the intermediary of any other founder, in immediate union with the essential holiness of the Church. May the religious who read these lines forgive us for saying that this state seems to us very noble, beautiful, exacting, and sufficient, without need of any modification or addition. To be a priest, to be only that and yet all of that,—this is a program, a definition, an honor, a grace to which, because of its very dignity, we do not want to add anything else.[2]

We have simply been trying to delve deeper into its rich significance. The demands of our epoch, the necessity of starting all over again to evangelize a people that has lapsed into paganism, the organic birth of Catholic Action—all these things have obliged us, as we have just said, to look in a direction to which the Masters of French spirituality, while not denying it, had given less consideration. That is not to say that we have abandoned the main road or the straight line. We believe we are still going forward in the same direction as our fathers, and also in accordance with our origin, which is truly the Cenacle and the period of the *Acts of the Apostles*. Now as then, it is by looking toward the

---

[2] "When Father de Faville had his visiting cards made last year, he enjoyed the gentle pleasure of enumerating the titles he could have had printed on it, from his gymnastics prizes won at the age of four, his studies at Polytechnic and in the School of Mines, up to his professorship of comparative science at Laval University and his honorary directorship at Saint-Sulpice in recent years. After he had thus joked for a while, he concluded: 'I shall have them put: Paul de Faville, priest. That is simpler.' And it was truer, too." (From the biography by Bishop René de la Serre, Pro-Rector of the Institut Catholique de Paris.)

bishop that the priest understands what he is and what he must be.

This vision of the priesthood, as it has appeared to us in the first part of this book, as a subordinate participation in the powers and graces of the episcopacy for the service of God and of Christians, offers us perspectives of spirituality, both ascetic and mystical, that lead in several directions. But precisely because these perspectives start from the bishop and find their way back to him, all these views are complementary. Each time, it is the verb *serve* that comes before our eyes, with different sets of rules born of as many different needs.

The priests are at the service of the bishop—or rather it is the bishop who invites them to help him in his services. We are here in the presence of the principle and the reason for being of a community, that can be looked upon from above, from below, or on its own level. The idea of the community, left in the shade during the earlier centuries, and somewhat repressed by the great individualistic syntheses elaborated since the sixteenth century, is now returning to the forefront of the doctrinal scene. It finds its place in all the ancient questions, coloring them in its own way. The Treatise on the Sacrament of Order, which just recently spoke of the bishop and of the priest in the singular and in an abstract manner, is now obliged to solve the problem of the diocesan community and to explain how the priesthood is a collaboration and a life in society as well as a grace and the possession of personal powers.

At the top is the bishop, the successor to the Apostles who were the heirs to Christ's priestly ministry. And by reason of this very fact, the poor priest finds himself in possession of a full-fledged mysticism which opens up vast possibilities of contemplation. He sees and feels himself to be a member of an institution which, without crushing him, makes him a participant in the noblest system that the world has ever known.

At the bottom are all the faithful and also all the unbelievers in whose service the priest is delegated. In giving the priest the noblest of occupations and enriching his life with the loftiest significance, they, too, make of him—through action this time, and not through contemplation—a candidate for the mystical life, by encouraging in him the passive attitude of submission to the real, to his brothers, and to God who is the principle of all apostolic activities, all zeals, and all initiatives.

Then there is the horizontal, social, or communitarian bond. In participating in the responsibilities of the bishop, the priest also attaches himself to his fellow-priests for the service of the body of the faithful.

The diocesan priesthood is eminently organic, with respect to the summits from which it descends as well as to the broad masses toward which it bends down. However, our theology may have run the risk of remaining too individualistic. We have told this story already. The moment has come, in a century entirely orientated toward social concerns, to draw practical conclusions from this communitarian theology which has been more clearly elucidated, that is, from this less individualistic definition of the priesthood.

Our last two chapters were concerned respectively with the spirituality of action and the spirituality of the community. A way must now be found of conjoining these two forms of spirituality, so that life, as if unfolds, may unify them. The mission should be a community, and the community should be missionary. This is the hope of many of our older priests as well as of many younger ones. One of the reasons why we have been groping so long is perhaps that, without willing it or knowing it and because of the swift progress achieved by earlier reforms, we have centered the community too exclusively on exercises of piety and asceticism. We have tended to neglect a much stronger bond, linked to the very essence of the diocesan priesthood, which unites all its members in the unity of service. This apostolic action, which is the normal subject of conversation in the missionary group, is likewise— and for much deeper reasons—the reason for the existence of the community. The two save each other by perpetually begetting each other through a reciprocal causality.

To conclude, let us turn back once again to Miletus, to Chapter 20 of the *Acts of the Apostles,* and reread the law of the origins of the diocesan priesthood, the spirit of its institution, its definition, the ordering of its life, the functions of its state. Modern exegesis and criticism have their good points. By restoring to the words *presbyter* and *episcopus* their full professional meaning, by showing that in this passage and elsewhere these names designate the same personages, and these personages are priests, collaborators of the founder-Apostle, they have brought back to us the full force of these texts that the Latin Vulgate had greatly diminished. How did St. Paul, in this farewell discourse which is perhaps the most emotional he has left us, look upon these mandatories whom he had secured by the imposition of hands, and also through fasting and prayer—as St. Luke points out in Acts 14:22? He charged them to take his place during his absence, not as founders but as heads and fathers. These ancients, if we are to keep to the etymology of their name, celebrated or rather co-celebrated the breaking of the bread. That is certain. And yet, it was not of this great mystery that St. Paul spoke to them on the eve of his departure, because their function went beyond, or rather sheathed and covered over the sacramental and Eucharistic rite over which they presided. This essential and total function was the function of the Apostle himself, in which they participated as delegates, unquestionably inferior to their father but still his collaborators and deputies: *"Take heed to yourselves and to the whole flock in which the Holy Spirit has placed you as bishops, to rule the Church of God, which He has purchased with His own blood. . . . Watch, therefore, and remember that for three years night and day I did not cease with tears to admonish every one of you."* [3]

---

[3] Acts 20:28-31.

It is with reference to this passage that the prudent and discreet Father Prat, S.J., wrote: "By virtue of the sacrament of Order, priests have also been established by the Holy Ghost to tend the flock, that is, to instruct, direct, and govern a portion of the flock of Christ, and for this reason they can be given the title of pastors."[4]

This is our whole thesis.

NOTE

A Thomistic theologian, using a tripartite division of the titles of the Word incarnate—priest, king, and prophet—which are found in all the manuals, chided us for having confused the last two of these attributes with the first. According to this author and several others as well, the sacrament of Order makes us participate in the *priesthood* of Christ, but not in His *kingship* or in His role as *teacher*. In consequence, it would confer only the power to celebrate sacrifice, and the priesthood of Christ would also be limited to this function. This would be the ruin of our whole thesis.

However, another Dominican, a student of the very delicate theology of the Christian laity, recently solved this difficulty for us. He explained how the simple faithful participate in a certain manner in the priesthood of Christ (this is the famous doctrine of the royal priesthood of baptized Christians, recorded in I Pet. 2:9). He showed further that in certain cases, the simple faithful participate in a subordinate, partial and imperfect manner in the teaching function, when, for example, a layman belonging to Catholic Action or a lay catechist, with or without any special mandate, explains to unbelievers the Christian conception of life; or when the father of a family, like the newly converted William Ward, taught Catholic theology in the major seminary of Saint Edmund. In fact, it was the latter instance that led the witty Pius IX to answer the

---

[4] *Dictionnaire de Théologie catholique*, under the word *"Évêque,"* col. 1659.

zealots who were protesting against this "abuse" by saying: "Your Excellencies, we were not yet aware that the fact of having received a sacrament of Holy Mother Church, which neither you nor I can receive, should prevent anyone from laboring at the work of God." [5]

But the religious who is the source of my inspiration in the present matter went further still. He showed that in a certain dependent and subordinate way, lay Christians participate in the government of the Church, and therefore in the kingship of Christ, by calling forth decisions on the part of authority, by respectfully asking for reforms, by creating customs, and also, alas! by making use of the power of inertia.

In short, both the clergy and the faithful participate in the three classical functions of Christ the Redeemer, their head, although they do so in very different ways. And the way in which priests and bishops exercise these functions is what we have called their priesthood throughout this book. For priests exercise the priesthood, the kingship, and the role of teachers differently from the laity; and it is in this that they are truly priests and that the simple faithful are not.

The word *"priesthood"* has therefore two meanings: a restricted sense in which it is distinguished from the kingship and the role of teacher. In general we have not used this sense in the present volume. The other sense of the word, at once broader and loftier, distinguishes the priesthood from the lay state in the celebration of sacrifice, in the exercise of authority, and in the responsibility of teaching. It therefore includes the sacrificial priesthood in the restricted sense plus the kingship and the teaching role, all three exercised from above on the superior and reserved level from which the priest rules as a responsible pastor over those who have been entrusted to his care before God. The faithful, for their part, are to be content to participate in a totally different way in these same functions,—a way that is inferior, subordinate, *"episcopated,"*

---

[5] Cited by Henri Brémond in *L'inquiétude religieuse,* Tome I, p. 182.

that is to say, supervised. Thus, it is the integral, total, even if specialized sense of the idea of the priesthood that we have proposed and utilized to establish our thesis. In this sense the priesthood is synonymous with the pastorate: *posuit vos epis-copos pascere gregem Dei.*

Whence the following schema:

THE PASTORATE or the priesthood in the plenary sense	1. The sacrificial priesthood of the priest, or the celebration of the Eucharist. 2. Pastoral rule. 3. Magisterial teaching.
THE LAY STATE	1. The priesthood according to I Peter, and participation in the Eucharist. 2. Catholic action. 3. Profession of faith.

GENERAL CONCLUSION

"What is the episcopacy, if not a servitude that charity imposes upon us to save souls?"

> Bossuet, *Sermon sur l'unité de l'Église,*
> 1681, end of the second point.

In his funeral oration for Father Bourgoing, Bossuet spoke of Cardinal de Berulle's *immense love for the Church* which "inspired him to form a society, to which he wanted to give no spirit but the spirit of the Church herself, no rules but the Church's canons, no superiors but her bishops, no bonds but those of her charity, nor solemn vows but those of baptism and the priesthood. There a holy freedom begets a holy obligation. . . ." Replace the word *"society"* in this heroic sentence by the old Christian word *"presbyterium,"* and every diocesan priest can recognize his state of life. And if we were to add that this state proceeds from a sacrament that makes its subjects participate in the powers, the duties, and above all in the grace of their bishops, we should possess the very definition of the priesthood just as Christ Jesus and His Apostles founded it: it consisted then and it still consists in *helping the bishop to serve God and men.*

SUPPORTING DOCUMENTS

I.

RESOLUTIONS OF THE ASSEMBLY OF THE CARDINALS AND ARCHBISHOPS OF FRANCE (1944), excerpts published in *Le Clergé Diocésain en face de sa mission actuelle d'évangélisation,* by His Excellency Émile Guerry, Coadjutor-Archbishop of Cambrai, (1944), p. 151:

1st Resolution: The Assembly resolves:

(1) That in the *Journées pour les Vocations Sacerdotales,*[1] in conferences given to college and youth movement groups, the vocation of the diocesan clergy be clearly presented, with its greatness, its demands, its own distinguishing marks, notably its irreplaceable mission as Pastor, its responsibility for evangelizing souls at all stages of life, and for assuring the ministry's stability and duration.

(2) That in the major seminaries, the treatise *"de Ordine"* be no longer left to the individual study of seminarians during the vacation period, but be the object of very thorough doctrinal teaching which will reveal at its center the priesthood of Christ in His two inseparable offices: His office of contemplation and prayer, as Meditator on behalf of men before God; His office of apostolate and testimony, as the

---

[1] i.e., days devoted to sponsoring religious vocations.

Mediator of God to men; to be followed by an explanation of the priesthood of the bishop, his spiritual fatherhood and his mission of sanctification; the study of the priesthood of the priest, bound to that of the bishop; and finally by the study of the sacrament of Order in its relationship to the life of the Church, the mystical body of Christ.

(3) That preachers of retreats for priests find their inspiration in the spirituality of the diocesan clergy, which is the spirituality of the Church, thus training souls to live intensely by the life of the Church, its doctrine, its liturgy, in filial and loving docility to the Sovereign Pontiff, a spirituality which is also apostolic, vivifying the souls of pastors, of apostles wholly given to Jesus Christ for the work of Redemption and who find their sanctification *in* and *through* the exercise of their pastoral ministry.

7th Resolution: (2) The Assembly judges that a very efficacious means of training seminarians in the apostolic spirit is to have them live as apostles in the major seminary, each one feeling, in his relations with the others, a responsibility for the souls of his brothers and a sense of oneness with them in the forward movement of the whole group. It is the duty of the body of professors to create this apostolic climate, by seeing that the clerics live under the law of charity, so that the seminary may be a real family, a unique and genuine community, in which no one turns his attention inward upon himself in a desiccating egoism, but where on the contrary each one is ready to give of himself to the various services and team projects, to collaborate actively in campaigns organized for the collective practice of a certain virtue or to instill respect for a given rule, and finally to live his seminarian's life as a member of a cohesive group. A communitarian spirit will thus be formed and the meaning of work in common will be learned, which will directly prepare these future priests for a collective apostolate organized as a community.

10th Resolution: The Assembly resolves that wherever their

Excellencies the Bishops judge it possible and useful, there be established in each deanery a pooling of the spiritual, intellectual, and apostolic activity of the priests, thus forming a community out of the deanery, by practical study meetings, days of spiritual recollection, and the organization of a common action throughout the deanery.

The Assembly likewise encourages the establishment of the communitarian life, properly so-called, with voluntary priests subject to the same rules, in certain sectors designated by the Bishop.

2.

Views of His Excellency Émile Guerry, Coadjutor-Archbishop of Cambrai, expressed in *Le Clergé Diocésain en face de sa mission actuelle d'évangélisation* ("The Diocesan Clergy and its current mission of evangelization"—a general report on its spirituality, its training, and its mode of life, based on the inquiry started by the Assembly of the Cardinals and Archbishops of France), included in the verbatim report of the Assembly of the Cardinals and Archbishops of France for February 15-17, 1944:

"In his little book on the eminent dignity of the diocesan priesthood, Canon Masure shows how the presbyteral priesthood consists in a subordinate participation in the religious and apostolic functions of the bishop. The priesthood does not stand alone: it is not an institution capable of perpetuating itself; it can be explained only by its dependence upon the episcopacy. Historically and theologically, the priesthood has sprung from the episcopacy: it is a participated, derived, subordinate priesthood. . . .

"He [the bishop] is himself in the state of perfection, because he is pledged until death to the service of charity, the loftiest charity, spiritual charity, which consists in saving souls. Priests are the immediate collaborators of their bishop in this apostolic ministry: they participate in the duties and responsibilities of their bishop, under his direction. The reason they must obey him is not primarily so that they may practice abnegation, but first of all to assure the unity of the diocese and because they exercise their powers, in this service of charity, only in dependence upon his mission of episcopal charity."

3. *Teamwork*

His Excellency Auguste Bonnabel, Bishop of Gap, published the following note that proves "teamwork" is the order of the day, in *Croix de Paris* for August 16, 1946:

"In answer to wishes that have been expressed to us, and compelled by circumstances—notably the lack of workers— we are trying to constitute a few groups of priests who are to work in teams. In view of the state of mind of our people who absolutely demand that their pastor be in effective and permanent residence in the parish, taking into account also the situation of those priests who have relatives with them or some elderly servant, we want to proceed slowly, and for the moment we accept that the realization of our plans remain incomplete. Likewise, we do not impose habitual life in community upon everyone, but we desire that there be at least one meeting each week for all members and that the work in common be under the direction of a head whose authority is to be accepted by all the members of the team.

"There is to be no modification in the constitution of the parishes. Each one has its responsible administrator who administers the finances, keeps records, assures visits to the sick, the administration of the sacraments, burials, etc. But all the members of the team have the delegated power to accomplish these functions and these duties in the absence of the one who is responsible for them and upon designation by the head of the team. Moreover, in carrying on the apostolate— preaching, catechizing, giving First Communion retreats and parish missions, holding cantonal reunions and the Sunday service—the work is done by several at once, making the best use of the aptitudes of each member of the team. We have reached the conclusion, which experience confirms, that it is better to have less frequent meetings that are well prepared and properly conducted by two or more priests than to have frequent gatherings in which the same worker has to be everything at once: the bell-ringer and the preacher, the choir boy and the celebrant, the precentor and the organist, the confessor and the guardian of order and discipline.

"We ask our priests and our faithful to understand this and to help us bring about the success of these efforts, even at the price of a change in the parish or of a modification in their personal habits and preferences.

"We note that the majority of our seminarians have asked that we use them in teams, when they applied for their call to Orders. With all due allowance for the obedience they owe and want to maintain, we have promised to use them in teams. For a number of them, this question will decide whether they enter the clergy of the diocese or turn to the religious orders or to the Mission of France.

"It would be a serious matter if we did not know how to keep them. Isolation in their residence and isolation in their work frighten them. We must parry this danger through teamwork."

4.

Report on the 1946 General Chapter of the Priests of the Heart of Jesus, by J. Anger, published in their Bulletin for October, 1946: "The principal wishes [presented to the General Chapter] by the group as a whole may be summed up as follows: to proceed further in the doctrinal synthesis of the constitutions on the priesthood; to lay greater stress on community with the bishop and with the diocesan colleagues; to bring out more forcefully the priestly sources of our spiritual life: the Mass, the breviary, the apostolate; as well as the unity that must exist between the interior life and the apostolic life. . . . In recent years, young priests have shown a desire to be called priests of a given diocese, and to understand the power and

the usefulness of the vital bond that binds them to their hierarchical head, the bishop, the father of the diocesan Church;
they take great delight in all that promises them a chance to
work in teams, a communitarian life. All these aspirations are
in line with the authentic intentions of the priesthood." (This
report was also published by Father G. Lemaître, the Secretary-General of the Society, in the *Bulletin Apostolique,* for
October-November, 1946, p. 296.

5.

Instructions given by His Eminence Cardinal Suhard before
the *Journée Sacerdotale des Vocations* for the Diocese of Paris,
on November 20, 1946 (published in *Croix de Paris,* for December 27, 1946):

"Many young men flee the diocesan ministry because they
are afraid of it, both from the point of view of their personal
perseverence and because they no longer believe in its power
to conquer.

"The hierarchy can take two possible attitudes in dealing
with these dispositions. One would be to take no notice of
their desires and to maintain existing traditions through their
authority alone. But such sternness would have little effect.
One can never make headway against life. The other attitude,
on the contrary, consists first of all in seeing and listening, and
then in prescribing: this will be our approach.

"It will consist above all in creating a climate.

"A climate of reason, to begin with.

"We must demonstrate that, on the level of doctrine as well
as in the light of history, the ministry of priests grouped
around their bishop for a common action in a well-defined
territory, the diocese, is both necessary and fruitful. This is
the preponderant action in the Church. It is even irreplaceable
and directly willed by God. Every other form of apostolate is
but the complement of this primordial structure. We must
prove that the ministry of the secular priest is possible: that it

is not beyond the powers of nature and that it leads to the most supernatural holiness; that this ministry has had its heroes and its saints, in the past as well as during recent years.

"We shall show how, through constant faithfulness to the humble duty of each day, through 'little things' offered to God for souls with great love, all the merits of the hidden life, all the daring and all the miracles of the public life are brought together in the receptive and generous soul of the true priest of Jesus Christ. By such testimony, we shall refute the accusation of 'mediocrity' which has been so irresponsibly hurled at a life that is wholly given to God.

"And yet, we must admit it, this is not enough. We must go beyond the acceptance of the mind, and 'speak to the heart': we must create an inviting climate!

"We must show that the diocesan priesthood is not foreign to the aspirations of our young men, but that it is attuned to their inclinations, and that it is capable of keeping them passionately interested for the rest of their lives.

"Do they dread solitude, accustomed as they are to live and to work in teams? Let us insist upon the community. You know how strongly we encourage this orientation and how much we are working in this direction. We should not judge we had lost our time in Paris if we had done no more than gain increasing acceptance for this communitarian climate among the ranks of our clergy. Already, these living, fraternal, joyous communities give daily proofs of their timeliness and their usefulness. In addition, they are the best nurseries for diocesan vocations.

"To all who reject the distorted picture of an *'administrative'* priesthood, we wish to point out the magnificent possibilities offered at the present time by the *missionary apostolate* in a diocese like Paris. If there is any place where the danger of conformism and of comfortable routine is banished from the priestly life, it is surely in these bold, daily contacts with the vast Godless masses. The labor priests, the chaplains of the Y.C.W., the suburban curates, the priests of the Mission of Paris can all bear witness, as of the past few years, to the superhuman task, but a task to impassion a priest of Jesus Christ, that summons them at every moment.

"These are the perspectives that open up to aspirants to the priesthood, as they stand on the threshold of life. Need it be said that in order to be inviting, these perspectives must be presented and often called to mind by those who are guiding souls? Beyond doubt, this role belongs primarily to the clergy. Everything predisposes it for this work: the duty of its state of life, its vocation. But the entire diocese must give its support to this task: parents, educators, militant laymen. They will remember that more often than not the child or the adolescent does not know the diocesan priest. He is ignorant of his mode of life, his activity, and his joys. We are thinking particularly of the students in our public schools and in our high schools and lycées. It is our wish that the directors of the days of recollection and retreats to be given in these schools should include not only religious but also priests of the diocese, preferably chosen from among the former students of the respective schools. Thus the testimony will be more personal, and the example more contagious."

6.

In the prefatory letter that Cardinal Van Roey, Archbishop of Malines, wrote for the book by Father Paul Fécherolle, Professor at the Seminary of Bastogne, Belgium, entitled: *Le Clergé diocésain aux avant-postes* (Tournai-Paris: Casterman, 1947), His Eminence expresses himself as follows:

ARCHBISHOPRIC OF MALINES

March 10, 1947.

Dear Professor:
We salute with joy and gratitude your penetrating study on the diocesan ministry. You are right in stressing the excellence

and the noble worth of the pastoral function exercised in dependence upon the bishop and in union with him. It is a very meritorious and most opportune task at the present time.

You are not the first to undertake it. From the days of St. John Chrysostom who, in his work on the priesthood, extolled the dignity and the action of the priest, the pastor of souls, even above the contemplative and penitent life of the monks of his own day, to Cardinal Mercier, whose views on the specific perfection of the diocesan clergy set forth in his book *La Vie Interieure* are well known, authorized voices have not been lacking to praise the singular beauty of the ministry of souls, which is the most perfect form of apostolic charity.

Nonetheless, the subject which you have approached with real mastery appears most timely to us! There is need of clarifying certain points of spirituality which have too often been left in the shade, and to redress certain obstinate prejudices that sometimes seek to elevate the religious to the detriment of the diocesan priest. Fortunately, in recent years various studies have tried, not without success, to restore the prestige of the diocesan pastoral ministry. The pages which you have written have the same purpose. They will be welcomed by all who are interested in the religious life of our dioceses and who understand the primordial needs of the Church at this moment. . . .

Have we not even seen the palms of martyrdom—which formerly seemed reserved for the pioneers of the faith in pagan countries—widely distributed among the ranks of the diocesan militia? . . . The diocesan clergy deserves to be highly honored, to be appreciated at its full value, to be "revalued," to use your very exact expression.

You have placed your pen, your talent, and your priestly experience at the service of a very real cause. We thank you.

J.-E. CARD. VAN ROEY
Arch. of Malines

* * *

7.

Tome II.
  No. 18

To the Clergy of the Diocese

Reverend and dear Cooperators,

Everything that bears on the priestly vocation is subject to the vigilance of the bishops. We therefore consider it our pastoral duty to invite the entire clergy of the diocese to read attentively the pontifical document that we are herewith publishing and to conform strictly to it in their teaching.

In a letter dated July 13, 1952, the Sacred Congregation of Extraordinary Ecclesiastical Affairs has transmitted to us, through the intermediary of the Apostolic Nunciature of Brussels, a detailed note from His Holiness in answer to requests for clarifications that had reached the Holy See from diverse sources.

We beg you to believe, reverend and dear cooperators, in our religious devotion, in our Lord and our Lady.

ANDRÉ-MARIE
Bishop of Namur

Namur, September 3, 1952.

Text of the Note from the Sacred Congregation of Extraordinary Ecclesiastical Affairs to the Bishop of Namur (Belgium), dated July 13, 1952:

1. When anyone says that a priest who wants to tend toward perfection must become a religious or at least a member of a secular institute; and when anyone tells a young man who is hesitating to choose between the secular priesthood and entrance into religion, that it is a question of generosity; when anyone declares that he

who decides in favor of the secular clergy proves that he is not generous enough to give himself entirely to the service of God; when anyone thinks that he cannot counsel a young man in this undecided state to enter the seminary rather than a religious institute; when anyone goes so far as to say that the Church "tolerates" the secular clergy as a last resort, but that the ideal would be for all priests to be religious: that is a false understanding and an erroneous application of the Holy Father's Allocution of December 8, 1950 (*Annus Sacer,* A.A.S., Volume 43, 1951, pp. 26-36). The Bishops have the right to oppose propaganda for the recruitment of religious societies which is based on incorrect theoretical premises and capable of leading into error, and which is at the very least lacking in practical loyalty; and they may establish just and strict limits for this propaganda by administrative decision.

2. The above-mentioned Allocution of the Holy Father had as its purpose the clarification of three questions:

  (a) What is the place of the regular clergy (clerus religiosus) with relation to the secular clergy (clerus saecularis) in the constitution that Christ gave to His Church? (pp. 27-29.) The answer was as follows: ". . . ordine a Christo statuto ob oculos habito, neutra peculiaris gemini cleri forma divini iuris praerogativam tenet, cum idem ius neque alteri alteram praeponat neque alterutram emoveat." (p. 28.)

  (b) What is the relationship of the "cleric" and the "religious" with respect to the "state of perfection" insofar as the evangelical counsels are concerned? The answer given was: "Clericus . . . non vi divini iuris evangelicis consiliis paupertatis, castitatis, oboedientiae devincitur; ac praesertim non eodem modo devincitur eademque ratione, qua ex votis publice nuncupatis in religioso statu capessendo huiusmodi obligatio exoritur. Id autem non prohibet, quominus

privatim suaque sponte clericus haec vincula susci-
piat. . . . Clericus vero regularis, non prout est clericus, sed prout est religiosus, evangelicae perfectionis
condicionem et statum profitetur." (p. 29.)

Moreover, it was expressly affirmed that even the
"Saecularia Instituta" realize the essence of the "state
of perfection," "propterea quod eorum sodales evangelicis consiliis observandis aliquo modo astringun-
tur," (p. 29.) If "clerics unite in such a secular institute, "tum ipsi quoque sunt in statu perfectionis
acquirendae, non utpote clerici sed utpote Saecularis
Instituti gregales." (p. 30.)

(c) What are the motives for embracing the religious
state (p. 30)? What is said in the Pontifical Allocution concerning the religious state in itself, as a state
of perfection, must not be identified—as certain religious societies do in their reprehensible manner of
recruiting—with the individual's vocation to personal
perfection, whether it be within the "state of perfection" or outside of it.

The three clarifications given above do not immediately
concern the individual person, but concern the state, its position in law and its intrinsic nature. Therefore they do not
deal with the individual's vocation to a determinate state in
the Church; nor with the vocation of the individual to personal perfection within his state; nor with the perfection actually attained by the individual in his state or in his vocation.

It is not the personal perfection of the individual that is
under discussion. This perfection is measured by the degree
of love, of "theological charity" that has been realized within
him. The criterion for the intensity and the purity of love is,
according to the Master's words, the fulfillment of the will of
God. The individual is thus in the eyes of God the more
personally perfect in the measure that he fulfills the divine
will more perfectly. In determining this, the state in which

he lives matters very little, whether it be the lay or the ecclesiastical state, and for the priest, whether it be the secular or the regular priesthood.

It follows that it would not be correct to say that the secular priest, with respect to his personal holiness, has a lesser call to perfection than the regular priest; or that a young man's decision to follow the vocation of the secular priesthood involves the choice of a lesser personal perfection than if he had chosen the religious state. It may happen that this is the case; it may happen just as well that the choice of a state other than the state of perfection will come from a greater love of God and from a nobler spirit of sacrifice than the choice of another to enter the religious state.

With reference to the priest and likewise to the candidate for the priesthood, it is thus not difficult to perceive that by reason of the dignity and the duties of the priestly function, he is called in a very special manner to personal perfection. This is true even when the person clothed with priestly perfection lives legitimately in the "state of marriage," as is the case in the Eastern Rites.

In conclusion, we must therefore say: the individual's vocation to holiness or to personal perfection, the adoption and the permanent exercise of this perfection is not to be confused with the question of the "state of perfection" in the juridical sense of the word. The state of perfection is so named and is such because by means of the three evangelical counsels it removes the principal obstacles to the effort toward personal holiness. To speak more precisely, this state by its very nature is suited to the overcoming of these obstacles. But it is not given to the individual religious, by the mere fact of embracing the state of perfection, to fulfill the virtualities of this state, or to be led effectively to holiness. That depends on the effort of the subject, on the measure in which, by cooperating with divine grace, he actualizes the evangelical counsels in his life.